IMAGES
of America

The Basques of Reno and the Northeastern Sierra

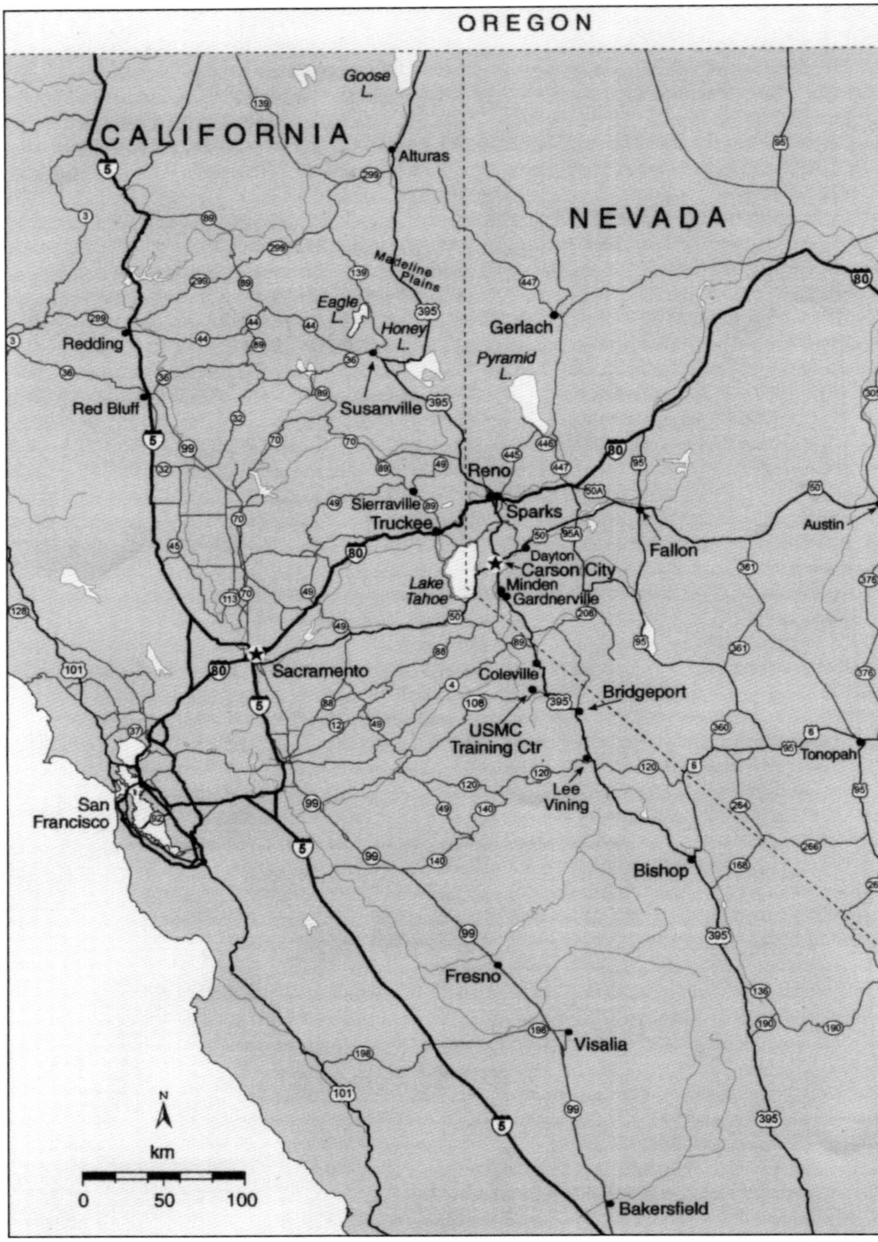

This map of the Reno area and the Sierra Nevada shows the locations mentioned in this book. (Map by Cam Sutherland.)

On the Cover: A mid-1930s Basque picnic takes place at Urtxel's Sheep Camp on Mount Rose near Reno. Individuals who can be identified in this image are Urtxel (to the right of the accordion player), which was probably a nickname; Josephine and Domingo Oroz (back right, with arms around one another); Martin Orriaga (with the overalls on); Marie Inda (to the left of Orriaga); and Antonia Saralegi (two over to the left from Inda), who later married sheepman Alfonso Sario. The rest in the group are unidentified Basques, probably celebrating the Fourth of July. Notice the sheepherder tent under the trees, a wooden structure, and a truck. (Courtesy Irene Arbeloa.)

IMAGES
of America

The Basques of Reno and the Northeastern Sierra

Joxe Mallea-Olaetxe

ARCADIA
PUBLISHING

ISBN 978-0-7385-6961-1

Published by Arcadia Publishing
Charleston, South Carolina

Printed in the United States of America

Library of Congress Catalog Card Number: 2008936545

For all general information contact Arcadia Publishing at:
Telephone 843-853-2070
Fax 843-853-0044
E-mail sales@arcadiapublishing.com
For customer service and orders:
Toll-Free 1-888-313-2665

Visit us on the Internet at www.arcadiapublishing.com

This book is dedicated to many unsung heroes of the North American Basque Organization, but primarily to local club members, who without fanfare perform the tasks that enable the survival of Basque identity, which enriches American diversity.

Contents

Acknowledgments

This is the first photographic book of the Basques in Reno, Nevada, and the surrounding area. The core of the Basque-speaking community remains attached to its cultural oral roots, and many individuals still remember past events and names. I am forever grateful to the many people and families who shared their time, hospitality, invaluable memories, and precious photographs with me.

I owe special thanks to the Landa families, LeRoy Arrascada, Irene Arbeloa, Lisa Corcostegui, and many others I cannot remember.

In Gardnerville, Nevada, I received much help from the Lekumberrys, Elbira Cenoz, the Izocos, Helen Chapell, and Jesus and Frances Pedroarena.

The Basque Library at University of Nevada, Reno (hereafter Basque Library, UNR) staff—Esti Ezkerra, Shannon Sisco, Brandon Scutt, and the librarian-in-chief, Marimar Ubeda—was most helpful in providing photographs and assistance, as was the staff of the Special Collections Department, University of Nevada, Reno, Library (hereafter Special Collections, UNR). I also wish to thank Kate Camino and Jill Berner at the Center for Basque Studies at the University of Nevada Reno (hereafter CBS), as well as Reno's Nevada Historical Society Museum (hereafter Historical Society.)

Hannah Carney, the first editor at Arcadia for Nevada, and her successor, Debbie Seracini, were always ready with helpful guidance. Finally, I am grateful to my wife, Sara Vélez, for her editorial skills and general support.

All photographs used in this book come from the author's collection, unless otherwise noted.

Glossary

Araba, Bizkaia, Gipuzkoa, Lapurdi, Nafarroa/Navarre, Behenafarroa, Zuberoa. The seven Basque regions, which straddle the Pyrenees in northern Spain and southern France.
Euskal Herria. The land of the Basque-speaking people.
Euskaldun(ak). Basque-language speaker(s).
Euskara. The Basque language.
Hegoalde. The southern region of Euskal Herria.
Iparralde. The northern region of Euskal Herria.
Zazpiak Bat. Basque motto: "The Seven [regions] are one."

Abbreviations

NABO, North American Basque Organization
CBS, Center for Basque Studies
UNR, University of Nevada, Reno

Introduction

If one were to open a history book of any country, France or Spain would be an appropriate example in this case, one of the first things seen would be a map because territorial sovereignty is the primary foundation of modern nation-states. If a historian today were to inquire on how those borders were drawn, he or she would be considered a reactionary at best. Such nation-states as France and Spain, with supposedly long pedigrees, do not want to venture there, and neither do their state historians.

However, if the person is a Basque, the question begs itself. Historians know that in 1659 the kings of Spain and France decided to settle their unending border wars by drawing a line in the Pyrenees, thereby effectively splitting the Basque Country in two. They knew what they were doing—divide and conquer—because they did the same thing to Catalonia, another region with a strong identity. Today, 350 years later, the Basques are as relentless as ever in their demands for home rule, but France and Spain evade the issue with the forged claim of the nation's "sacred indivisibility."

Many perhaps have never heard of the Indians of Europeans, the first Europeans: the Basques. That is because for centuries France and Spain have refused to acknowledge the existence of minorities within their borders. There are 11 languages or dialects spoken in France and four in Spain; all are Latin-derived except one, Euskara (Basque), which linguists call a mystery language.

DNA research indicates that the Basques are very probably the oldest Western Europeans, having lived in their present-day homeland for over 30,000 years. Even before the DNA revelations, the proud Basques knew that, compared to them, the French and Spanish nations were born yesterday. The Basques can be viewed as museum artifacts, which explains two anomalies: their language, unrelated to any other in the world, and their unusual blood type that has a high incidence of Rh-negative. Experts have traced the Basque DNA to Central Asia as far back as 30,000–35,000 years ago. The Basques and Celtic people share ancient kinship.

The early Basques (also known as Cro-Magnon) lived for millennia, undisturbed in a place called Euskal Herria ("the Land of the Basque-Speaking People"). During the Paleolithic Ice Age, the caves were their homes, which they decorated with realistic wall paintings of bison, bears, horses, and other animals; it is safe to say they created the first art in that part of the world.

The many years spent dwelling in caves have left a deep mark in the Basque collective memory and in their legends. They reflect a culture dramatically different from the "civilization" that emerged much later in the Middle East, one that later spread into Europe. City dwellers invented organized religion and the idea of external gods, who live somewhere in the sky and who issue commandments; the Basque deities—if they can be called that—on the other hand, never felt they needed to leave the security of the earth. For them, the supreme god figure is female, and she lives, not in the sky, but in a cave. She is more woman than a traditional deity; she does not claim omnipotence or omniscience, and she did not create the world, but she does have certain rules, for example, about lying. She makes a living with the "yes" and the "no" of the people; that is, if a person claims to have 100 sheep when in reality the number is 150, she takes the 50 for herself. She does not have angels to assist her, but she does have a ram. She mates with humans but also with Suar, the male serpent. She predates the sky deities, and she is attached firmly to the earth. Ancient Basque tales, preserved in Euskara (the Basque language), are full of beings who live in caves and forests, where the people also once lived. More significantly, they reflect a more egalitarian world than the one observed in other civilizations, whose religions and legends have made humans the pawns of omnipotent, invisible, outsider gods.

One day, some 8,000 years ago—nobody knows exactly when—large numbers of people speaking Indo-European languages came from the east and eventually overran most of Euskal Herria. After initial clashes, Basque-speaking populations accepted the foreign languages (Erdara) of the newcomers, but not before lending them some of their own vocabulary. When the Greeks and Romans arrived in Europe, many rivers, mountains, and places had names already. Yet many today still think the Greeks and Romans invented all of their vocabulary. This would be like believing that Lakota, Apache, and Cherokee come from English. Recently Theo Vannemann, as others before him, has argued that European languages were built over the foundation of proto-Euskara. The original Euskal Herria was renamed or changed to Europe, which nevertheless still retains the first two letters of "Eusk," the root of Basque. Through the millennia, the native language kept losing ground, and today only one million people speak Basque, which survives in the "reservation" of the Pyrenees Mountains and in areas of the Americas, like Nevada and California.

The Basques call themselves Euskaldunak, the people who speak the language of the Eusk. Their country, Euskal Herria, is defined by language and not by territory, as is the norm in western civilization. In the Basque mind, the language is the primary cultural marker, one that cannot be forged, like an ID card or a passport can.

In spite of such early origins, the Basque people have never cared much for political unity. They know unity means one ruler, such as a king, and that means inequality, higher taxes, and less freedom for the average individual. Lack of political unity, however, does not mean lack of solidarity, especially when the Basques—and additionally the Irish—find themselves abroad as immigrants. The traditional motto is *Zazpiak Bat* (The Seven Are One), meaning that the seven historic regions of Araba, Bizkaia, Gipuzkoa, Lapurdi, Nafarroa, Behenafarroa, and Zuberoa are one unit. Today the revised motto claims *Zortziak Bat* (The Eight Are One) to include the diaspora Basques, who number some three million worldwide.

The Basques survived the Roman Empire, the Barbarians, and the Moors. In 778, Charlemagne—a hero of France, but in reality a warmonger—crossed the Pyrenees on his way to negotiate with the Moors of Zaragoza. Without provocation, his army destroyed the walls of Iruñea, the main city of the Basques, but a bigger tactical mistake was his decision to return home by the same route. The Basques, waiting in the mountain passes, inflicted on Charlemagne the only defeat of his long military career, but they did not bother to write about it. However, the Frankish chroniclers did, admitting to the defeat some 50 years later and giving rise to the epic *Song of Roland*.

To counter the threat of the Franks and the Moors, around 824, the Navarrese elected Eneko Aritza, nicknamed "Menditarra" (the Mountain Man), as king of Iruñea. He and his successors collaborated with the dukes of Vasconia in the north, and by the year 1000, the kingdom grew to the point that Antso Aundia (Sancho the Great) may have been the first king of all the Basques. His influence reached as far as Leon and Catalonia, and he elevated Castile and Aragon into kingdoms and put his sons in their thrones. In 1512, King Ferdinand of Aragon invaded Navarre without provocation and then tried to coerce the pope into legitimizing the aggression with letters. The conquest did not affect Navarre's home rule, but it affected its culture with the forsaking of its native Basque.

Araba, Bizkaia, and Gipuzkoa had economic and political ties with Castile, a landlocked country that since the Middle Ages needed the Basque ports and ships to export the prized merino wool to northern Europe. In 1379, the lord of Bizkaia became king of Castile, and since then, the two countries have been brought closer together. However, Bizkaian law required its lord to swear to uphold Lege Zaharra (the ancient local laws) as a precondition to be accepted as *jaun* (lord).

True to their distaste of a vertical society, Bizkaians limited the lord or lady's powers severely; he or she could not dictate any laws without the approval of the *batzar* (assembly) of Bizkaia that met under the Oak Tree of Gernika. Historians praise the Basque laws for their democratic spirit, modernity (such as the habeas corpus clause), relative equality regarding the sexes, and minimum bureaucracy (thus low taxes).

The proximity of sea and the mountains influenced Basque history and culture dramatically. While sheepherding was a major occupation in the rural areas, oak forests, iron mines, and the foundries allowed the Basques to build ships and sail the world. They became the first commercial whalers in Europe, and some claim they discovered the fishing banks of Newfoundland before 1492.

In spite of the efforts by the governments of France and Spain to undermine the Basque way of life, Araba, Bizkaia, and Gipuzkoa managed to keep their ancient laws until 1876. Lapurdi, Behenafarroa, and Zuberoa in Iparralde (the northern Basque regions) lost theirs in the aftermath of the French Revolution. Ironically, while the revolutionary motto was "Liberty, Fraternity, and Equality," the Basques were promptly forced to speak French, pay taxes to Paris, and serve in the French army. With the rise of modern nation-states came more centralization, compulsory public education that taught only French and Spanish, military service, and a relentless campaign to discredit local patois languages—all in the guise of enlightenment.

But many Basques were used to resisting assimilation. When the 1936 Spanish Civil War broke out, they sided with the popularly elected republic of Spain against the rebel Spanish generals. That year, they gained self-governance with their first *lehendakari* (president), José Antonio Agirre Lekube, but only briefly. The Nazis, allied with the fascist Spanish generals, firebombed Gernika, killing over 1,000 civilians. Subsequently, General Franco unleashed a repressive policy against all things Basque that lasted until his death in 1975, at which time Hegoalde regained autonomy again. Today Araba, Bizkaia, and Gipuzkoa make up the Autonomous Government of Euskadi; their parliament creates its own laws, collects taxes, runs schools, and manages welfare programs. There is also a Basque police force but no army. Navarre, because of its history, has its own autonomy. The three Basque regions in the north are much smaller and less populous and as a consequence have no autonomy yet.

No modern account of Basque history would be complete without mentioning the terrorist group ETA, an acronym for *Euskadi Ta Askatasuna* ("Basque Country and Freedom"). It emerged as a group of freedom fighters against the terrorism that the Basques were suffering under Franco's dictatorship. Today most Basques wish ETA would stop the violence, which for years has been sporadic. The Spanish media characterizes ETA as a serious "terrorist" threat, yet after Ireland, Euskal Herria is the safest country in Europe. Criminal activity in the Spanish state is 10 times higher than in the Basque region.

There would be no Basques in Nevada and California today if in the 1800s unemployment in their homeland was 3.4 percent or if they had ranked third in purchasing power in Europe, as was the case in the Basque Country in 2007. The Basques lead the world in cooperatives, and within a few years, Eroski Supermarkets and the Arrasate/Mondragon Cooperative consortium will be the largest in the world with some 50,000 worker-owners. For 2008, Euskadi, with a population of about 2.6 million, approved a budget of 10,000 million Euros, which benefits a society that enjoys one of the highest life expectancies in the world.

In the near future, France and Spain will be pressured to renounce their outdated idea of nation, which was achieved by invasion and through the rapacity of absolute kings. Only then will the European Union be able to implement its constitution. Only then will the Basques and other minorities be able to decide their destiny.

One

Basques in North America

The tiny Basque homeland is mountainous and does not produce sufficient foodstuffs, forcing many to seek their livelihood abroad. Freedom to trade by sea, written into the medieval law code, allowed Basque ships to arrange commercial ties with their neighbors and engage in active trade. Basque merchants established themselves in Seville right after its conquest in 1248 and became a powerful economic block. In 1492, Columbus sailed to discover America in the *Santa María*, a Basque ship with a sizable Basque crew. The Basque Country, located on the Atlantic, has long been a land of ships and sailors, and recent research indicates that without the Basques Castile could not have conquered or held its empire for 300 years.

There were many prominent Colonial figures of Basque descent, such as Juan Oñate, who colonized New Mexico in 1598 and introduced domesticated sheep to the Southwest. Franciscan friars Fermin Lasuen and Vicente Sarria built at least 10 missions in Alta California. In 1775–1776, Juan Bautista Anza journeyed across the Mojave Desert, bringing colonists to San Francisco. *Arizona* apparently is not a Papago word but Basque, meaning *aritz ona* (good oak tree). Finally, between 1792 and 1845, California had five Basque governors, namely Jose J. Arrillaga, Diego Borica, Pablo V. Sola, Jose M. Echeandia, and Manuel Micheltorena.

The 1849 California gold discovery spurred a fresh round of Basque immigration, this time as sheepherders and ranchers. Soon they spread out into the Great Basin following the 1859 mining strike in Virginia City, Nevada. The city of Reno began as a railroad town in 1867 and soon dubbed itself "The Biggest Little City in the World." It became America's capital for quick divorces and in 1931 the mecca of legal gambling as well. However, until the 1960s, Reno remained small and never far from the range.

Today more than 50,000 people in the United States claim to be Basque American, which is probably a low number. The largest concentrations are in San Francisco, California, and in Boise, Idaho.

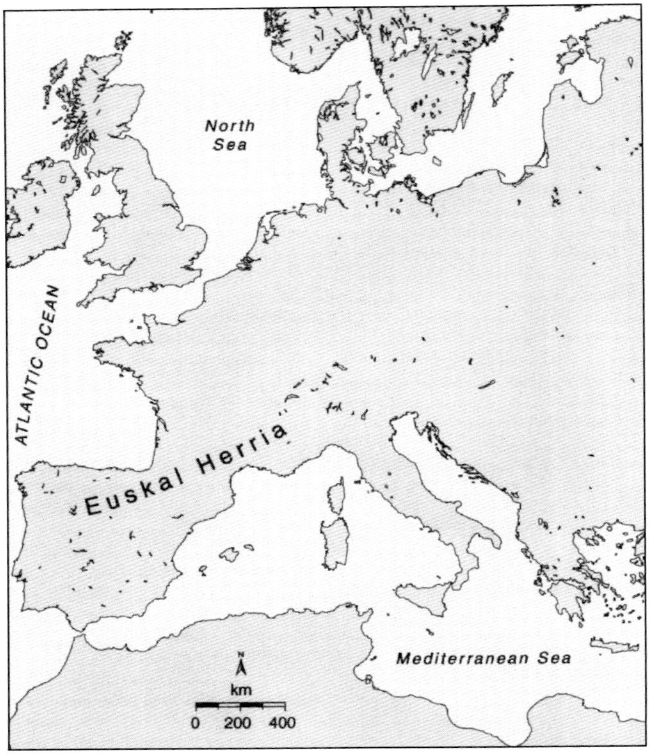

This is Euskal Herria (the land of the Basque-speaking people) from 10,000 to 30,000 BP (before the present). Though readers may not have seen a map like this before, DNA data and linguistics make it very plausible. It was much later when the continent was renamed Europa and only relatively recently when France and Spain emerged as they are now known. (Map by Cam Sutherland.)

The Basque Country has seven historic regions: Araba, Bizkaia, Gipuzkoa, Lapurdi, Nafarroa, Nafarroa Beherea, and Zuberoa. The total land area is 20,494 square kilometers with a population of over three million. The region faces the Atlantic Ocean, which the English call the Bay of Biscay. (Courtesy 2008 *HABE* calendar.)

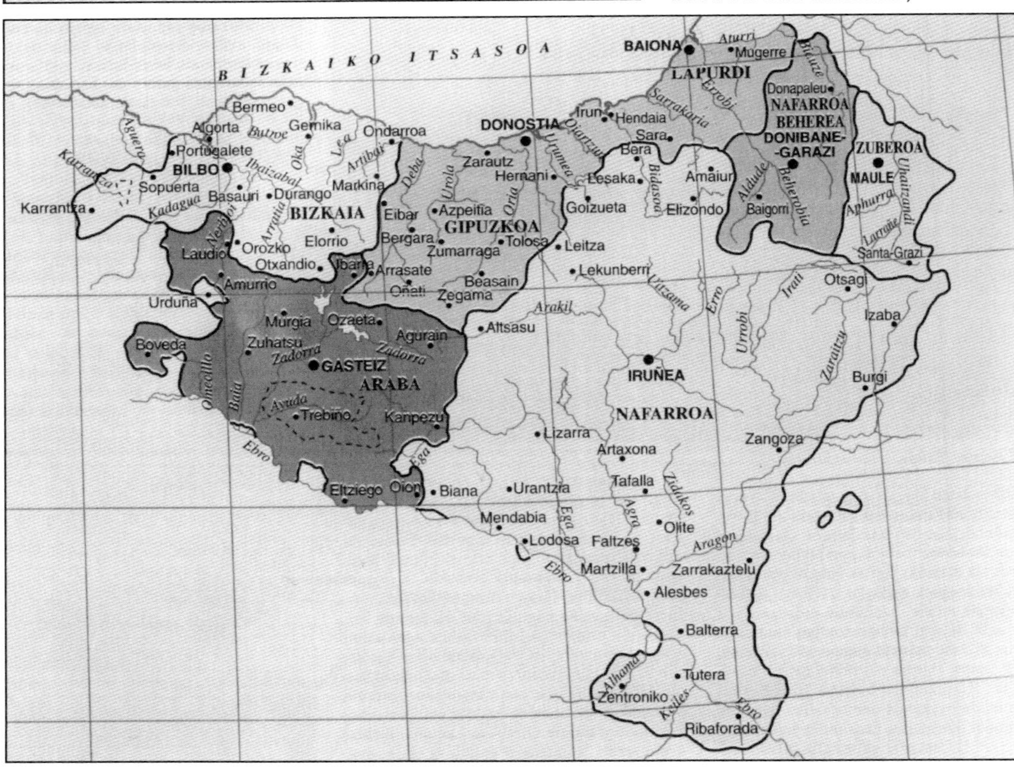

The major Paleolithic cave painting sites are found inside the line that generally encompasses the Pyrenees. The story is compelling because the Basque Country is at its geographic center. The paintings are usually attributed to the Cro-Magnon people, of whom relatively little is known when compared to the Basques, so why don't they or their ancestors get any credit for the cave paintings?

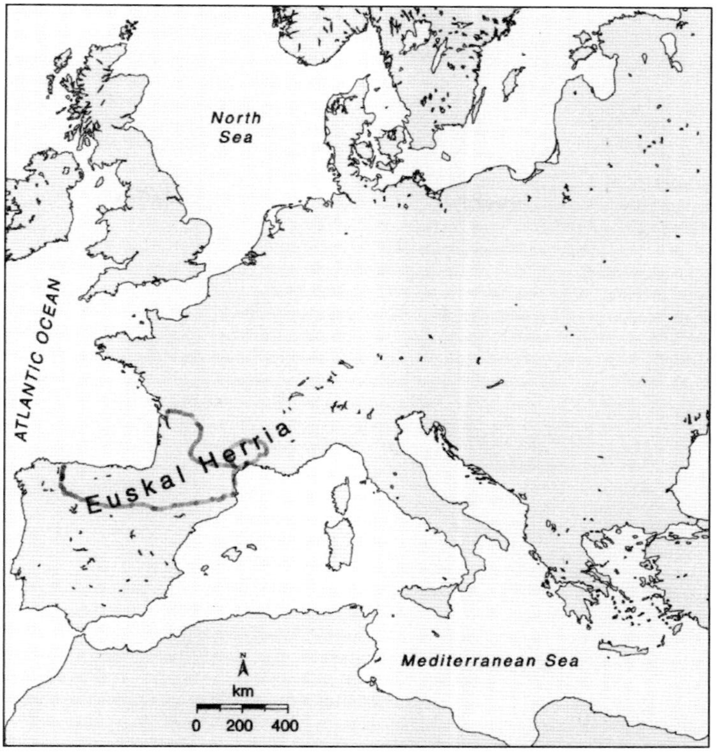

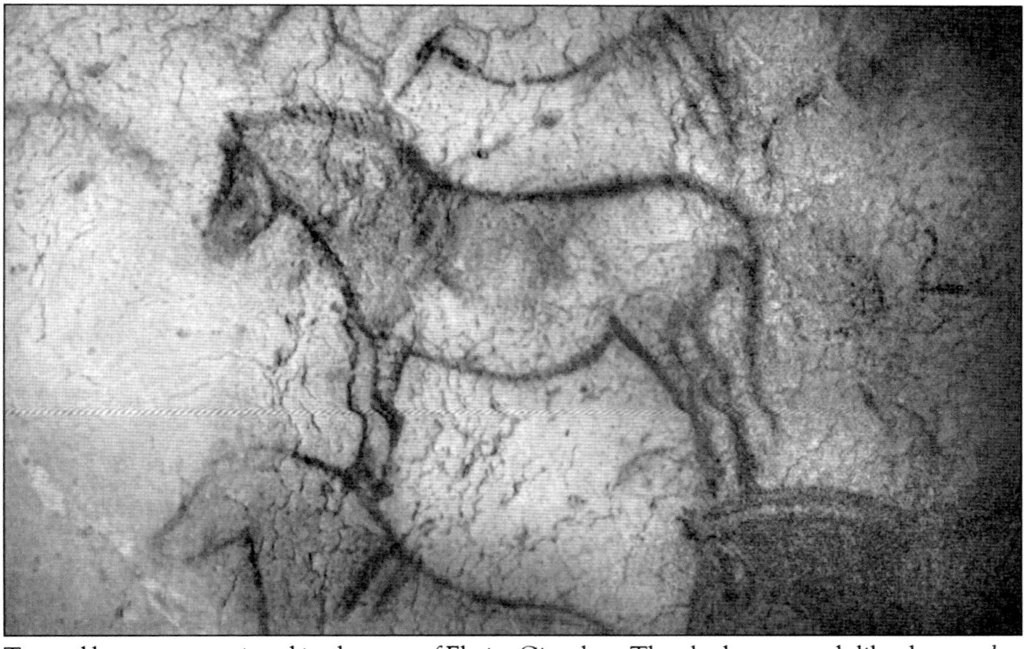

Two red horses were painted in the cave of Ekain, Gipuzkoa. They look very much like the *pottoka*, the red horses that still roam the Pyrenees. The date of these paintings is usually given between 10,000 and 15,000 years ago, but other paintings are thought to be 30,000, which matches the DNA chronology. (Courtesy *Lur Enziklopedia Tematikoa*.)

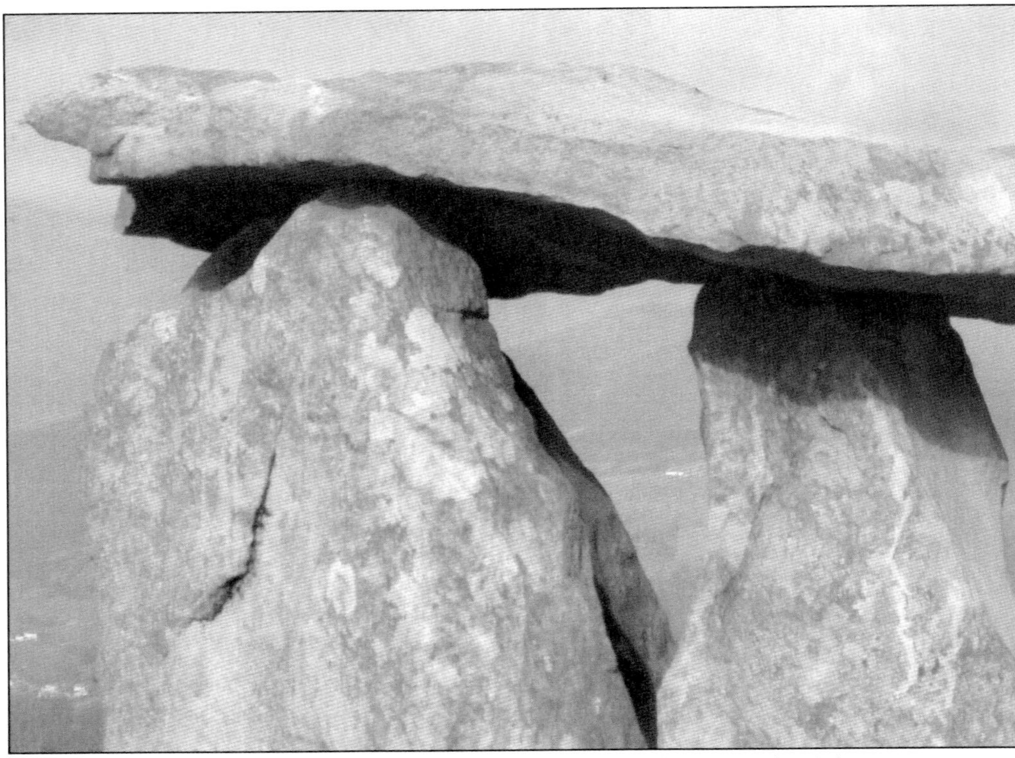

There a lot of dolmens on the Atlantic coast of Europe, but in the Basque Country, they are found in sheepherding mountain areas, and anthropologist Joxemiel Barandiaran believed they were burial sites. Their generic name is *trikuarri*, but some sites are known as *sorgin etxe* (witch's house).

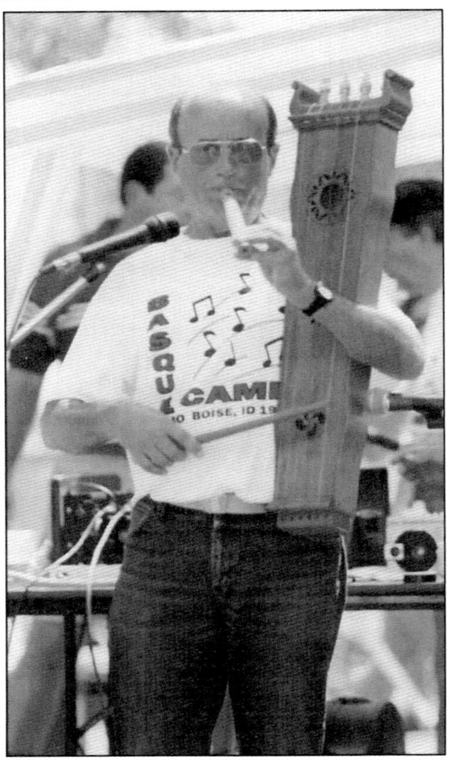

Singing and dancing are two Basque characteristics. Martxel Tillous is the *xirulari*, a flute player from the region of Zuberoa. A three-hole flute (*txistu*) common in the rest of the Basque Country is probably a prehistoric instrument, as the three-hole bird bone found in the Paleolithic cave of Izturitze in Lapurdi indicates. (Courtesy NABO Calendar 2008.)

Here are the Basque flag—*ikurrina*—and the coat of arms of the seven historic regions. Araba was known as the land of castles; Bizkaia had the Oak Tree; Gipuzkoa had its seafaring tradition; Lapurdi and Zuberoa are represented by the lions; and King Antso Azkarra earned Navarre's chains in the 1212 battle against the Moors in southern Spain.

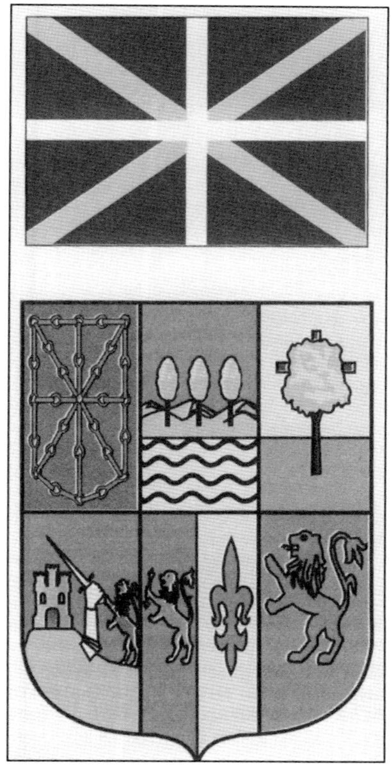

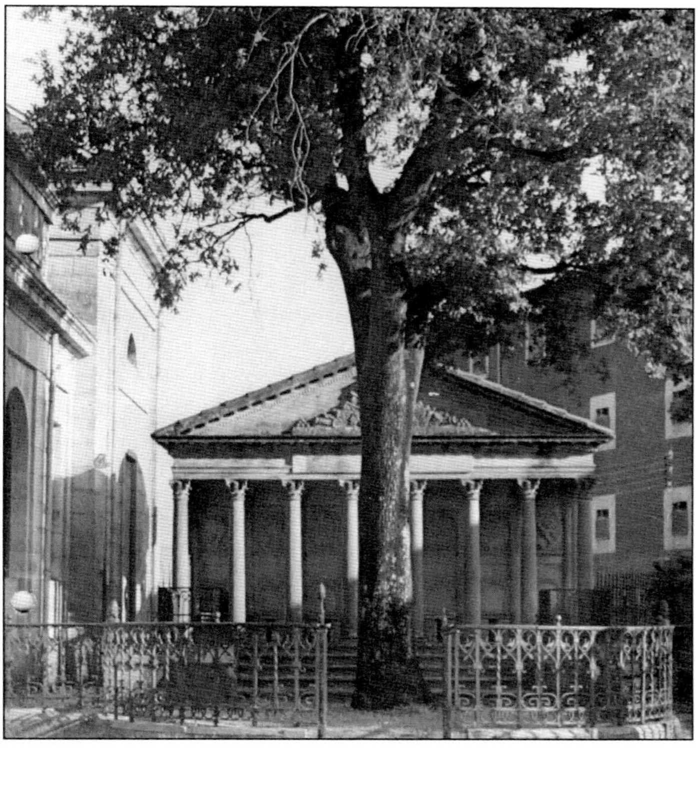

This is the symbolic Oak Tree of Gernika that stands as the beacon of Basque liberties and representative government. The Nazis and the Italians destroyed Gernika in 1936—just to try out their new war technology—but it was Picasso's immortal painting of the heinous massacre that brought the event to a world audience.

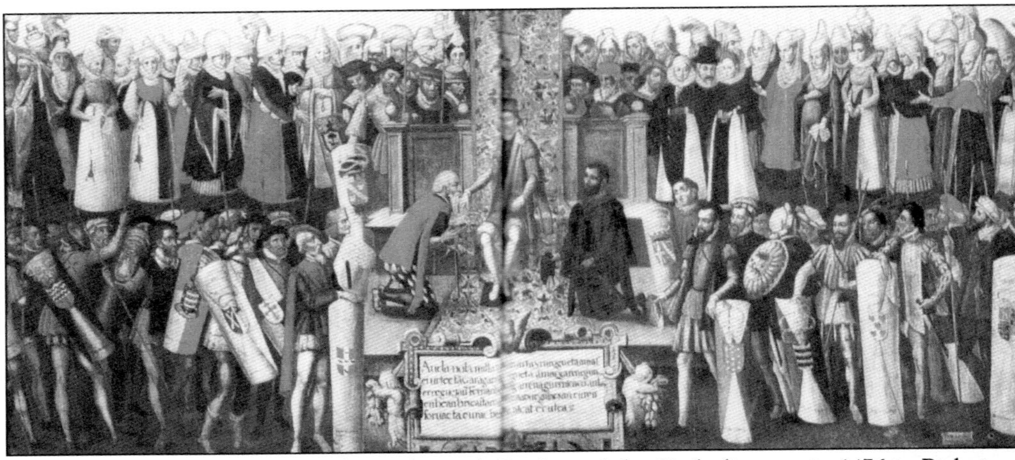

Francisco Mendieta's painting shows the oath Ferdinand the Catholic gave in 1476 in Bizkaia—instead of the Lady of Bizkaia, Queen Isabella of Castile—to uphold the law of the land, which was the condition sine qua non she would be accepted as lady. In theory, the law of Bizkaia was by the people, for the people. (Courtesy *Bilbao y Bizkaia.*)

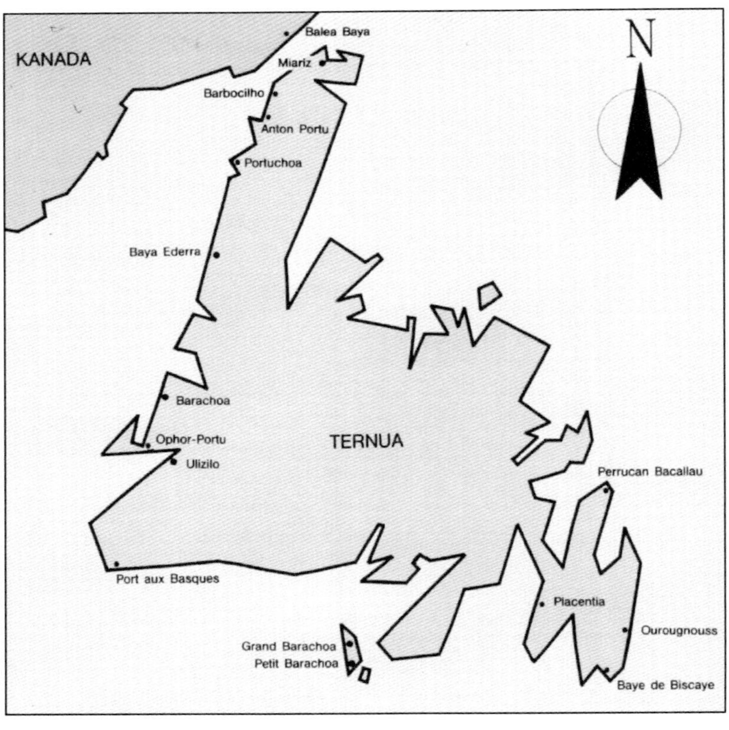

On this map of Ternua (Newfoundland), Basque toponyms, such as Baya Ederra, Portuchoa, Opor Portu, and Ulizilo, abound on the coast. The Basques arrived here in search of whales and cod. They built whale-oil rendering stations and taught Newfoundland natives a Basque-Indian pidgin. (Courtesy *Euskara Euskaldunon Hizkuntza.*)

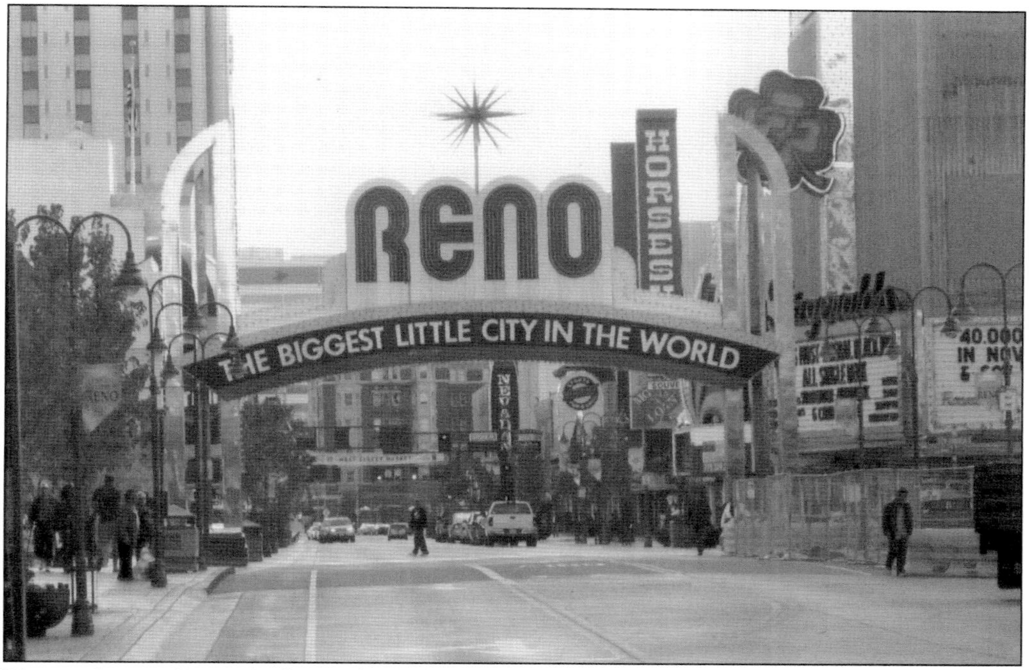

This is the new Reno Arch as it looked in 2007 straddling Virginia Street in downtown Reno. The original arch was erected in 1926 with the logo "The Biggest Little City in the World," which still is Reno's trademark.

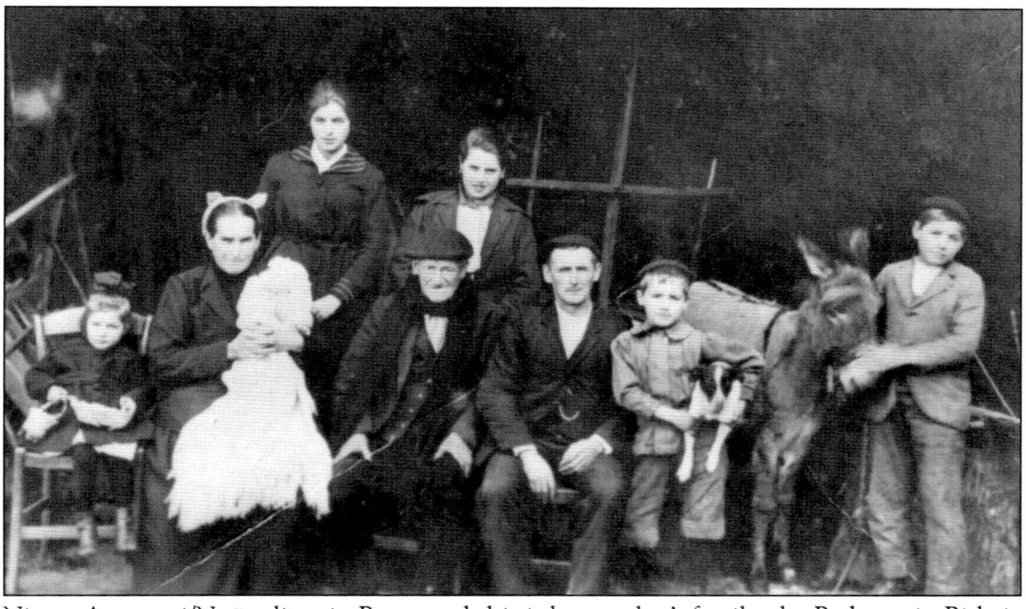

Nieves Arostegui/Nuñez lives in Reno, and this is her mother's family, the Badayas, in Bizkaia in the 1920s—an excellent photograph of a peasant family. From left to right are aunt Felisa, grandmother (holding a baby), aunt Lucia, great grandfather, Maria (Nieves's mother), grandfather, uncle Valentin Badaya (with dog), and Pedro (with donkey). (Courtesy Nieves Arostegui.)

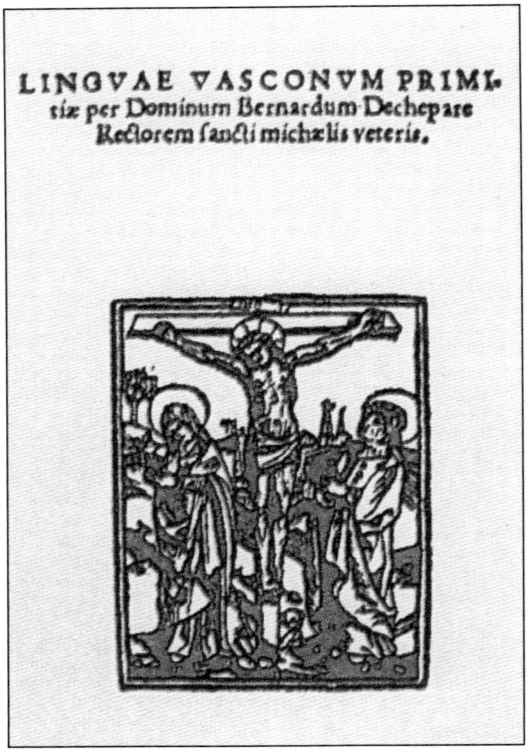

In 1548, Bernart Etxepare, the parish priest of Garazi, wrote the first book in Basque, which was published in Bordeaux and was appropriately titled *Linguae Vasconum Primitiae* (Latin for "The first [book] in the Basque Language"). In it, he encouraged the ancient language to get out to the public square and into the world.

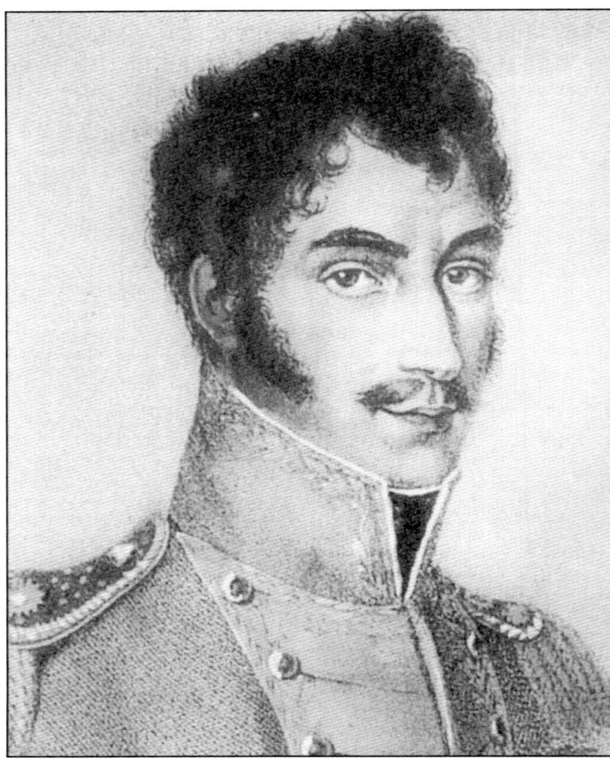

Simon Bolivar (1783–1830), known as El Libertador and considered the George Washington of South America, descended from Bolibar, a village in Bizkaia. He freed Panama, Colombia, Venezuela, and Ecuador from Spanish rule, and—with Gen. Antonio José de Sucre—Peru and Bolivia, which was named after him.

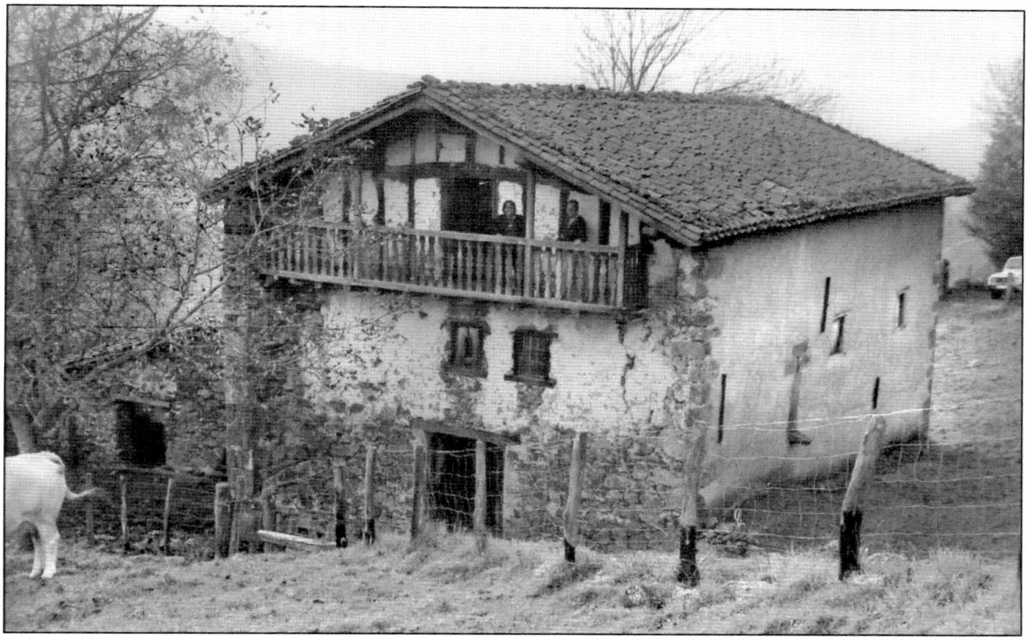

The *baserri* or *borda* (Basque farmstead), regarded by many as the foundation of the Basque way of life, housed both people and farm animals. Traditionally it was indivisible and passed down to one heir chosen by the parents. Other siblings had the right to stay, but they had to leave if they wanted to marry.

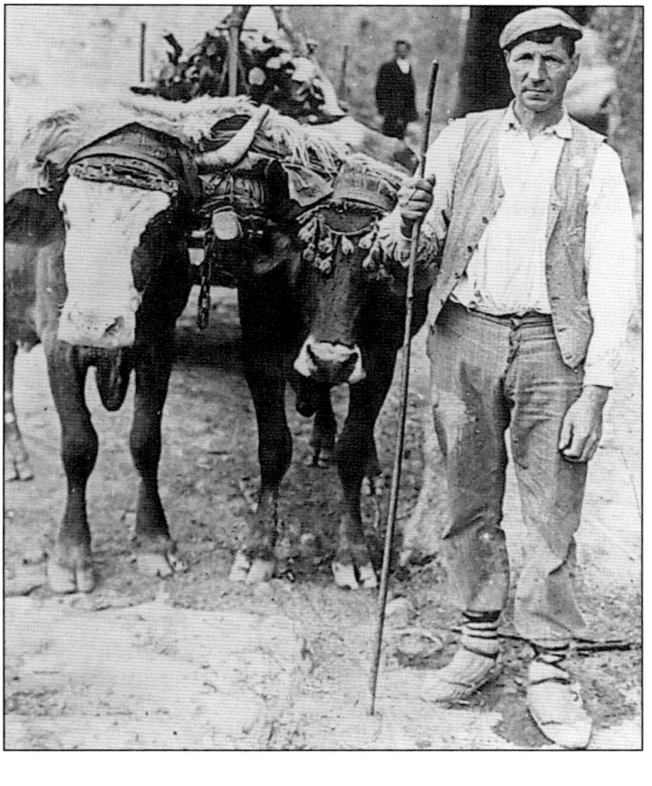

An early-20th-century Bizkaian *baserritarra* (farmstead dweller) is dressed in typical everyday garb. His *abarkak* were shoes made from cow leather, and the sheep provided the wool for his socks. The cart was made from wood except for the outer wheel rings. He holds the *akulu* (goad), made from a hazelnut sapling. (Courtesy *Lur Enziklopedia Tematikoa*.)

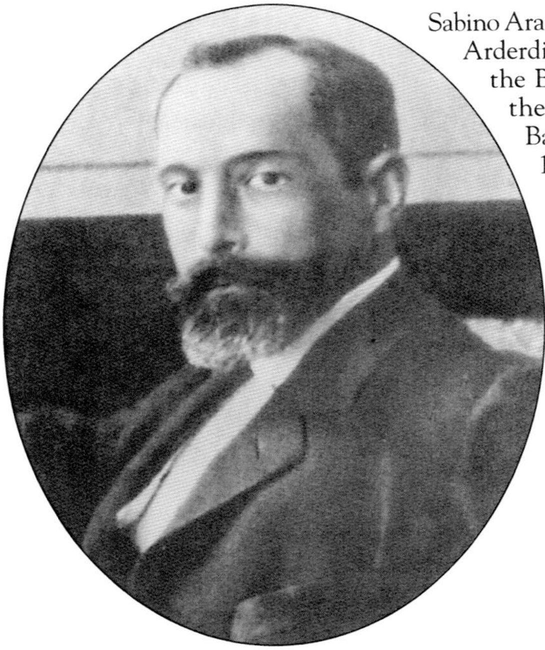

Sabino Arana Goiri (1865–1903), founder of Eusko Jeltzaile Arderdia (Basque Nationalist Party—BNP) taught the Basques that Euskadi was their country and the *ikurrina* was their flag. Arana influenced Basque politics and language considerably. In 1936, the first Basque president-elect was of the BNP, which is still in power today. (Courtesy *Euskara Euskaldunon Hizkuntza*.)

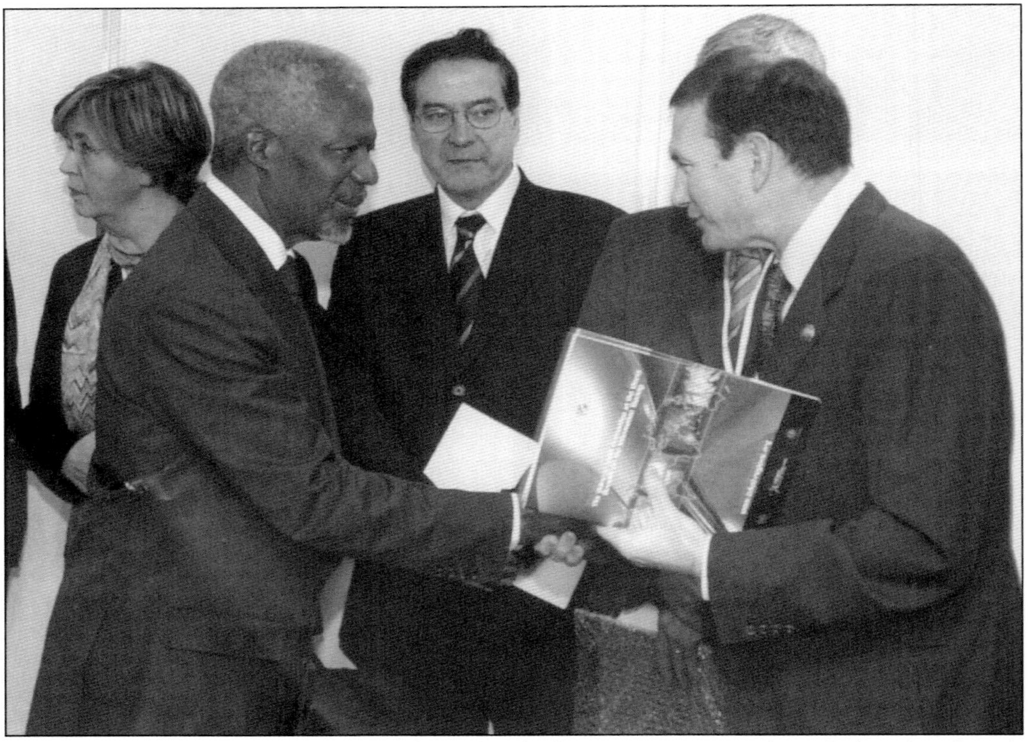

Juan Jose Ibarretxe (far right), the president of Euskadi since 1999, is seen here shaking hands with Kofi Annan, the secretary of the United Nations. In October 2008, he was charged for having held talks with Batasuna, a party linked to ETA. Ibarretxe wants the Basque people to speak and declare their opinion, but Madrid says that is illegal.

In the 1590s, Basque historian Geronimo Mendieta wrote that Christopher Columbus received information about unknown lands from a dying pilot, who also handed him the ship's log. Mendieta's source was probably Gonzalo Fdez. de Oviedo (1535) and added that the pilot's ship was either "Basque, Portuguese, or Andalusian." (Courtesy *Historia Eclesiastica Indiana.*)

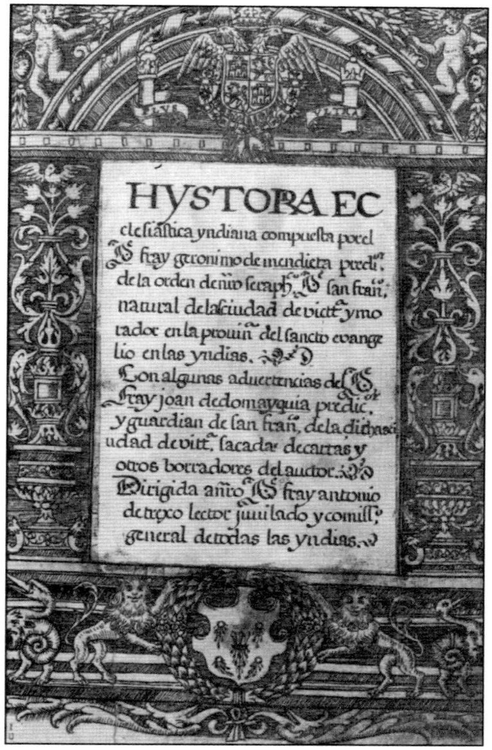

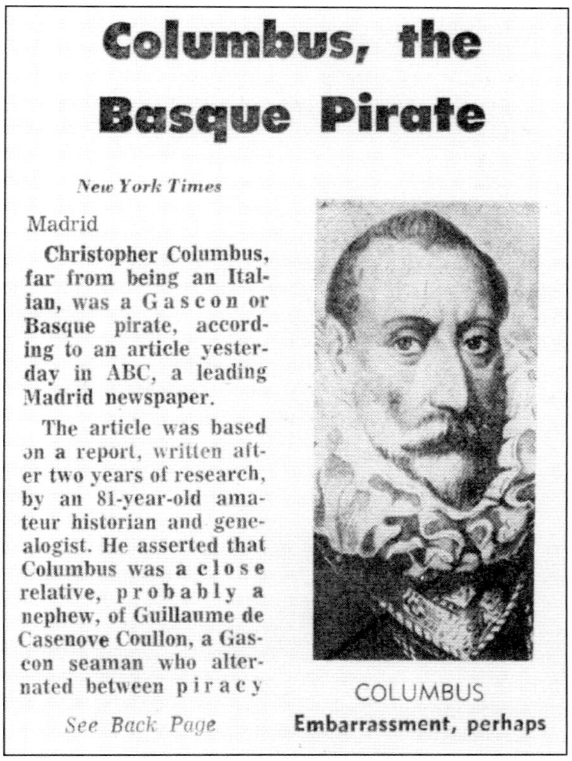

Columbus, the Basque Pirate

New York Times

Madrid

Christopher Columbus, far from being an Italian, was a Gascon or Basque pirate, according to an article yesterday in ABC, a leading Madrid newspaper.

The article was based on a report, written after two years of research, by an 81-year-old amateur historian and genealogist. He asserted that Columbus was a close relative, probably a nephew, of Guillaume de Casenove Coullon, a Gascon seaman who alternated between piracy

See Back Page

COLUMBUS
Embarrassment, perhaps

Though most historians agree that Christopher Columbus was from Genoa, there is little definite documentation to back it up with. Apparently he did not speak or write in Italian, so questions linger about his birthplace. Was he Portuguese, Norwegian, Catalan? Or perhaps he was Basque.

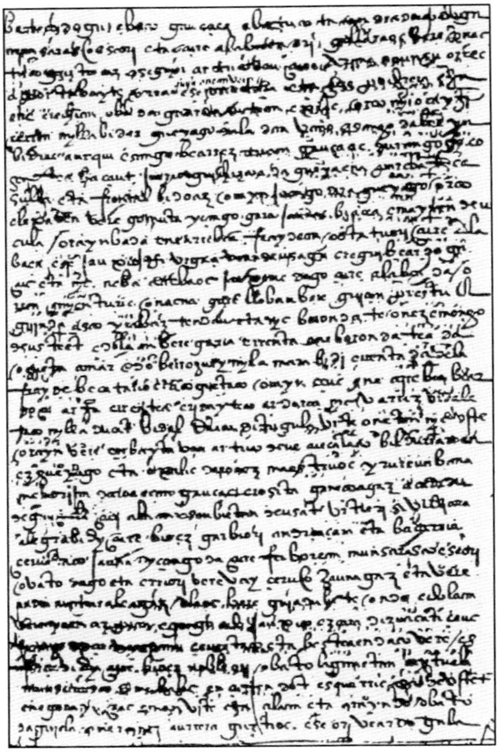

The Bizkaian Joan Zumarraga (1472–1548) was the first bishop of North America. He had available at home the first printing press in the New World and published the first books. In 1537, he wrote a letter in Euskara because he did not want the Spaniards to understand its contents. Zumarraga owned a ranch with over 8,000 sheep and bred donkeys for the natives.

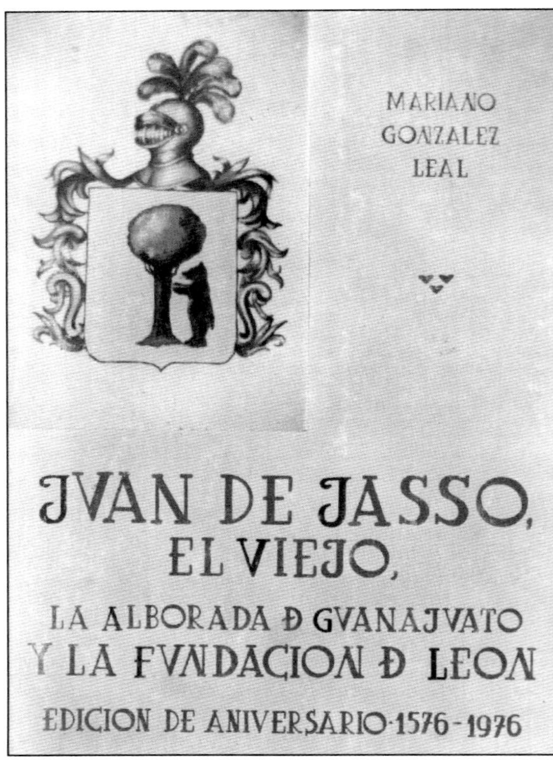

In the 1540s, Joanes Jatsu (written Juan de Jasso) owned a roadside inn on the wild road to Zacatecas, where the Basques Kristobal Oñate, Juanes Tolosa, the Zaldibar brothers, and Diego Ibarra owned mines. One can imagine that they appreciated Jatsu's hospitality and after a hearty meal they sang old country songs, as centuries later the Basques in Reno still do.

The Colonial push into northern Mexico was spurred by Zacatecas mining, where Diego Ibarra became wealthy. In the 1560s, his nephew Frantzisko Ibarra opened and established Nueva Vizcaya with Durango as its capital city under the Law of Bizkaia. Not surprisingly, the king of Spain rejected that. (Courtesy *The Course of Mexican History*.)

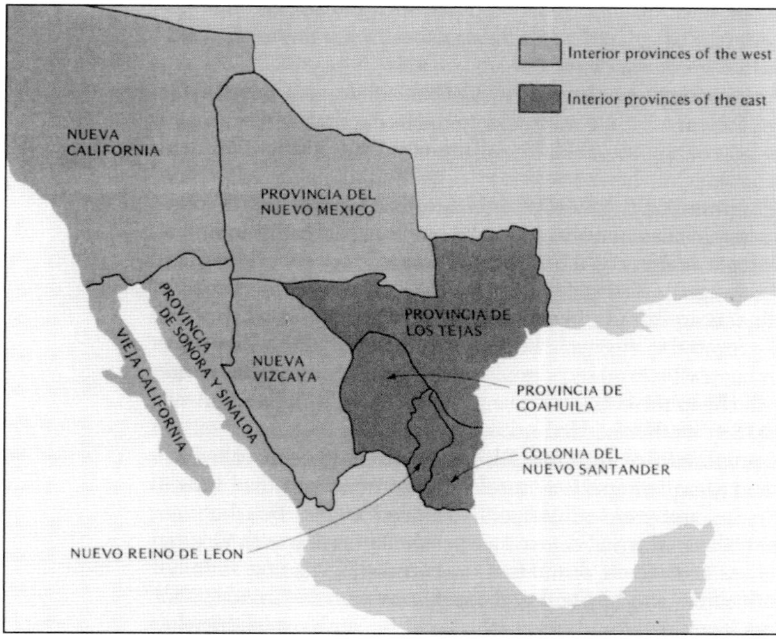

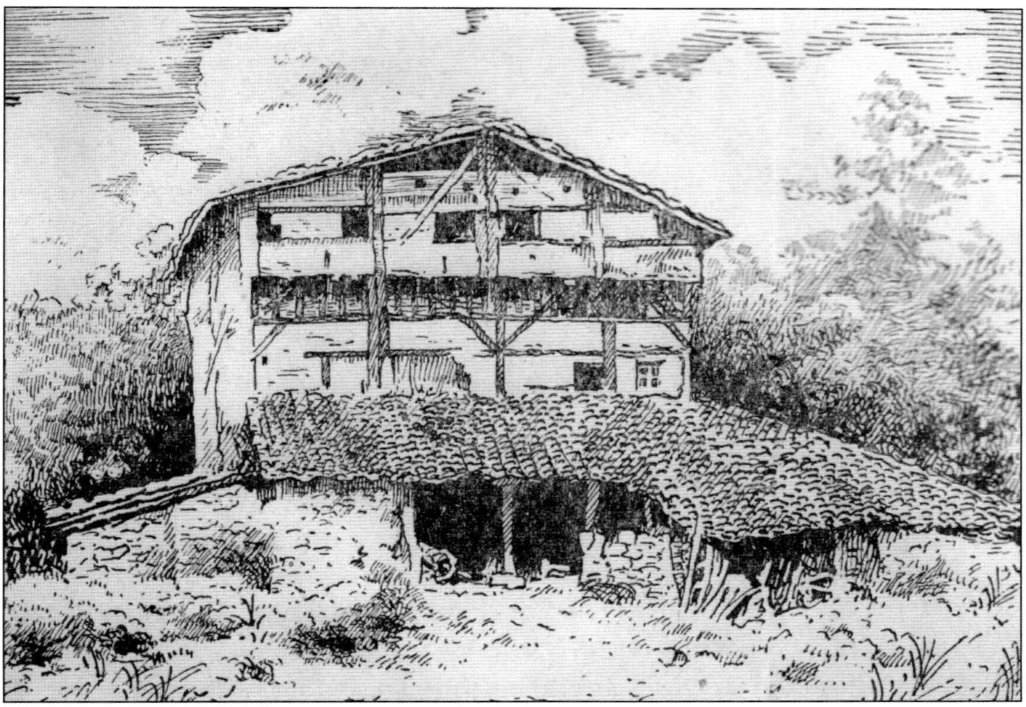

Miguel Lopez Legazpi colonized the Philippines for the Spanish Empire in 1565, but his Spanish competitors accused him of securing the contract through his Basque connections. Legazpi chose his compatriot Andres Urdaneta as his navigator, who discovered the return sea route from the Orient to Mexico. The drawing illustrates the ancestral Legazpi Manor. (Courtesy Jose Sanz y Diaz.)

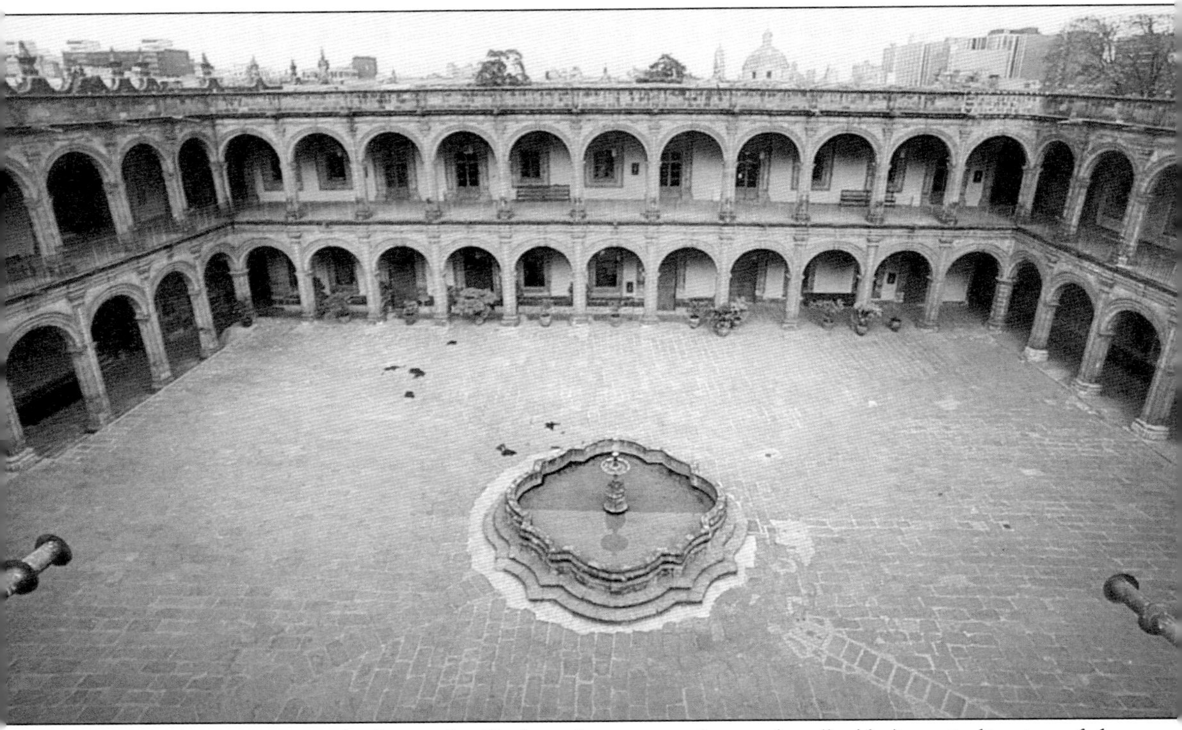

With the exception of a few verbs, Euskara has no gender marker (he/she), an indicative of the high equality among the sexes. In 1734, the Basque colony of Mexico built a sumptuous college for the needy women among them—probably one of the few such institutions in the world. Known popularly as Colegio de las Vizcaínas, it was finished in 1752, when a heated struggle began to secure for the college a lay constitution, free from ecclesiastical jurisdiction. In a 1752 letter between two leading Basques of Mexico, Manuel Aldako writes to his friend Ambrosio Meabe that he would rather burn the building down than accept Church supervision. In the end, after appealing to the king and all the way to the pope in Rome, they obtained independent status for the college. (Courtesy *Los Vascos en Mexico y su Colegio de las Vizcainas.*)

Fortun Ximenez Bertandona may have been the first to discover "California" in 1533. In 1602–1603, Sebastian Vizcaíno identified the future sites of San Diego and Monterey, while his countrymen Juan Francisco de la Bodega y Quadra and Bruno de Hezeta explored the coast up to Alaska in 1775. Hezeta discovered the mouth of the Columbia River.

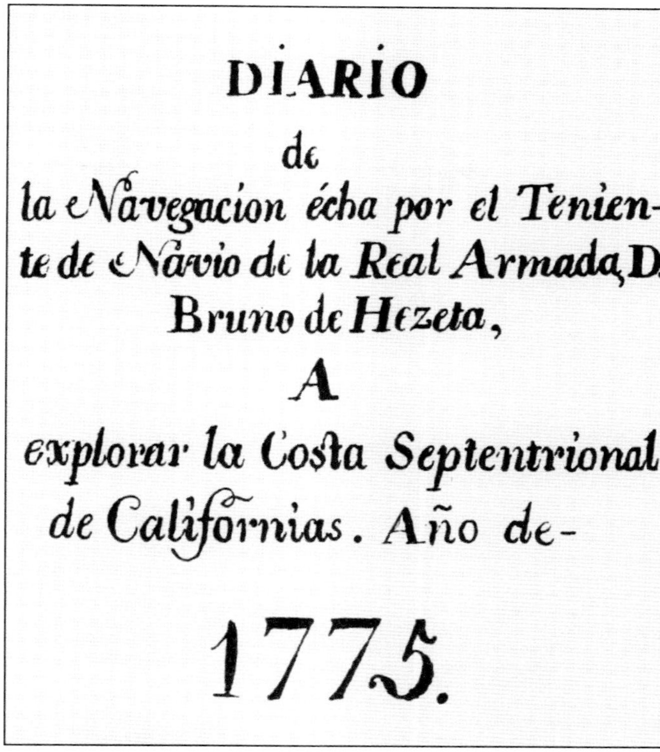

DIARIO
de
la Navegacion écha por el Teniente de Navio de la Real Armada D. Bruno de Hezeta,
A
explorar la Costa Septentrional de Californias. Año de-
1775.

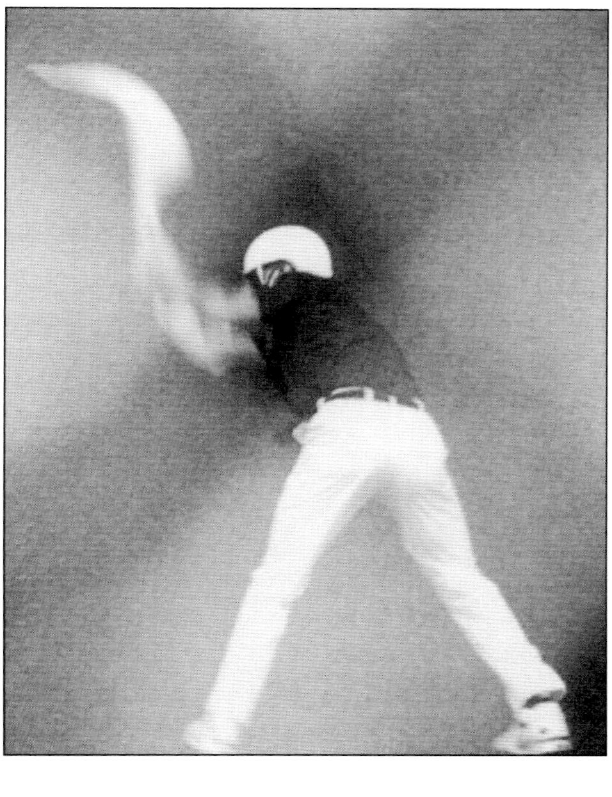

Jai alai is the fastest game in the world, as the ball, hard as a rock, travels at 160 miles per hour, hurtled from an elongated wicker basket tied to the wrist of the player. The sport was invented in the Basque Country, where *jai alai* means "cheerful holiday." Reno's Grand MGM Casino featured *jai alai* games from 1978 to 1980.

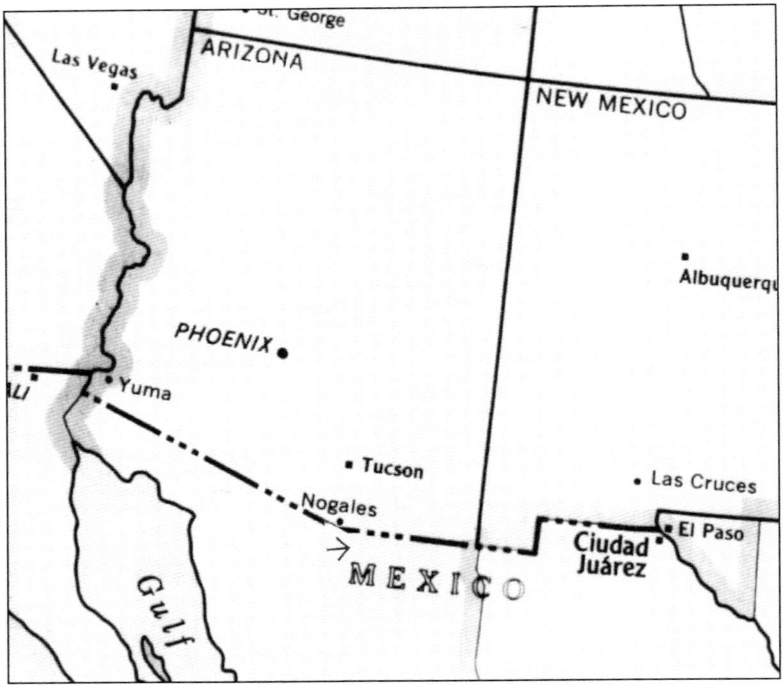

In 1979, William A. Douglass was the first to ask whether the origin of the name *Arizona* was Basque, and in 2003, Donald T. Garate put the question to rest. The original Arizona site (arrow) in Sonora, Mexico, was a mine within a ranch owned by the Basque Bernardo Urrea. The name means *aritz ona* (good oak tree[s]), like Bedarona (good grass), a town of Bizkaia.

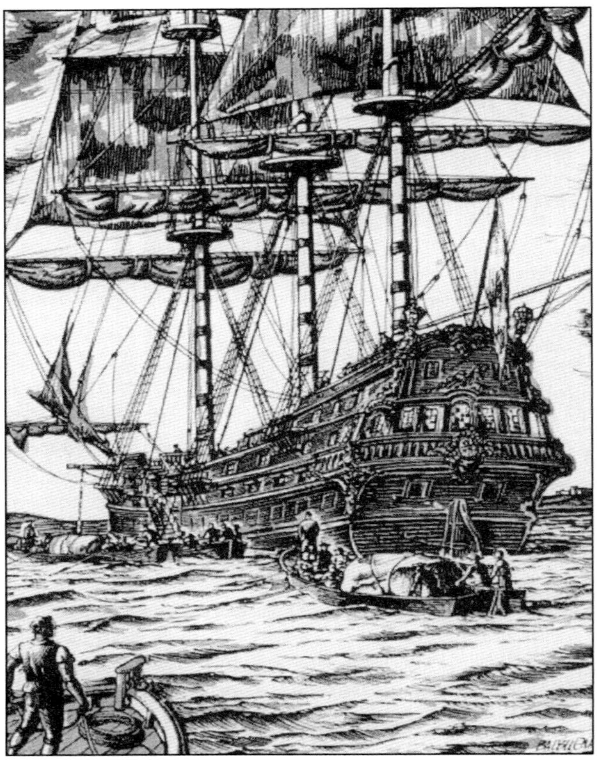

The Basques aligned with the Castilian/Spanish monarchy because of the availability of government jobs and opportunities in America. The monarchy in turn benefitted from Basque ships, sailors, and iron implements of all kinds to hold on to its far-flung colonies for three centuries. The galleon was the workhorse that tied the Philippines to Mexico and Mexico to Spain.

In 1821, Col. Agustin Iturbide proclaimed the independence of Mexico. During his short tenure as emperor, he put people of Basque descent in high places: Manuel Zozaya was the envoy to Washington, D.C., and J. A. Echaverri was in charge of the troops. It has been said that the people from Extremadura conquered America for Spain, but the Basques freed it.

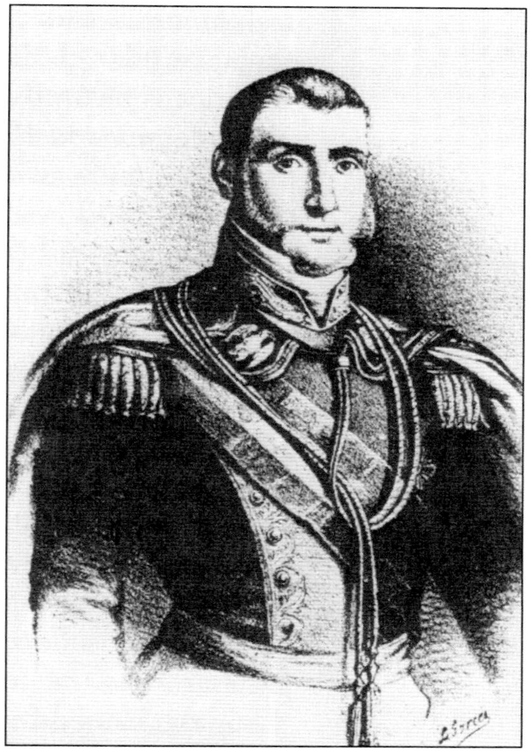

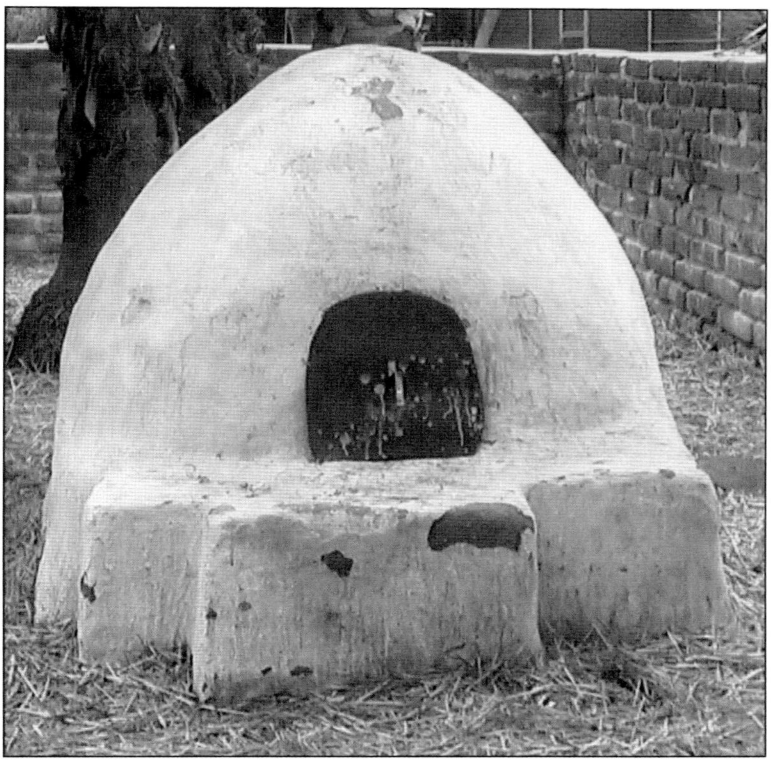

The building of Los Cerritos, which houses the Historical Society of Long Beach, California, dates from 1844 according to its curator, Steve Iverson. Originally it was a sheep ranch with Basque herders, though it is usually assumed that Basque sheepherding dates from the Anglo-American period. The old rancho included this bread oven.

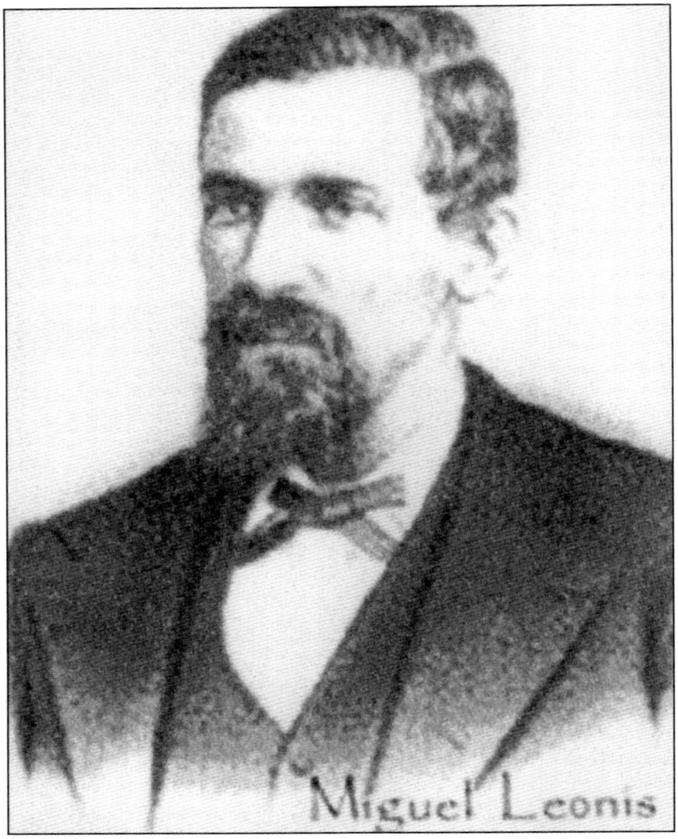

Miguel Leonis—the "King of Calabasas"—was born in Iparralde and was a striking figure of the 1870s and 1880s. Though Leonis had armed men to help defend his extensive California land claims, he suffered frequent lawsuits. One of his lawyers was Jean Pierre Goytino, who wrote to him in Basque, "Miguel, what would us lawyers do without people like yourself?" (Courtesy www.calabasashistory.com.)

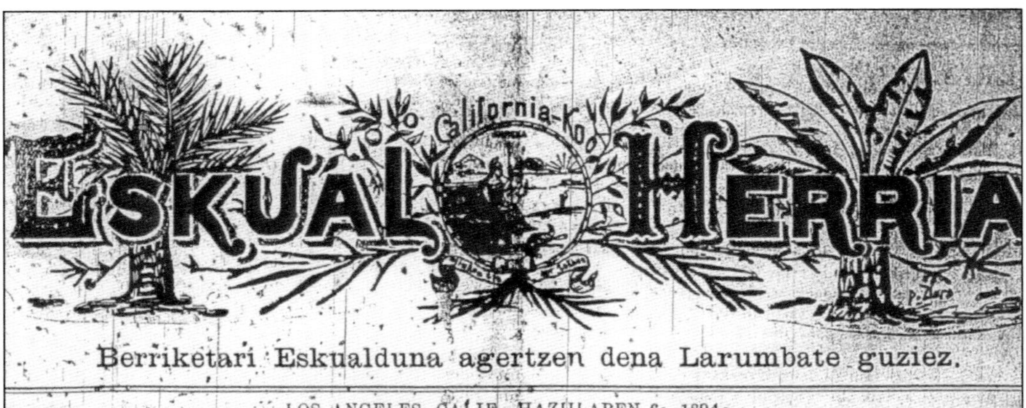
California-ko
ESKUAL HERRIA
Berriketari Eskualduna agertzen dena Larumbate guziez.
LOS ANGELES, CALIF., HAZILAREN 6a 1894a.

Joseph Agostin Xaho (1811–1858) published the first Basque weekly, *Ariel, Uscal Herrico Gaseta*, in Baiona (Lapurdi), but the next two such media emerged far away, in Los Angeles, California. *Escualdun Gazeta* only lasted three issues, but Jean Pierre Goytino's weekly *Californiako Eskual Herria* endured from 1892 to 1898. (Courtesy Basque Library, UNR.)

The brothers Pedro and Bernardo Altube immigrated first to the Pampas of Argentina and then to California in 1849. In 1871, Pedro bought 3,000 head of cattle in Mexico and drove them to Elko County, Nevada, where they established a huge cattle and sheep empire. Pedro "Palo Alto," photographed here, was inducted into the Cowboy Hall of Fame in 1960. (Courtesy *Elko Free Press*.)

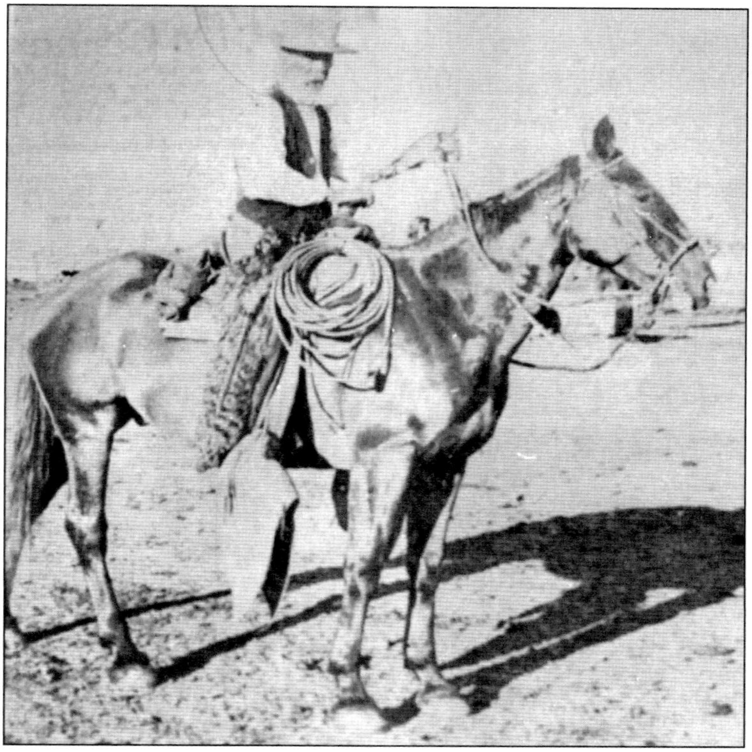

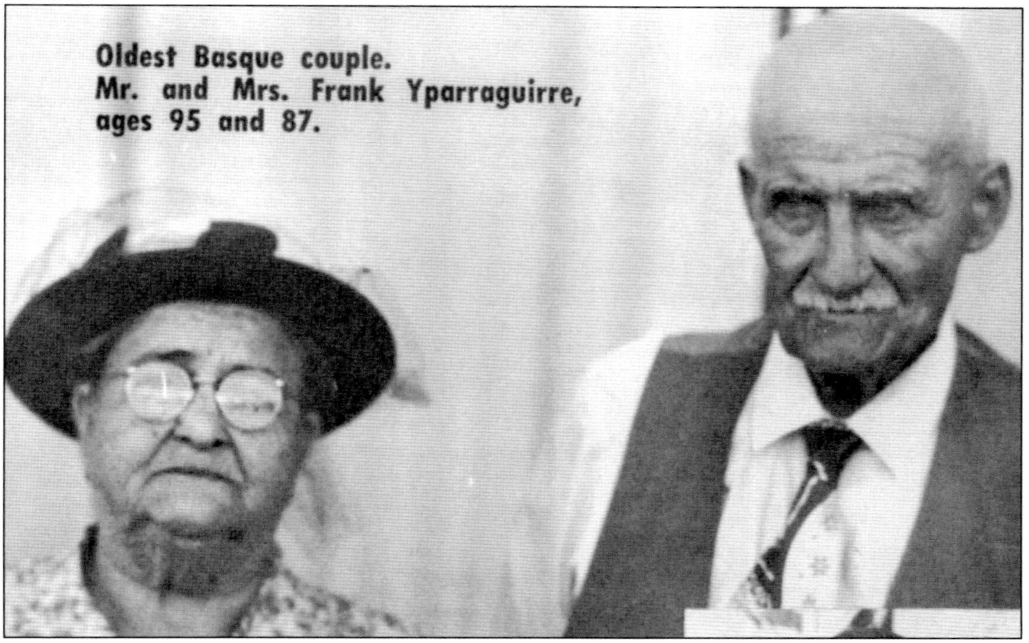

In the mid-1880s, three Yparraguirre brothers purchased the Sweetwater Ranch in Lyon County, Nevada, and turned it into a large sheep operation, which attracted many countrymen, who worked for shares instead of wages. Pictured here are Frank Yparraguirre and his wife, Josephine Arriet. (Courtesy Basque Library, UNR.)

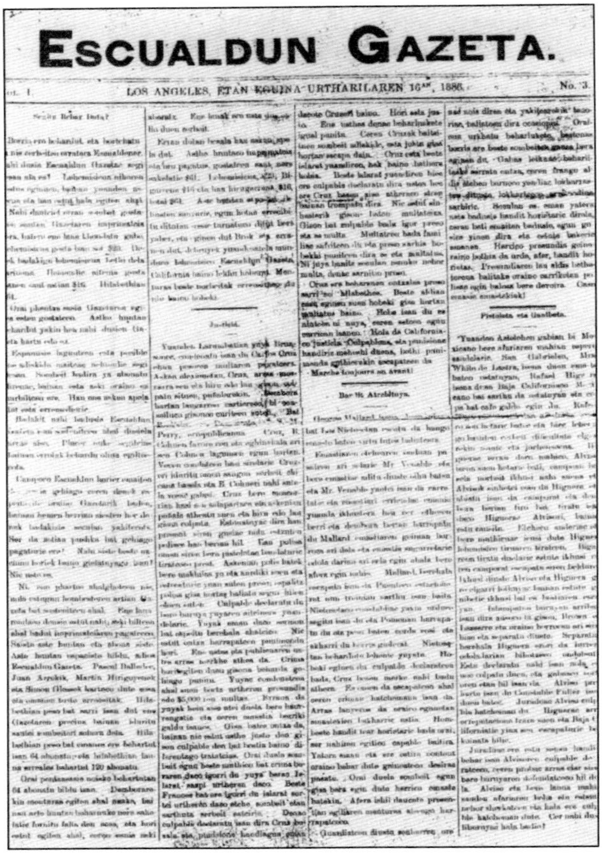

ESCUALDUN GAZETA.

LOS ANGELES, ETAN EGUINA-URTHARILAREN 16an, 1886. No. 3.

Escualdun Gazeta was Martin Bizcailuz's brave attempt in a brand-new territory—Basque media. The first issue of the weekly came out on December 24, 1885, and in the masthead of the third issue, Bizcailuz asked his few readers, "*Segida behar duta?*" (Should I continue?) That was the last issue. (Courtesy Basque Library, UNR.)

For many years, Carson City, Nevada, was the smallest capital city in America. Mining had given it life, but ranching provided more stability. In the summer months, thousands of sheep pastured in the nearby mountains while cattle fattened in the valley below. This early-1900s photograph looks west from the capitol. (Courtesy Nevada Historical Society.)

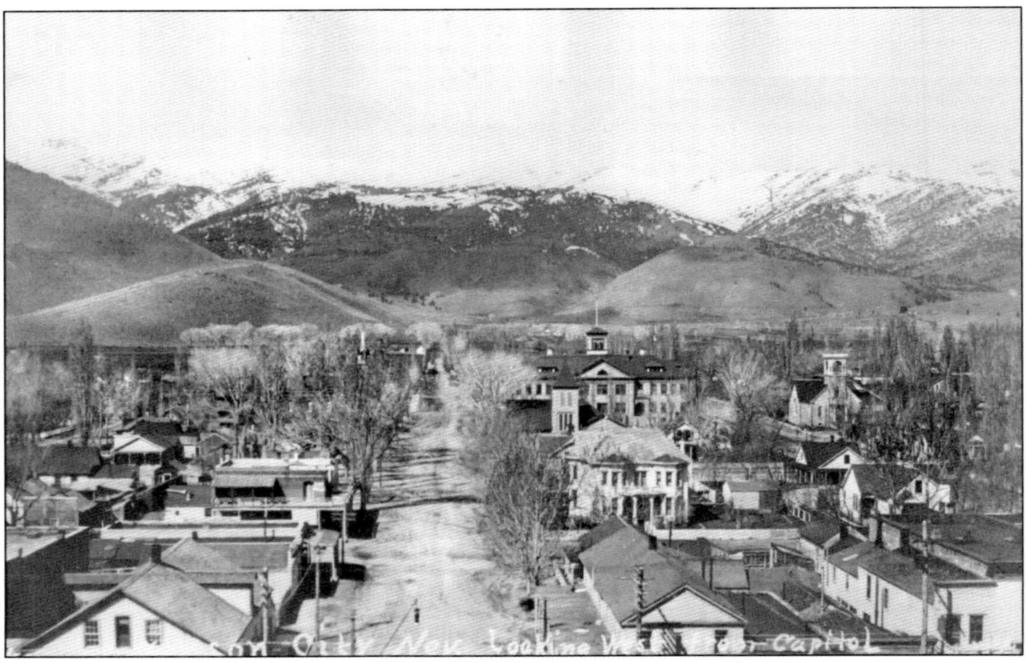

Two

Sheepherders of the Greater Reno Area

The area of study (see map on page 2) includes from Bridgeport in the south to Susanville in the north, both in California. The Basque settlement pattern did not conform to that of most other immigrant groups. They settled in towns, but as sheepherders, the Basques had to avoid urban centers altogether. Until the 1930s and 1940s, relatively few of them lived in town, and that was true about Reno and environs.

Imagine coming from a land-starved homeland to an open territory like the Old West (Nevada is still 85 percent publicly owned). The Basques recognized the West's potential for raising sheep, and they knew that a herd could be purchased with little capital. More importantly, miners needed to eat a good protein diet, as Nevada sheepman Fred Fulstone is fond of saying. It seemed like an ideal situation for determined immigrants, but they had to overcome linguistic and cultural barriers. The Old West was big but, alas, not big enough, and sheepmen and cattlemen quarreled over grazing land, especially before the U.S. Forest Service and the Bureau of Land Management came onto the scene in 1905 and 1934 respectively.

In the 1870s, the Altube brothers created the largest ranching empire in Nevada, and a few years later, the Yparraguirre brothers settled in their Sweetwater Ranch east of Bridgeport. Sheep business was relatively good until the Great Depression; however, by 1940, there was an acute shortage of herders, and associations of sheep owners sponsored Bill S.2549 to import 500 Basque sheepherders. In 1952, Sen. Patrick McCarran's bill institutionalized Basque sheepherder importation into the West, but by 1980, Basque immigration had all but ceased.

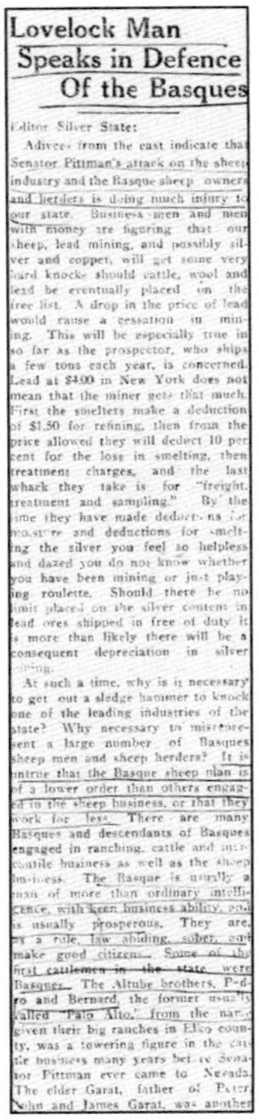

Lovelock Man Speaks in Defence Of the Basques

Editor Silver State:

Adivces from the east indicate that Senator Pittman's attack on the sheep industry and the Basque sheep owners and herders is doing much injury to our state. Business men and men with money are figuring that our sheep, lead mining, and possibly silver and copper, will get some very hard knocks should cattle, wool and lead be eventually placed on the free list. A drop in the price of lead would cause a cessation in mining. This will be especially true in so far as the prospector, who ships a few tons each year, is concerned. Lead at $4.00 in New York does not mean that the miner gets that much. First the smelters make a deduction of $1.50 for refining, then from the price allowed they will deduct 10 per cent for the loss in smelting, then treatment charges, and the last whack they take is for "freight, treatment and sampling." By the time they have made deductions for moisture and deductions for smelting the silver you feel so helpless and dazed you do not know whether you have been mining or just playing roulette. Should there be no limit placed on the silver content in lead ores shipped in free of duty it is more than likely there will be a consequent depreciation in silver mining.

At such a time, why is it necessary to get out a sledge hammer to knock one of the leading industries of the state? Why necessary to misrepresent a large number of Basques sheep men and sheep herders? It is untrue that the Basque sheep man is of a lower order than others engaged in the sheep business, or that they work for less. There are many Basques and descendants of Basques engaged in ranching, cattle and mercantile business as well as the sheep business. The Basque is usually a man of more than ordinary intelligence, with keen business ability, and is usually prosperous. They are, as a rule, law abiding, sober, and make good citizens. Some of the first cattlemen in the state were Basques. The Altube brothers, Pedro and Bernard, the former usually called "Palo Alto," from the name given their big ranches in Elko county, was a towering figure in the cattle business many years before Senator Pittman ever came to Nevada. The elder Garat, father of Peter, John and James Garat, was another

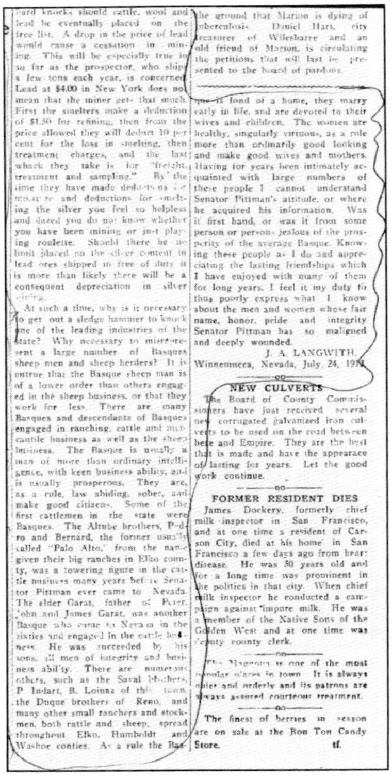

hard knocks should cattle, wool and lead be eventually placed on the free list. A drop in the price of lead would cause a cessation in mining. This will be especially true in so far as the prospector, who ships a few tons each year, is concerned. Lead at $4.00 in New York does not mean that the miner gets that much. First the smelters make a deduction of $1.50 for refining, then from the price allowed they will deduct 10 per cent for the loss in smelting, then treatment charges, and the last whack they take is for "freight, treatment and sampling." By the time they have made deductions for moisture and deductions for smelting the silver you feel so helpless and dazed you do not know whether you have been mining or just playing roulette. Should there be no limit placed on the silver content in lead ores shipped in free of duty it is more than likely there will be a consequent depreciation in silver mining.

At such a time, why is it necessary to get out a sledge hammer to knock one of the leading industries of the state? Why necessary to misrepresent a large number of Basques sheep men and sheep herders? It is untrue that the Basque sheep man is of a lower order than others engaged in the sheep business, or that they work for less. There are many Basques and descendants of Basques engaged in ranching, cattle and mercantile business as well as the sheep business. The Basque is usually a man of more than ordinary intelligence, with keen business ability, and is usually prosperous. They are, as a rule, law abiding, sober, and make good citizens. Some of the first cattlemen in the state were Basques. The Altube brothers, Pedro and Bernard, the former usually called "Palo Alto," from the name given their big ranches in Elko county, was a towering figure in the cattle business many years before Senator Pittman ever came to Nevada. The elder Garat, father of Peter, John and James Garat, was another Basque who came to Nevada in the sixties and engaged in the cattle business. He was succeeded by his sons, all men of integrity and business ability. There are numerous others, such as the Saval brothers, P. Indart, B. Loinaz of this town, the Duque brothers of Reno, and many other small ranchers and stockmen, both cattle and sheep, spread throughout Elko, Humboldt and Washoe conties. As a rule the Basque is fond of a home, they marry early in life, and are devoted to their wives and children. The women are healthy, singularly virtuous, as a rule more than ordinarily good looking and make good wives and mothers. Having for years been intimately acquainted with large numbers of these people I cannot understand Senator Pittman's attitude, or where he acquired his information. Was it first hand, or was it from some person or persons jealous of the prosperity of the average Basque. Knowing these people as I do and appreciating the lasting friendships which I have enjoyed with many of them for long years, I feel it my duty to thus poorly express what I know about the men and women whose fair name, honor, pride and integrity Senator Pittman has so maligned and deeply wounded.

J. A. LANGWITH.

Winnemucca, Nevada, July, 24, 191

the ground that Marion is dying of tuberculosis. Daniel Hart, city treasurer of Wilesbarre and an old friend of Marion, is circulating the petitions that will last be presented to the board of pardons.

NEW CULVERTS

The Board of County Commissioners have just received several new corrugated galvanized iron culverts to be used on the road between here and Empire. They are the best that is made and have the appearace of lasting for years. Let the good work continue.

FORMER RESIDENT DIES

James Dockery, formerly chief milk inspector in San Francisco, and at one time a resident of Carson City, died at his home in San Francisco a few days ago from heart disease. He was 50 years old and for a long time was prominent in the politics in that city. When chief milk inspector he conducted a campaign against impure milk. He was a member of the Native Sons of the Golden West and at one time was deputy county clerk.

The Magnolia is one of the most popular places in town. It is always quiet and orderly and its patrons are always assured courteous treatment.

The finest of berries in season are on sale at the Bon Ton Candy Store. tf.

Nevada senator Key Pittman attacked the Basques because he said they worked for less than others. J. A. Langwith of Winnemucca wrote to the *Silver State* and defended the Basques as sober, industrious, and good citizens and reminded the senator that the Altubes and the Garats had arrived in Nevada long before he had. (Courtesy Basque Library, UNR.)

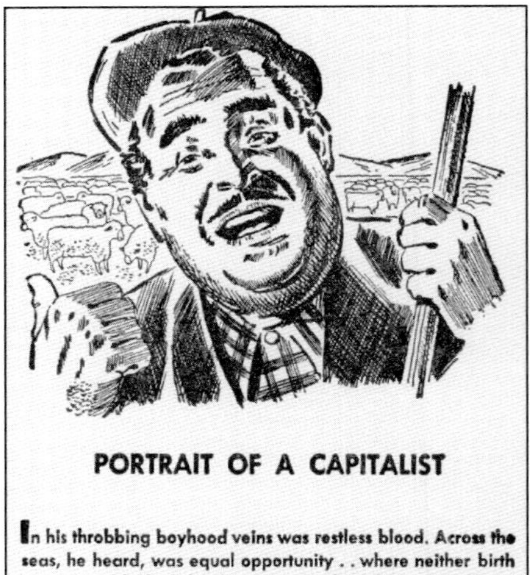

Boy, things have changed, haven't they? The Bank of America would likely not run this advertisement today. It doesn't say this capitalist is a Basque, but the beret and the sheep leave no doubt about his identity. The advertisement ran on the first page of the 1952 *California Livestock News*. Perhaps this is what Senator Pittman was really talking about. (Courtesy Basque Library, UNR.)

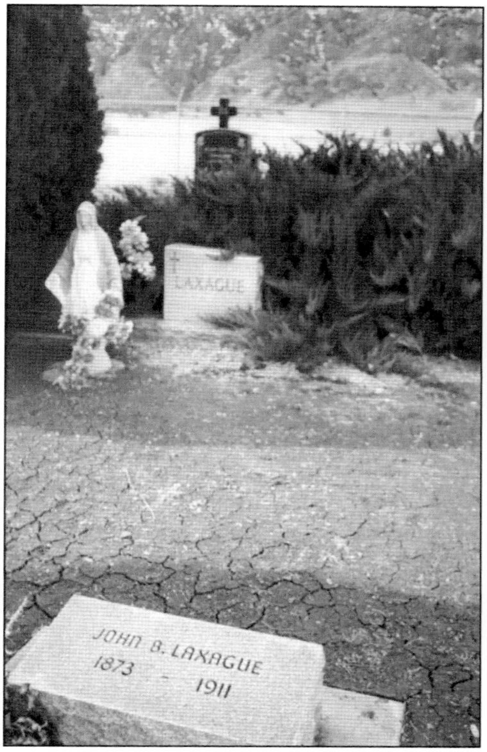

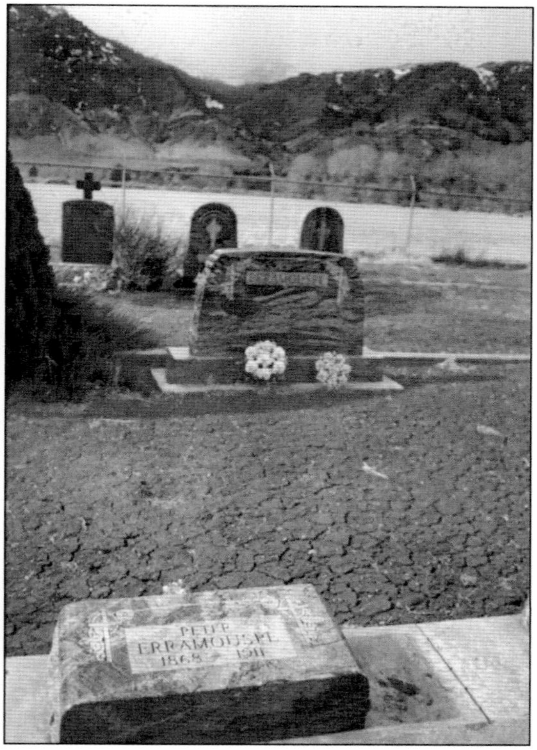

Three Basque sheepherders—Pete Erramouspe, John Laxague, and Bertrand Indiano—killed in January 1911 in northern Washoe County, rest side-by-side in the Eagleville, California, cemetery. A bit farther lies Englishman Harry Cambron, who was also killed. History knows the incident not as "sheepherders murdered" but as "the Last Indian Massacre." Indeed, a party of Shoshone Indians was blamed for the crime, chased by a posse, and almost totally exterminated near Golconda, Nevada. However, some Nevada historians suspect the perpetrators may have been cowboys.

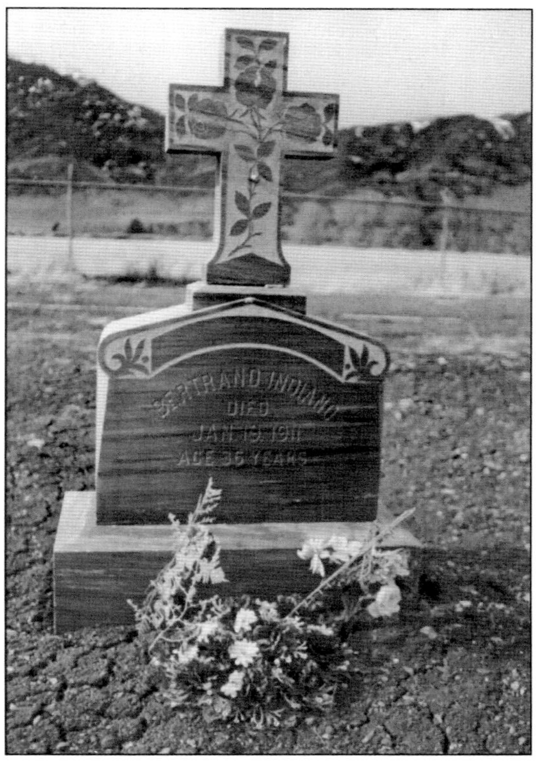

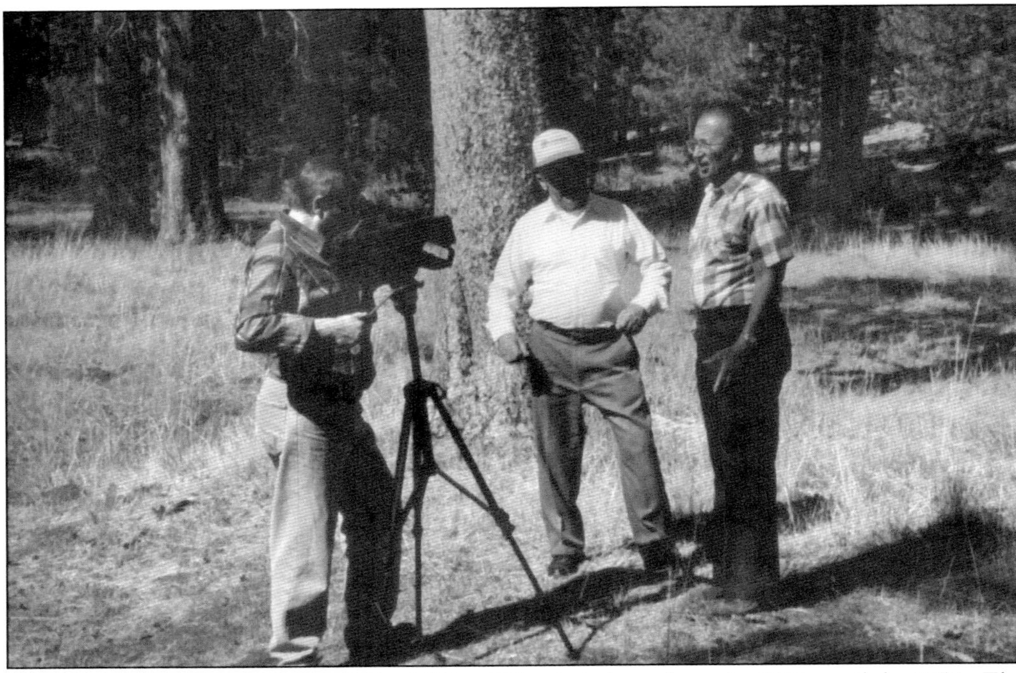

Martin Gallues of Reno managed "Uncle" Dan Wheeler's sheep from the 1910s until the 1950s. The sheep camp at Kyburz Flat north of Truckee, California, had three buildings, a year-round spring, scales, and an oven. It was the summer home for the Gallues family. In this 1992 photograph, Al Gallues (right), son of Martin, and Hilario Ortabe (middle) are being interviewed at the camp by the author. (Courtesy Tahoe National Forest.)

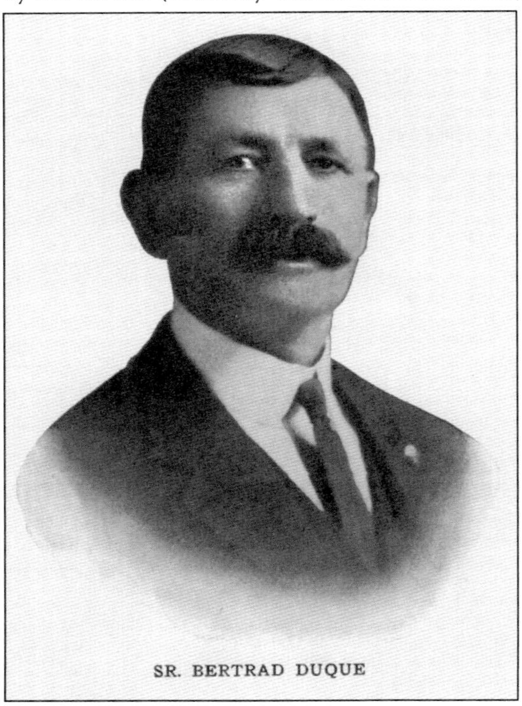

Bertrand Duque was born in Zuberoa on December 25, 1860, and in 1885, he landed in New York City from where he proceeded west. After working at a sheep ranch near San Francisco, in 1889, he left for Elko, Nevada. Having accumulated more capital, he established a large ranching operation 90 miles north of Reno. In 1905, he married Catherine Miramon, and they had two children. (Courtesy Sol Silen.)

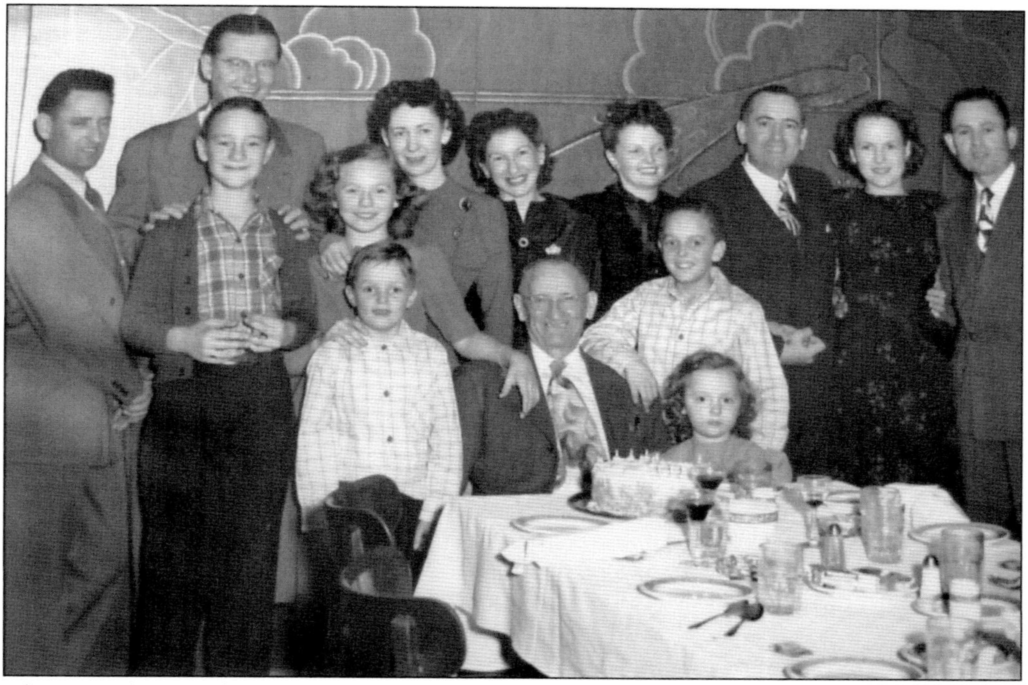

This 1949 photograph of the Gastañaga family shows, from left to right, (first row) Jose Gastañaga (G.), grandpa Jose V. G., Harvey G., and Marylynne Walker; (second row) Richard Zuroff and Joanne Brackett; (third row) Gene Gastañaga, Dr. Wally "Doc" Walker, Bernie G., Ellen G., Lola G., Martin G., Louise G./Walker, and Jake G. (Courtesy Eugene Gastañaga.)

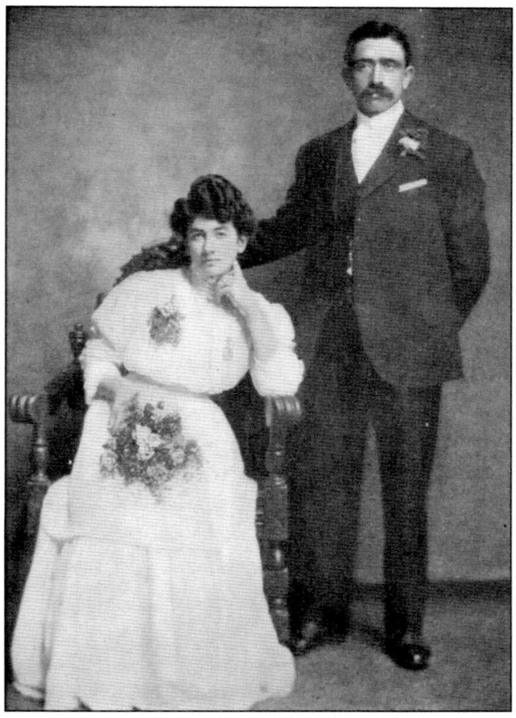

Antonio Saralegui was born in Navarre on February 21, 1874, and at 22 years of age he came first to California and then Nevada. After years of hard work, he was able to own a 5,000-acre sheep and cattle ranch north of Reno—still known as Saralegui Ranch. In 1907, he married Carmen Errecart, and they had three sons and one daughter. (Courtesy Sol Silen.)

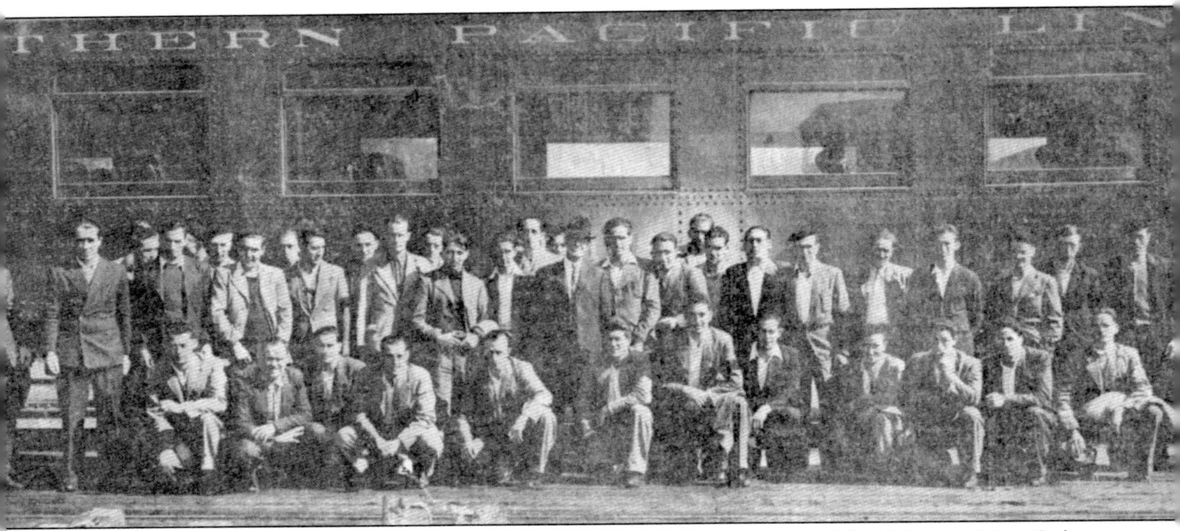

These 44 Navarrese sailed from Bilbao and arrived in Reno on June 22, 1944, via New Orleans. After posing, berets and all, for a historic photograph, they proceeded to the Santa Fe Basque Hotel and Restaurant for a hearty breakfast, and then without further ado, they each departed to their employer's ranch. By the following day, many of them were herding sheep, alone, and shocked by life's swift turn. They were recruited by the Nevada Range Sheep Owners Association, presided by Fred Danger of Minden and their agent Martin Goñi in Navarre. (Courtesy *Reno Evening Gazette*.)

This cancelled U.S. passport hangs from the wall of Arrascada and Arrascada Law Office in Reno. Dated 1922, it belonged to Leroy Arrascada's grandfather Ignacio. That year he took his family to the Basque Country, but when they entered Spain, an annoyed immigration agent destroyed his American passport (notice the hole in the seal) as he yelled at him, "You are not American, but Spanish."

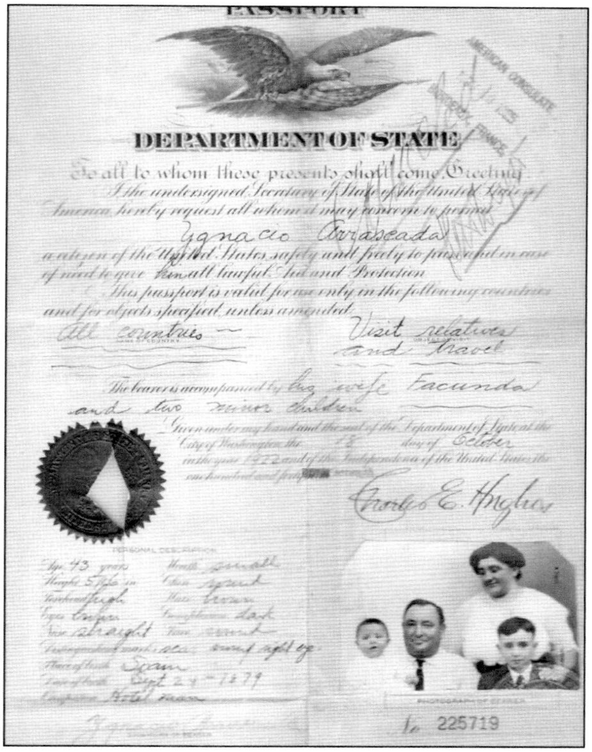

DEPARTMENT OF STATE

To all to whom these presents shall come, Greeting:

I the undersigned Secretary of State of the United States of America hereby request all whom it may concern to permit Ygnacio Arrascada a citizen of the United States safely and freely to pass and in case of need to give him all lawful Aid and Protection

This passport is valid for use only in the following countries and for objects specified unless amended

All countries — Visit relatives and travel

The bearer is accompanied by his wife Facunda and two minor children

Given under my hand and the seal of the Department of State at the City of Washington the day of October in the year 1922

Charles E. Hughes

Age 43 years

Place of birth Spain

Date of birth Sept 24 – 1879

Occupation Hotel man

No. 225719

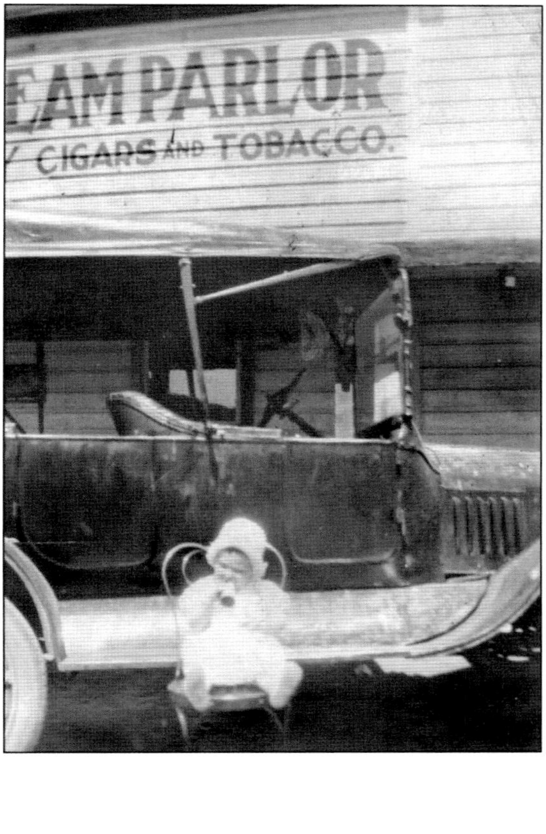

Martin Orriaga, after herding sheep for more than 10 years, set up an ice cream parlor in Wellington, Nevada, with his wife, Josephine. Photographed here is their daughter Irene in 1923 in front of Martin's Buick. The business advertised "Candy Cigars and Tobacco," but during Prohibition sometimes such establishments were fronts for bootlegging, Irene (Orriaga) Arbeloa said.

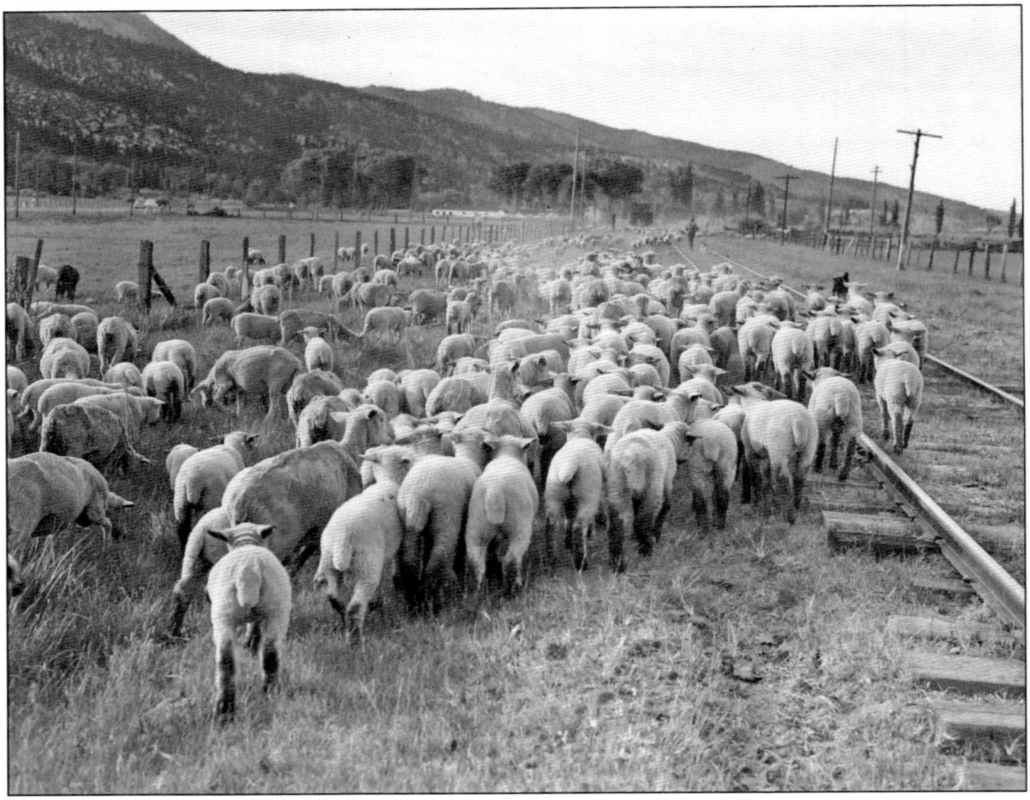

Nature was at times the sheepherder's adversary, but this photograph captured a moment many dreaded—crossing the railroad tracks. Trains ran more often in the old days; they appeared without warning, and their brakes could not stop fast enough. Meanwhile, some sheep were in trouble. (Courtesy Special Collections, UNR.)

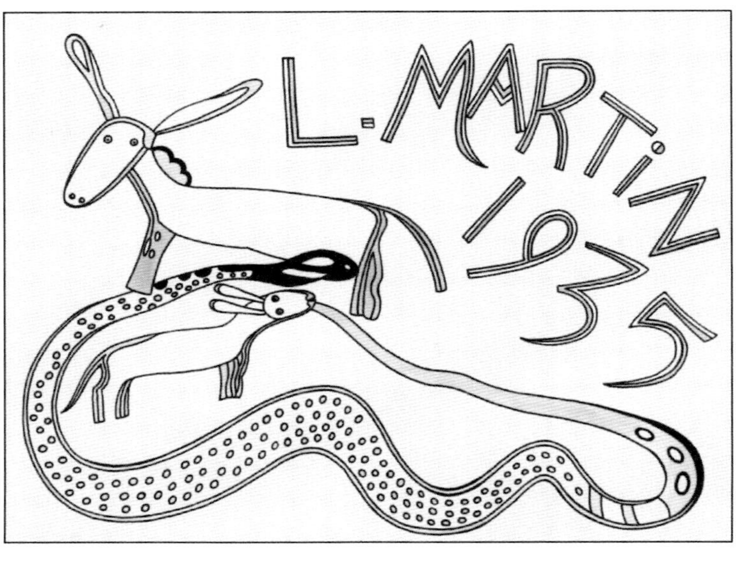

Some may wonder if the carver of this singular depiction—a donkey nursing a large snake—was deranged. He was simply evoking his ancient culture. As a child growing up in the Basque Country, this author was told of cows nursing snakes and more, such as snakes taking advantage of sleeping women. The drawing is by Frances Wallace and Hans Reiss. (Courtesy Special Collections, UNR.)

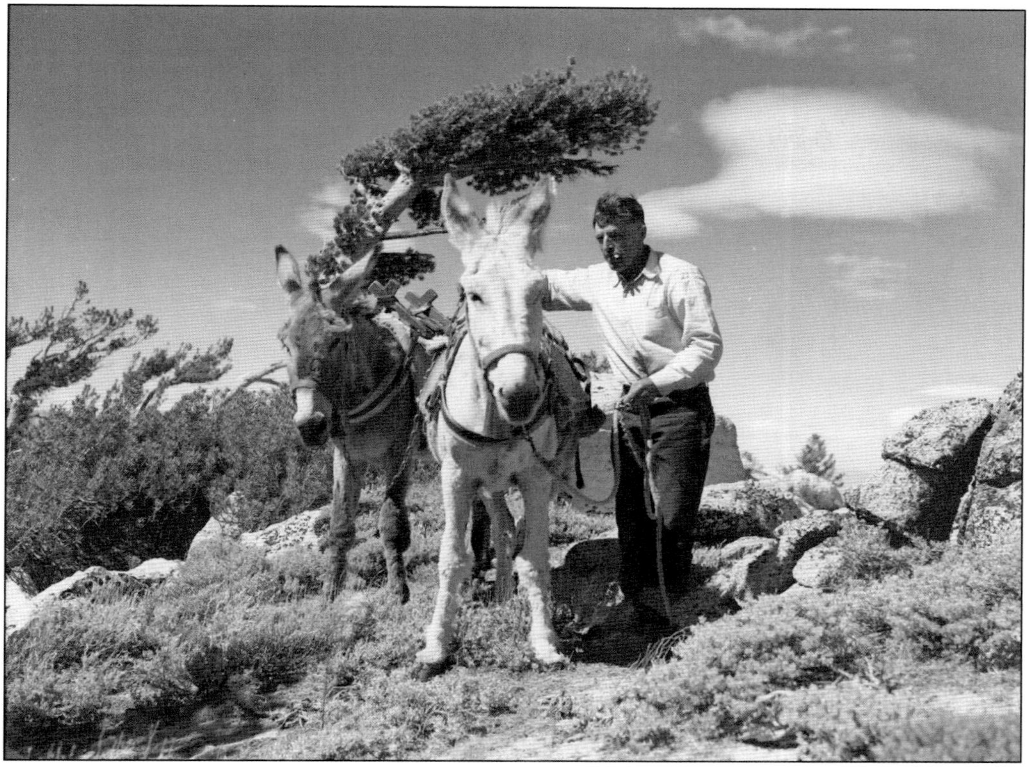

This image of Pierre Laxalt, Dominique Laxalt's brother, with pack mules high in the Sierra above Lake Tahoe, is dated probably to the 1930s. In a rugged and roadless terrain, mules were the best haulers, followed by donkeys. In the Mount Rose area, there is a place called *astozulo* (donkey hollow) where donkeys lost their footing sometimes.

A sheepherder carved this road sign, interpreted by Frances Wallace and Hans Reiss. This type of information (12 miles to Truckee, California) was very important to herders who were new to the area. Truckee, the railhead for shipping the lambs in the fall, was an important destination in the sheepherder's world. (Courtesy Special Collections, UNR.)

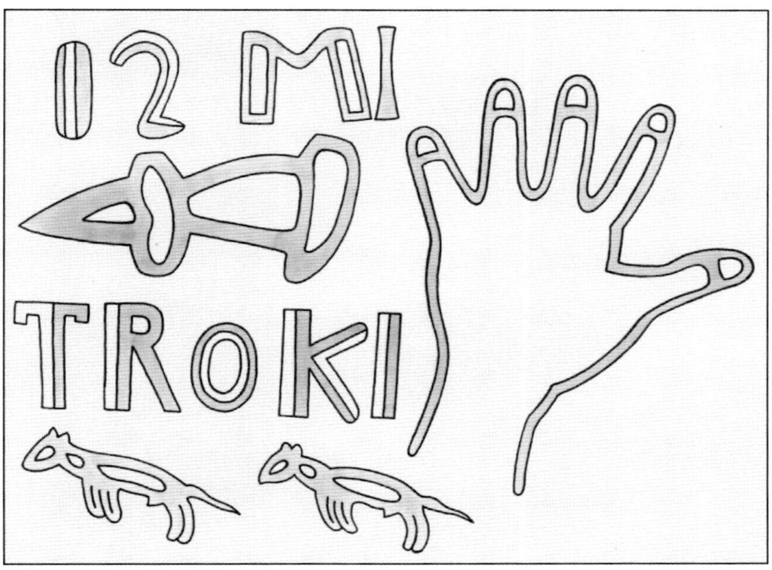

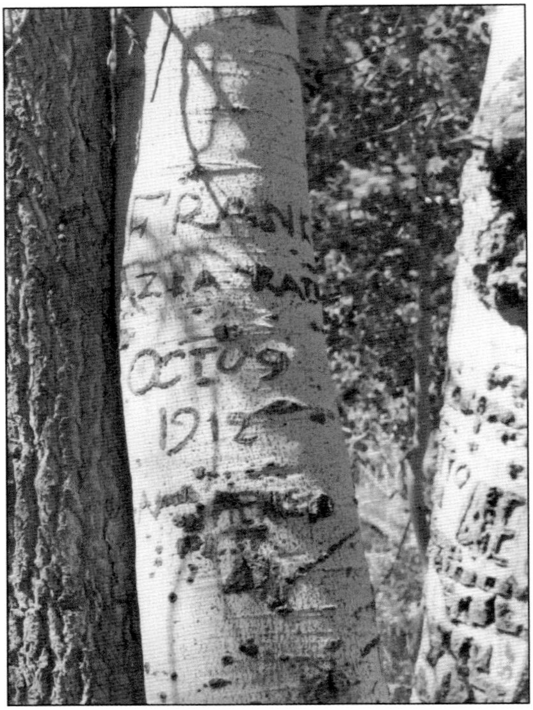

Frank Azkarate carved this into an aspen in 1912. At the time, and even later, little did he suspect that one day in the 1930s he would own a sheep ranch on the Truckee River, a few miles east of Sparks, Nevada. In 1967, Joe Conforte, a Sicilian immigrant, bought the ranch and turned it into the world-famous bordello the Mustang Ranch, still in business. (Courtesy the Landa family.)

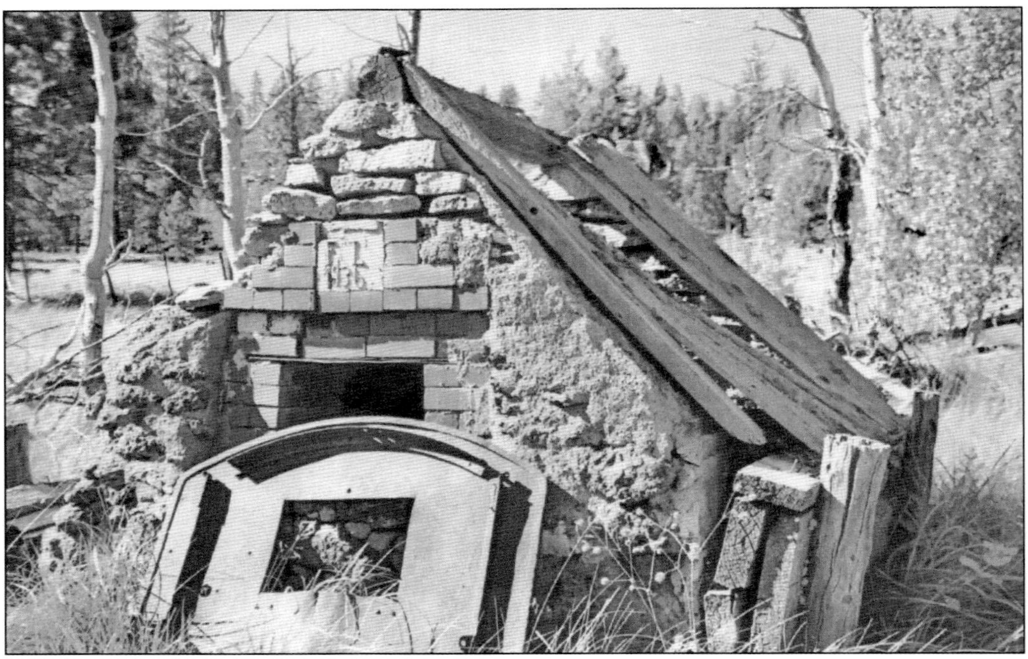

This Basque oven at the Red Clover Sheep Camp, Plumas National Forest, California, was built by F. L. in 1936. Some people call it the Poko Sheep Camp, after sheepman Juanes Poko, whose earliest tree carving recorded in the Modoc National Forest is dated 1892. Poko moved to Reno and built a fine house where the Wells Fargo Bank is located today on California and Arlington Streets. (Courtesy Judy Snyder.)

The Peyron brothers, Daniel L. (center) and Henry B. (right), natives of the French Alps, have a story worth telling. In 1911, Daniel created a beautiful aspen carving in Douglas County, Nevada, and in 2003, his daughter from Virginia and her daughter from Arizona brought their families and had an unforgettable day hiking and finding the carving. The visit was repeated in 2008 with an expanded group of siblings. (Courtesy Charlotte Harmon.)

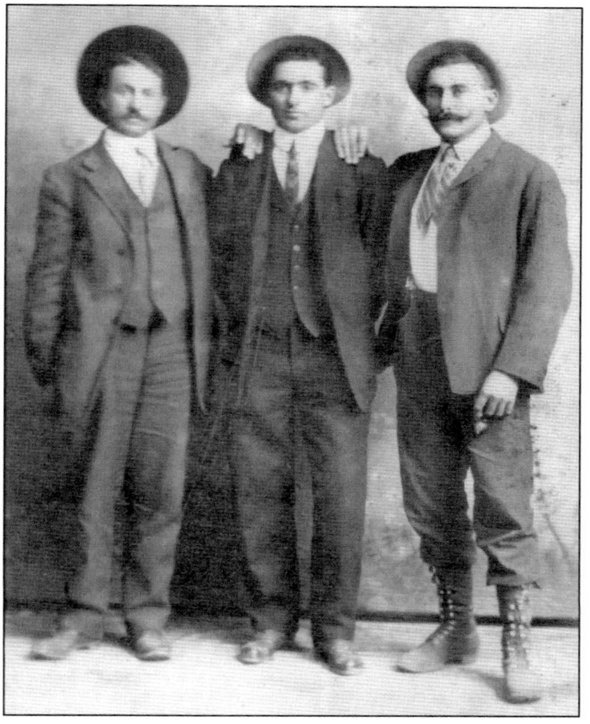

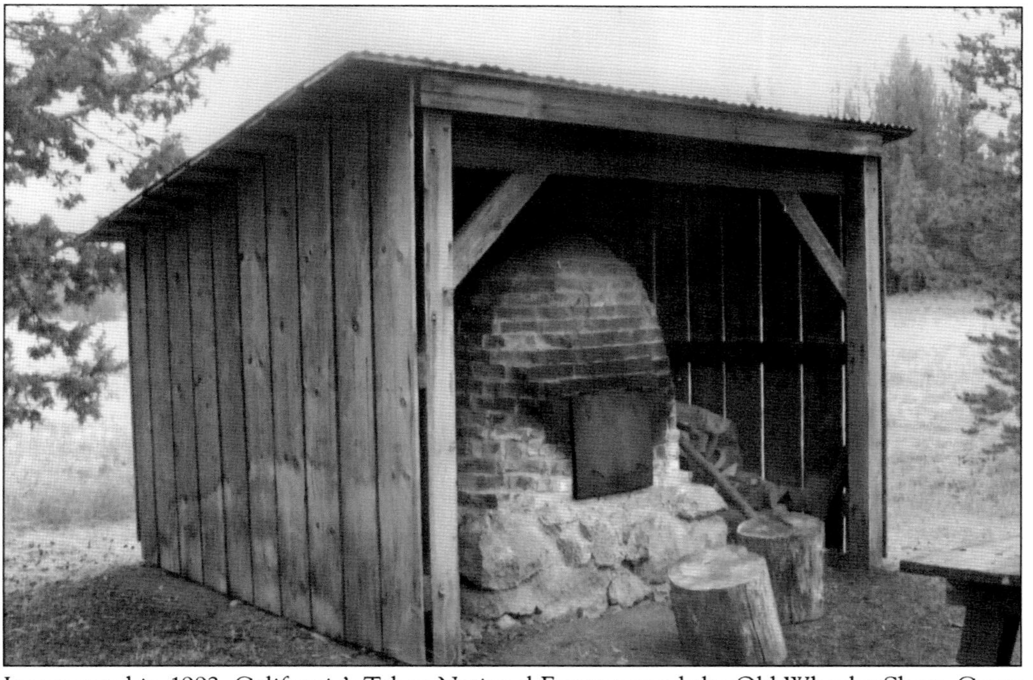

Inaugurated in 1992, California's Tahoe National Forest turned the Old Wheeler Sheep Camp at Kyburz Flat into an interpretative area. Petroglyphs, and the site of a 1860s roadside inn found nearby, are part of the cultural area. The 1929 bread oven at the sheep camp had been reduced to rubble, but in 1992 it was rebuilt by an army of volunteers.

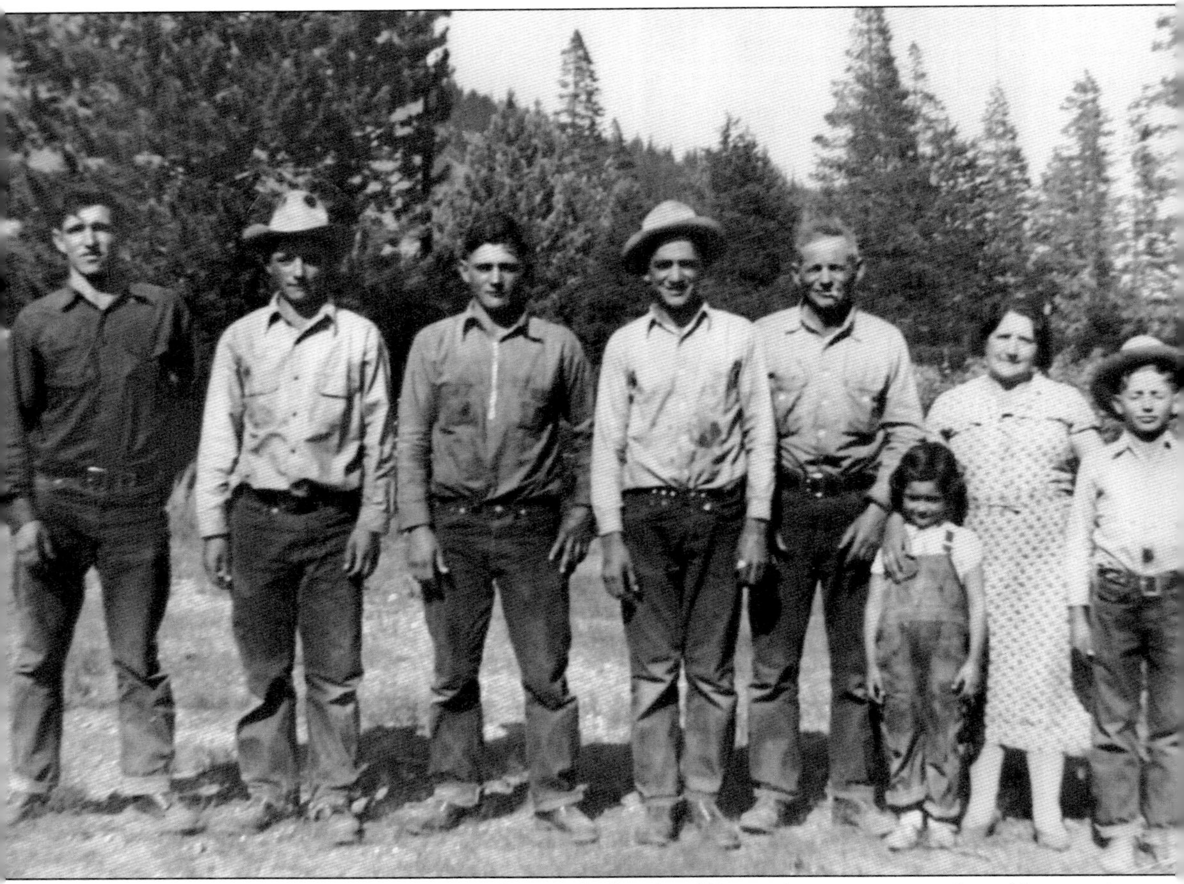

A proud family of true sheepmen is the Landa family of Reno. Anastasio came from Navarre in 1896, and his wife, Juanita Arrupe, came from Bizkaia to work in Reno's Hotel Español, where they met and were married in 1912. They raised five sons and one daughter; from left to right are Steve, March, Joe, John, Anastasio, Julia, Juanita Arrupe, and Anastasio "Anas" Jr. (Courtesy Anas Landa family.)

Three

Aspen Carvings

How likely was it that a small group of largely uneducated immigrants, known in their homeland for their little inclination for writing, would in the host country embark in a widespread record-keeping effort? How likely was it that sheepherders, stranded with their sheep in the high country, would create and sustain a tradition of carving aspens? In the process, they left half a million or more very personal documents of their wanderings throughout the American West.

Perhaps it was destiny because for thousands of years the ancestors of the Basques painted and carved the walls of Paleolithic caves. Perhaps their ancient artistic light rekindled itself in the remote Sierra, and in a monumental circle they reconnected prehistory with history. Paper was foreign to these Basques, while wood and stone were an integral part of their Pyrenean culture. Their Stone Age ancestors used stone tools, while the sheepherder used a pocketknife to carve trees, as well as a nail, a sharp stone, or the point of a bullet. The soft, smooth bark of the aspen is compliant, and the trees became the keepers of the herders' most intimate secrets.

Though tree carving is a universal activity, the sheepherders created a unique phenomenon. Perhaps 30,000 "arborglyphs" have been recorded in the Western states (the author has videotaped 27,000), the great majority of them in Nevada and California. It is the biggest little secret of the American West. European Basques transmitted culture orally, but in the United States, they switched to the written medium. It was yet another example of profound change that can occur when a culture is introduced to a new environment.

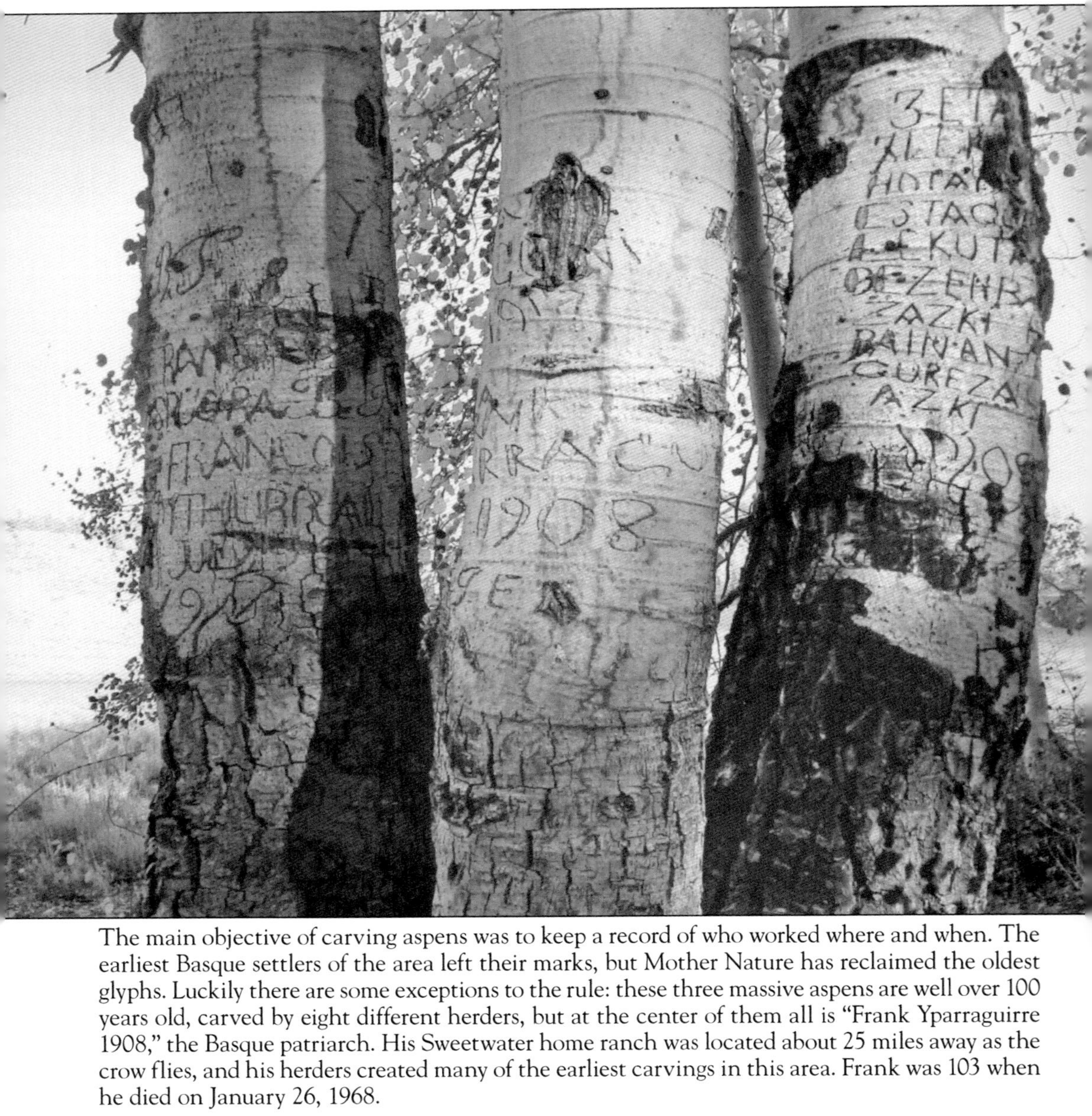

The main objective of carving aspens was to keep a record of who worked where and when. The earliest Basque settlers of the area left their marks, but Mother Nature has reclaimed the oldest glyphs. Luckily there are some exceptions to the rule: these three massive aspens are well over 100 years old, carved by eight different herders, but at the center of them all is "Frank Yparraguirre 1908," the Basque patriarch. His Sweetwater home ranch was located about 25 miles away as the crow flies, and his herders created many of the earliest carvings in this area. Frank was 103 when he died on January 26, 1968.

The herders used the aspen trees as paper and their pocketknives as pens. One would not pick a dirty and wrinkled paper to write on. Similarly, the herders picked mature yet smooth-barked trees to carve. Every person had his own distinct style, but the chief idea was to leave behind an impression of the herder's passing. Here it is carved, "*Kadet Kurutchet 1932 1933.*"

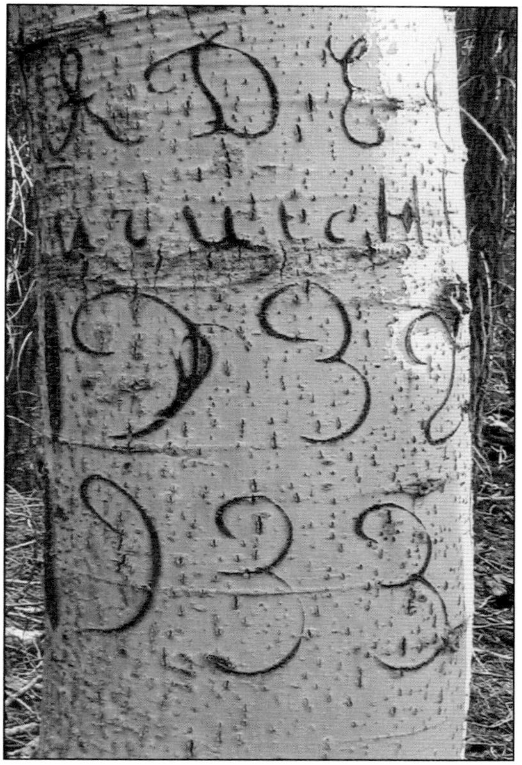

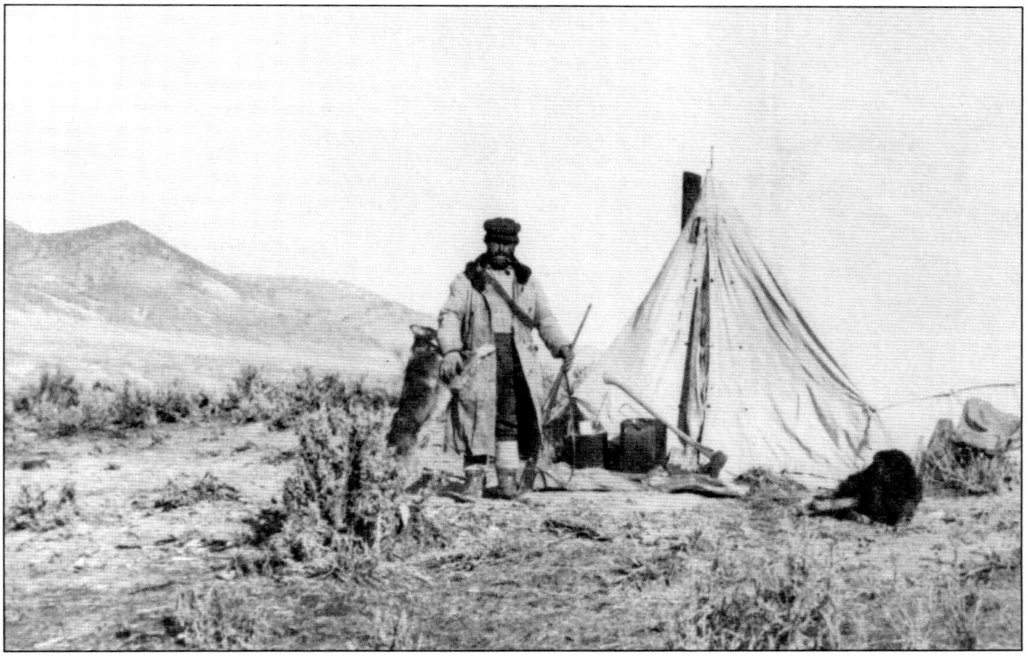

Talk about an image that conveys isolation. Look at the worldly possessions of Ramon Arrizabalaga of Araba, here herding sheep in the winter of 1911. Yet he has the aura of strength and self-reliance; all he needed was a rifle, his dog, tent, axe, and the stove. (Courtesy Joan Arrizabalaga.)

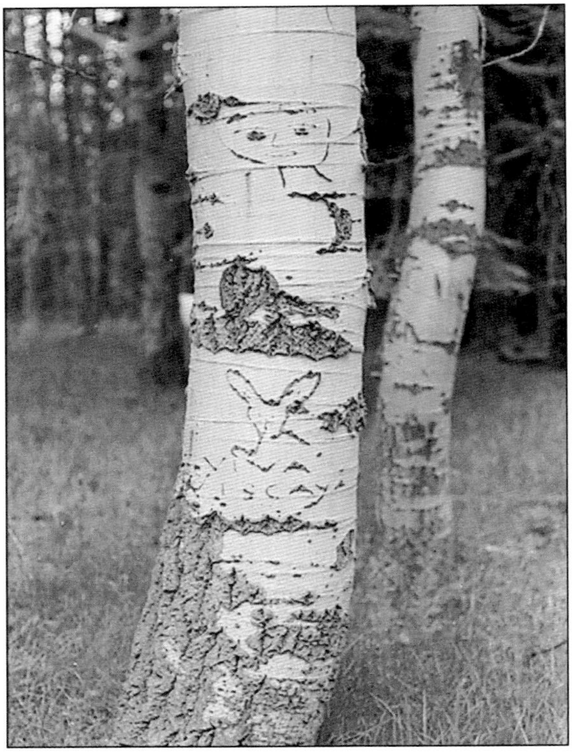

This unidentified carver started his work with a female face, then a cute rabbit, and ended it with "*Viva Viscaya*" (Long live Biscay), a nostalgic statement, while the female face is indicative of what else was on his mind. He was a Bizkaian with some artistic talent.

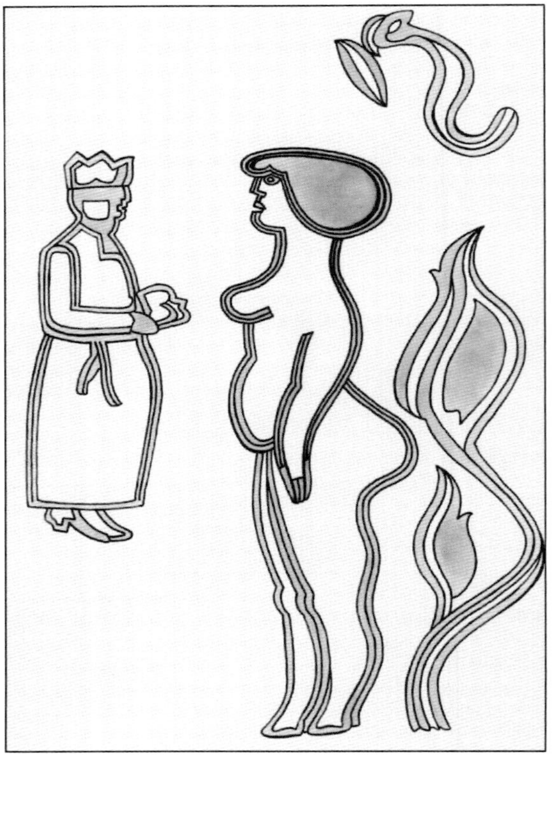

This 1930s carving is one of the most unusual ever found, faithfully enhanced by Frances Wallace and Hans Reiss. The naked woman is already burning in hell, but the chubby priest facing her, armed with the holy book, will save her. Or perhaps he is condemning her to hell for her sexual sins, underscored by her nakedness. (Courtesy Special Collections, UNR.)

This and the previous image were found on the Nevada side of Lake Tahoe. The photograph reveals a typical representation of the female body, with ample curves and high heels, but armless. The sheepherders deliberately accentuated the male and female bodies.

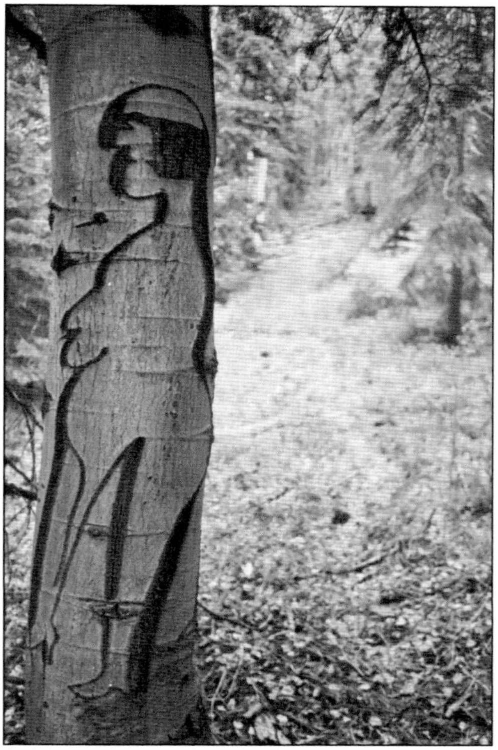

The carvings are dated mostly in Spanish, and unless one knows Basque surnames, the viewer might take *dia* as meaning "day," which by the way would fit well with the rest of this carving; but in reality, *dia* is the ending of Francisco's last name, Ezcurdia. He dated it August 26, 1911, his fourth year on the range.

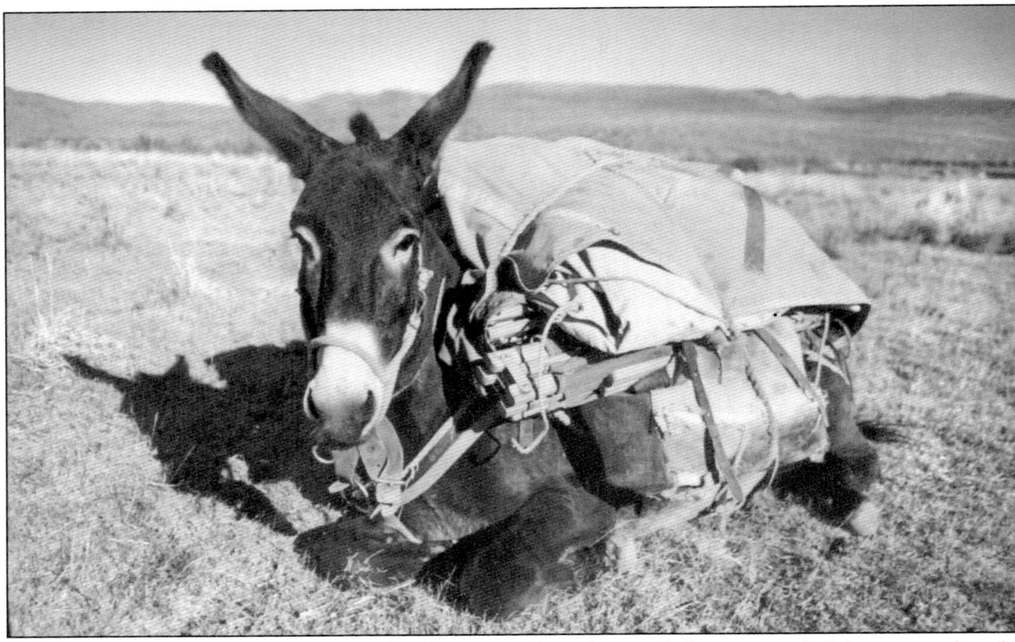

This is the sheepherder's "transport," hauling everything he needed to accomplish his one task—the care of 1,500 ewes and their lambs. Mules are incredibly strong and reliable, but they can be utterly stubborn as well, and nobody seems to know why. Here this smart animal sees a chance to rest his weary legs and pose for the photographer. The herder's cot is visible under the tarp.

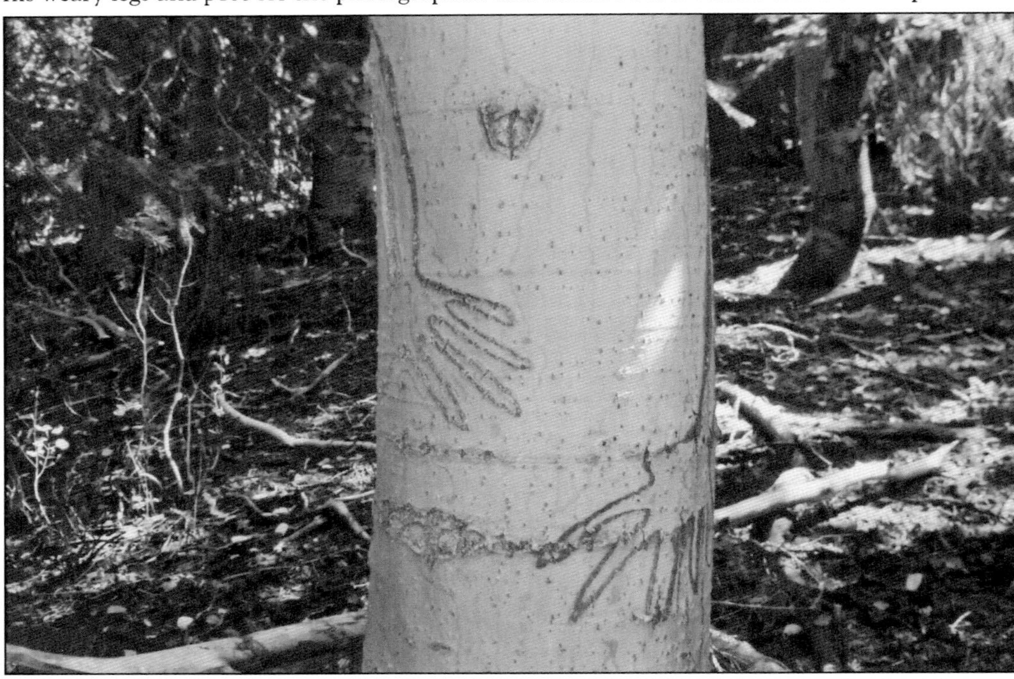

An unknown herder left this carving, which 50 years later could have inspired a "tree hugger." The author is mystified by the strange findings on trees from California to Minnesota and from Texas to Washington State and beyond. Was this the work of uneducated sheepherders?

Some unknown sheepherder carved this *ikurrina* (Basque flag), by which he made a political statement of adherence to the *Zazpiak Bat* (The Seven Are One) slogan. Interestingly, this motto rings truer among Basque Americans than among their European kin, who remain divided between autonomies and two centralized nation-states.

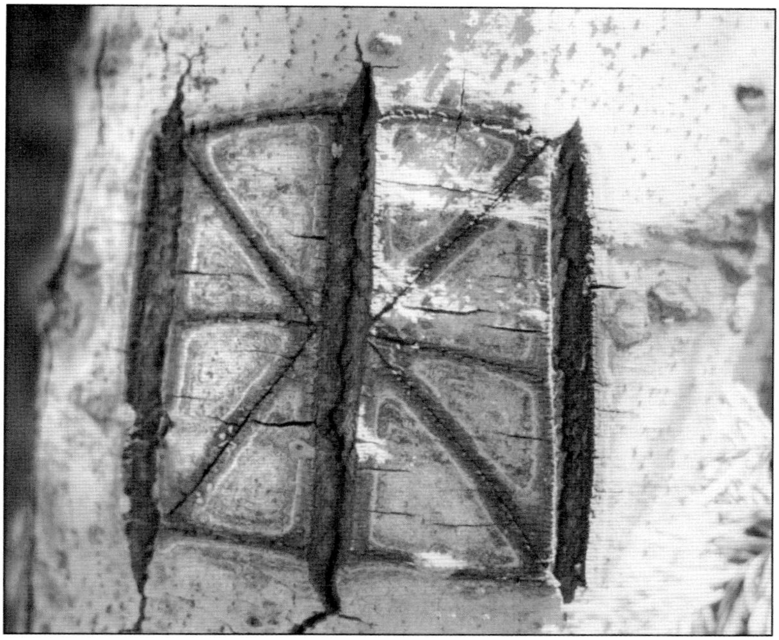

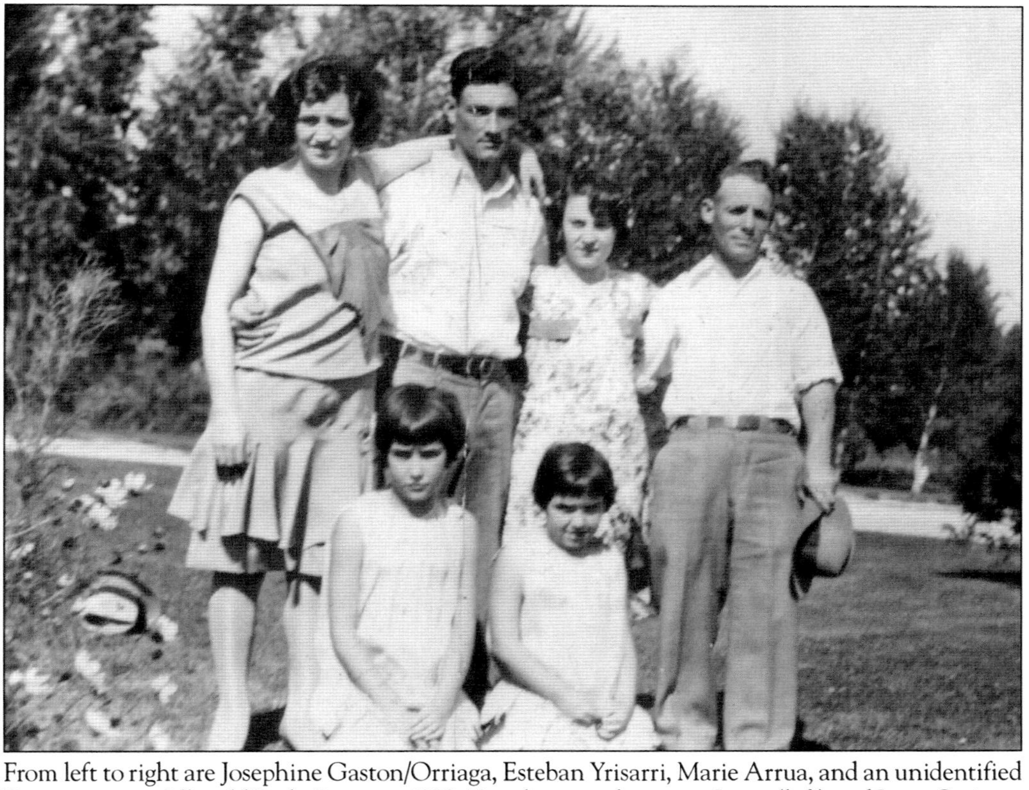

From left to right are Josephine Gaston/Orriaga, Esteban Yrisarri, Marie Arrua, and an unidentified Basque man in Idlewild Park, Reno, in 1933. Kneeling are the sisters Irene (left) and Lucy Orriaga. In the 1930s, in just one small mountain range, Yrisarri carved his name over 100 times. (Courtesy Irene Arbeloa.)

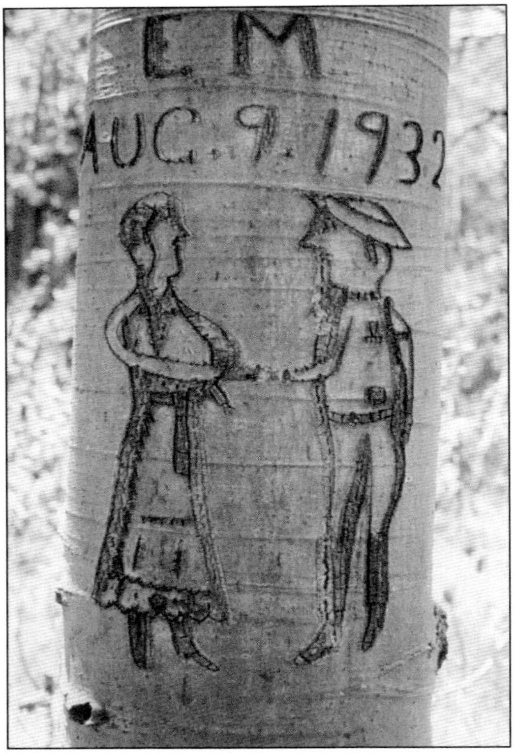

E. M. (Etienne Maizkorena) was a master carver of male and female figures with detailed clothing, animals, and horsemen. He did not carve nudes. The couple at left represents two dancers in Basque folk costume. The nude woman below, by Jose Mitjana, is a much more typical pursuit by lonely sheepherders. Asked why he carved, one herder answered, "To kill the time." (At left, courtesy Ana Parker.)

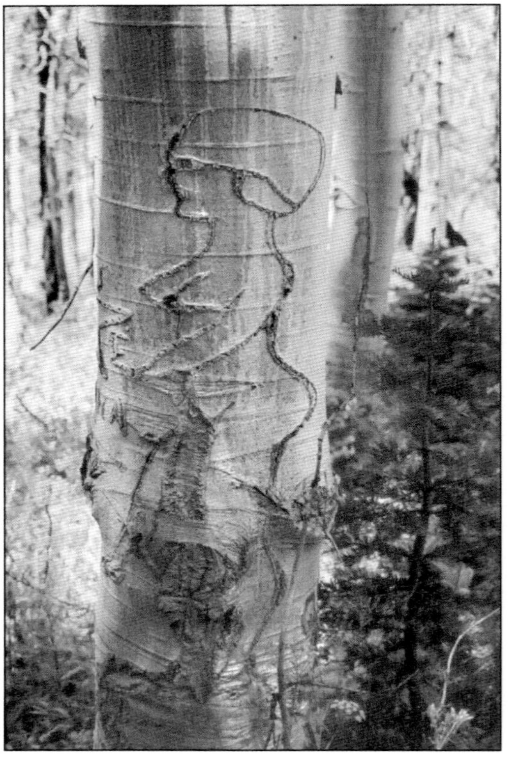

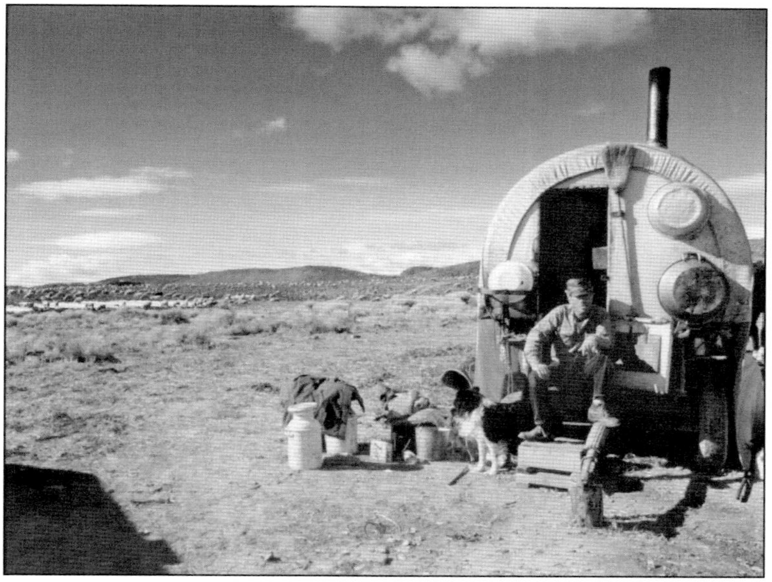

Lorenzo Alakano and his dog enjoy the late-1960s afternoon sun on the winter range (notice the snow bank) in Nevada. The two important items inside the sheep wagon were the bed and the fireplace. The largest hanging pan was used to wash clothes, dishes, or whatever. The cans contained water and the bucket grain. (Courtesy Basque Library, UNR.)

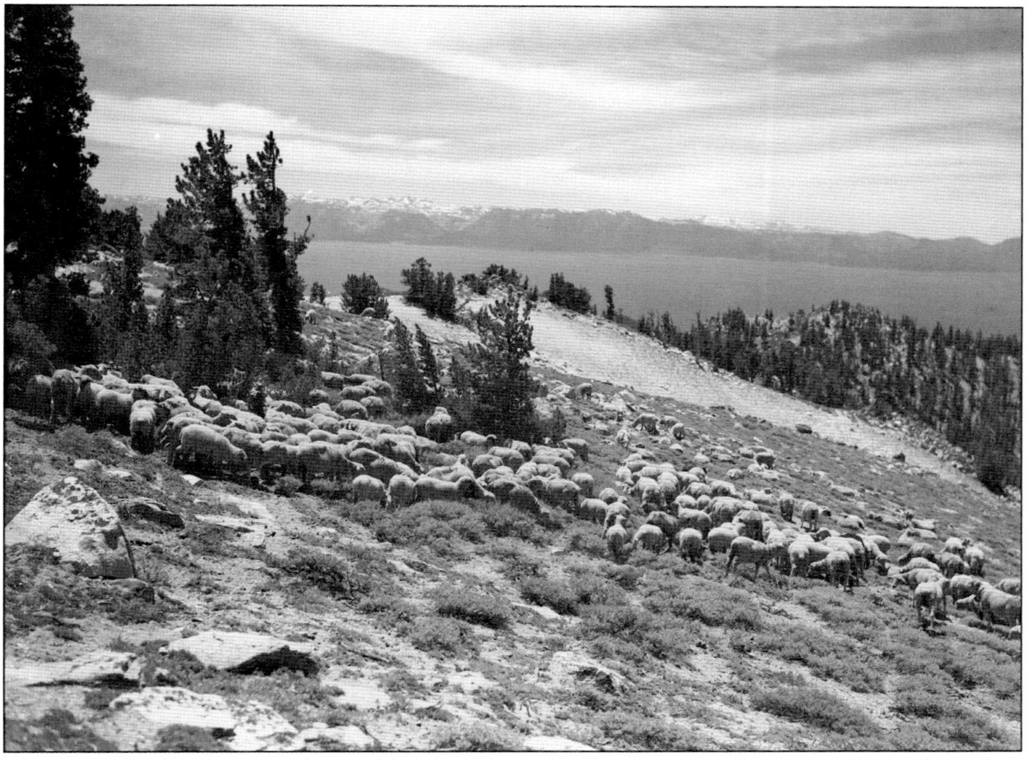

The camera is facing west at beautiful Lake Tahoe. People pay money for the privilege of spending time in the High Sierra, but did the sheepherders enjoy the great outdoors? Yes, of course, but one can also get tired of eating steak every day. Loneliness was their number one issue, and they preferred to be at the bar with friends than here enjoying the view. (Courtesy Special Collections, UNR.)

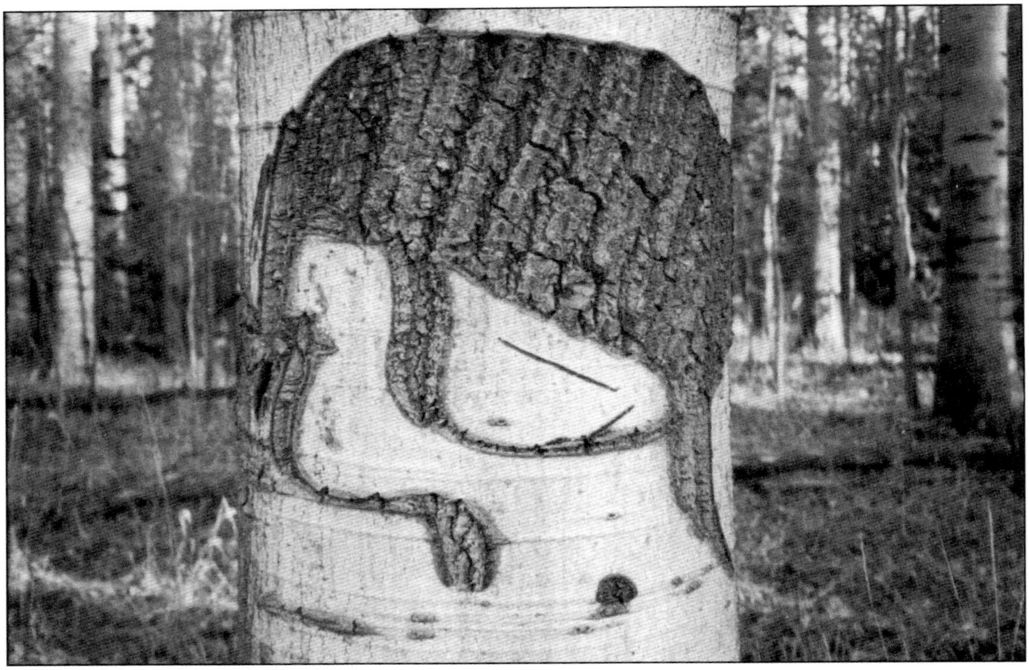

One sheepherder was in love with this woman, whose image he carved dozens of times, always with the same features: the strong chin, the hairline, and the flapper haircut covering her ears. It appears she "worked" in Reno and several herders had eyes for her. The earliest figures of the lady begin in 1929 and proceed unabated until the 1950s.

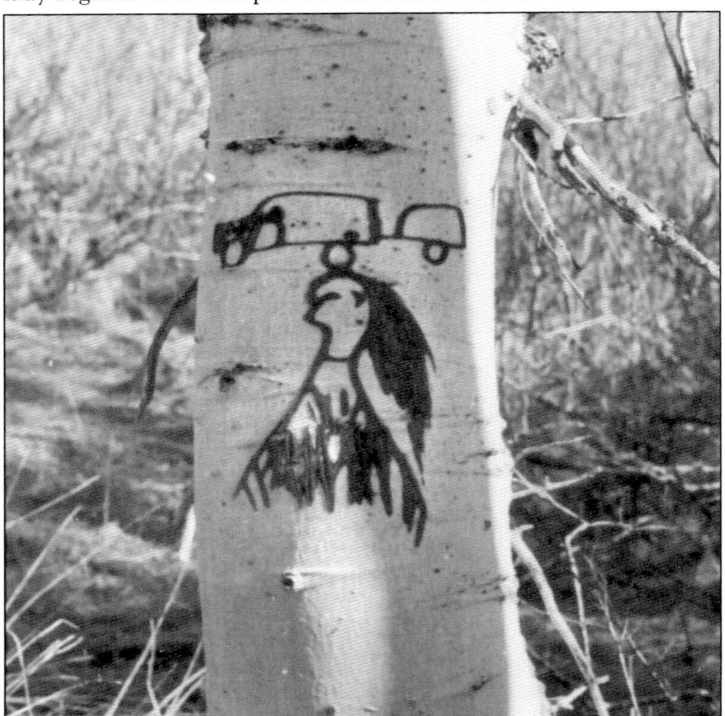

This sheepherder knows what he wants. One day, he is going to leave the sheep and the mountains and buy a pickup with a little trailer. He is going places; anywhere would be better than being alone here, he thought. But of course, the grand prize was the charming woman with long black hair.

Carved at right and below is "*Boz fini hau duc mizeria Jean 1936*" (Boss, this is it; what a miserable life, Jean 1936.) The carving wraps around the tree—a common occurrence—and two photographs were needed to record it entirely. This message must be one of the most gut-wrenching admissions by a herder who simply had had it with the job. It was in moments like these when they were likely to vent their frustrations by carving. Just by impressing the bark with their painful messages made them feel a little better. The good thing was that tomorrow it would be a new day, and dutifully, the herder would rise before daylight, pet his dogs, make his coffee, and lead the sheep to pasture.

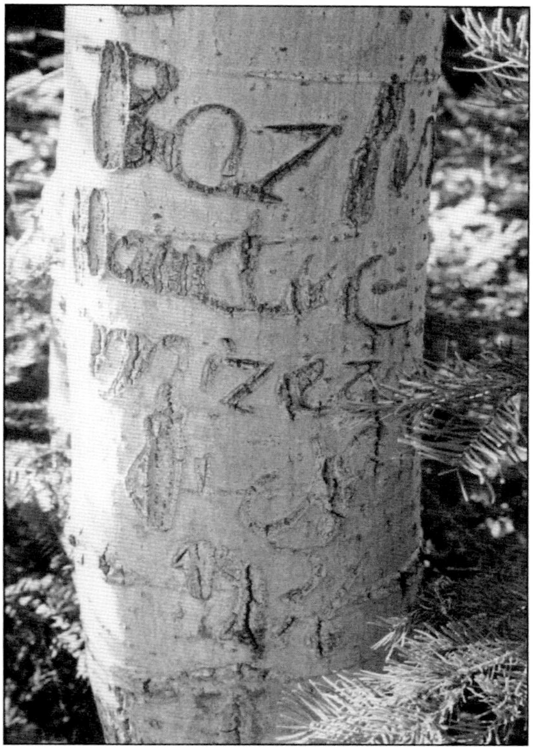

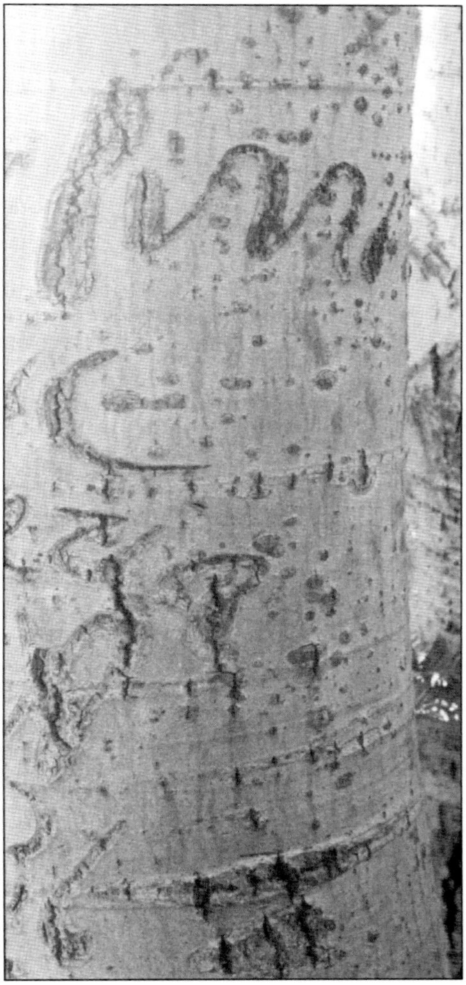

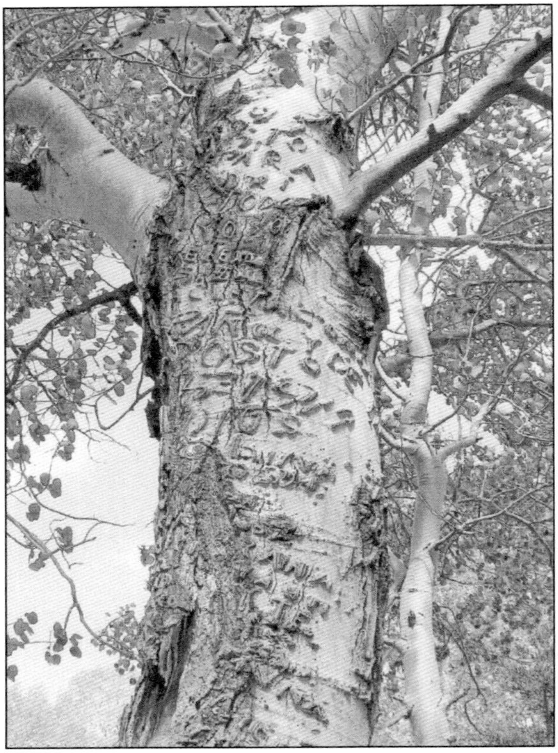

This grand old aspen is carved all around by three different herders, beginning 15 feet up and dated 1911, 1916, and 1917. It contains a total of 83 words, which is more than any other single tree ever recorded anywhere. The photograph shows the top half of the tree. Two of the messages are similar: the anguish of heartache over women.

When this drawing was young, it surely looked nice and clean, but it is 110 years old, and time has distorted it considerably (the double lines reveal the growth of the tree). A sheepherder's life and tastes gravitated between women, money, and booze. Seen here are a bottle and a glass carved by Pedro Urreltz Sabala in 1898.

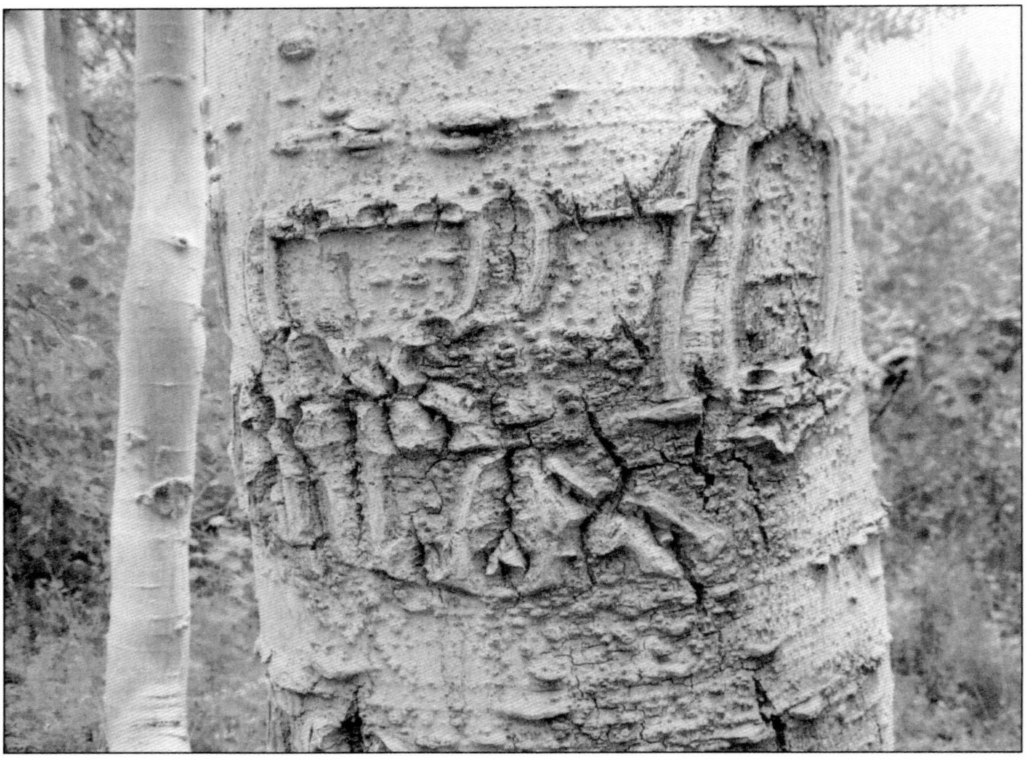

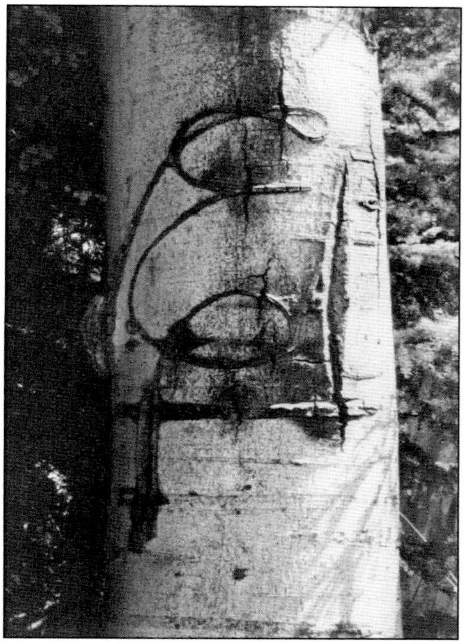

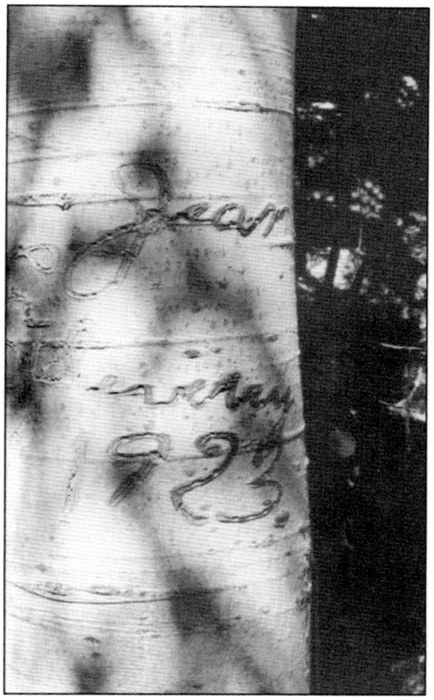

Two sides of a tree show a striking example of calligraphic carving by Jean Etcheverry in 1923. The northern Basques were particularly adept at this art, and they concentrated their efforts on the initials, as can be seen here. Block letters are the easiest to carve and calligraphic and script the most difficult.

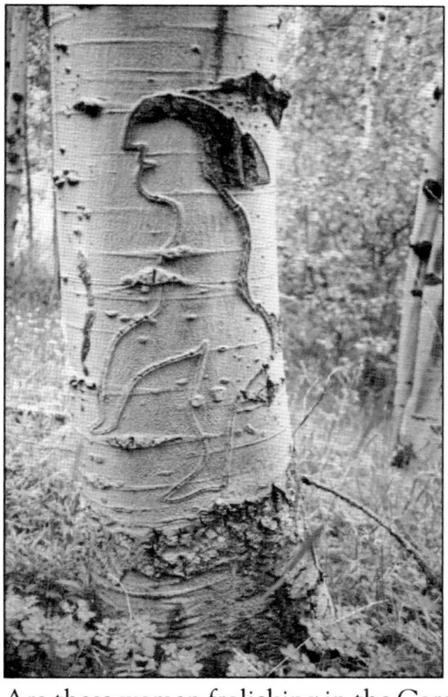

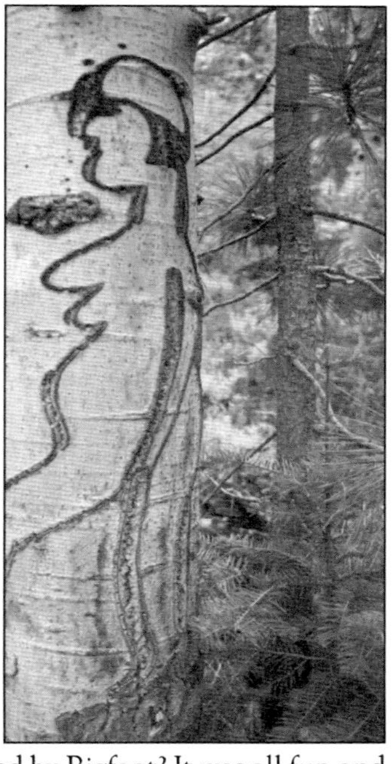

Are these women frolicking in the Garden of Eden or being chased by Bigfoot? It was all fun and games for this sheepherder artist with time on his hands, a little entertainment to shake off his two great enemies—isolation and boredom. Humor was fundamental to retain sanity, and sexual fantasies were one aspect of it.

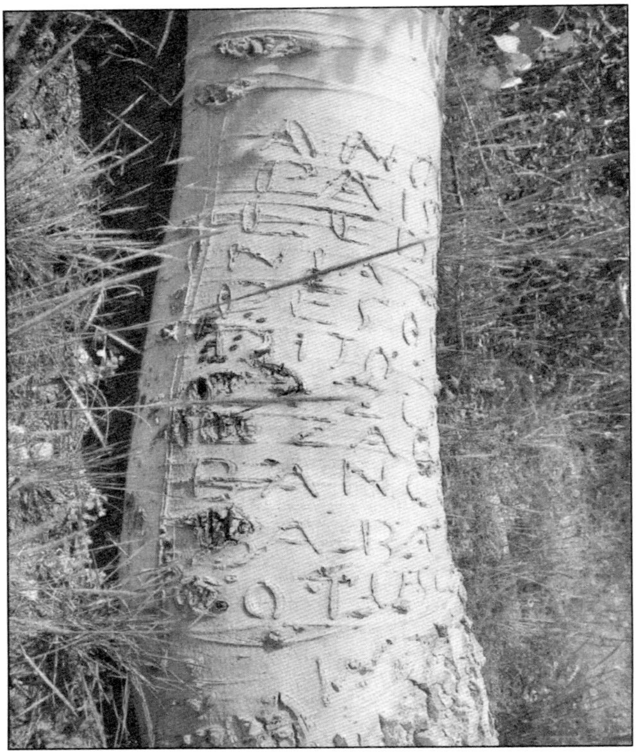

In 2007, this trunk was taken to the Nevada State Museum in Carson City. The 1929 message begins in Spanish: "I have been in this country three years and I told my girlfriend that I had 3,000 pesos, and she said [here he switches to Basque], 'Send it over. My uncle says to put it in the bank.' [The herder's reaction to him and to her] That big mouth; two greedy people."

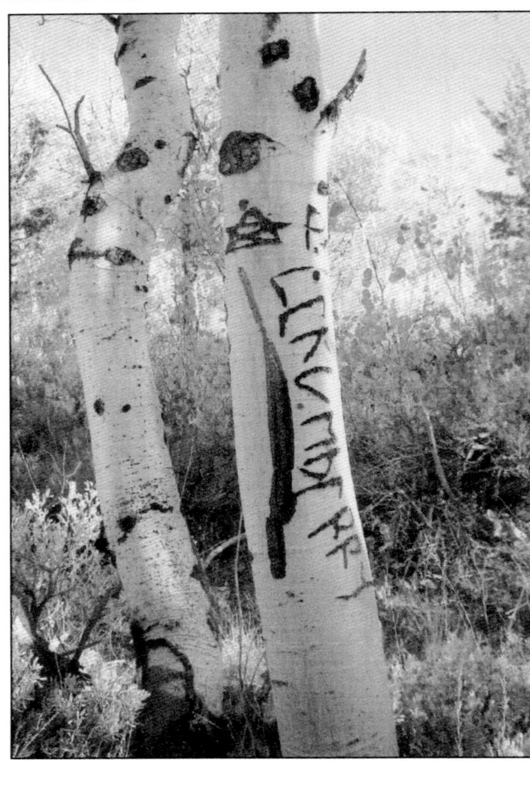

Nobody knows why the star was the preferred symbol of the sheepherders, but the technique for carving it differed. The most appealing figures were traced by one continuous movement rather than by pieces. Here P. Lekumberry succeeded halfway. He was a brother to Jean Lekumberry of Gardnerville, Nevada.

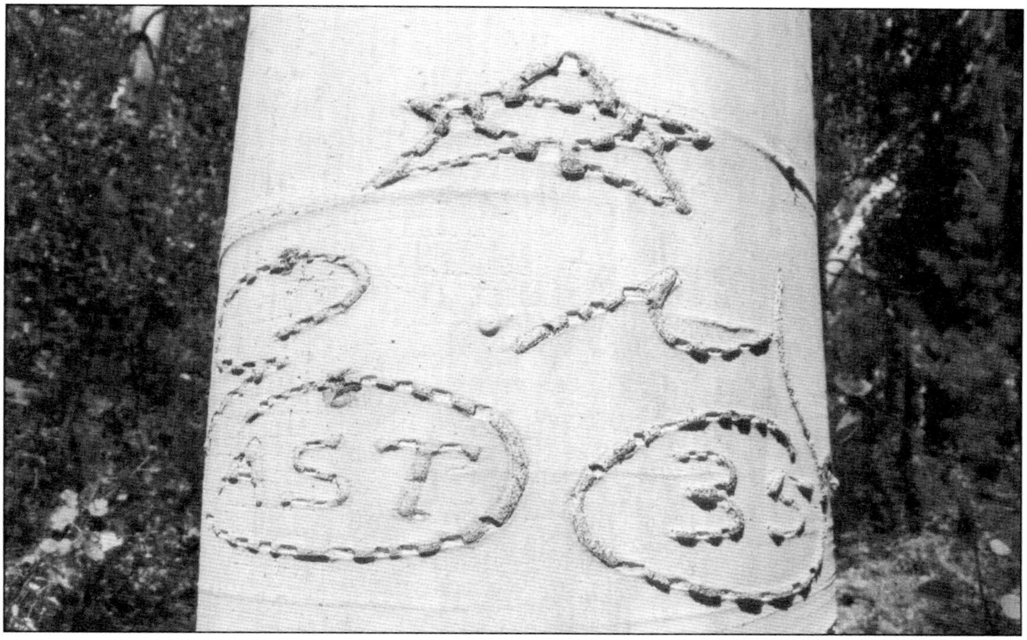

This is an exquisite sample of Esteban Yrisarri's sophisticated carving technique. Under the neat star, his elegant initials serve as cartouches for the date, "*Ast*" (August) and "35" (1935). Yrisarri and the Yparraguirres were born in the same village in Navarre. People who knew him say he had a somewhat negative outlook on life.

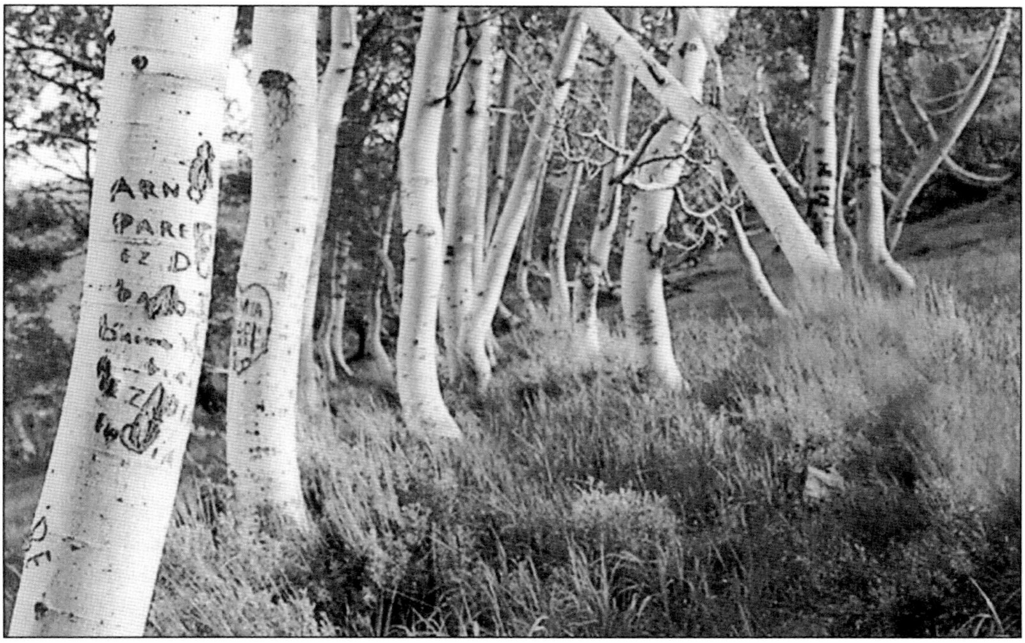

"The good wine has no equal; two glasses are better than one. However, the truth certainly is even better." This rare statement carved in Iparraldean Basque indicates that the carver had an appreciation for philosophy, wine, and truth. He carved it for his fellow herders and probably for someone in particular.

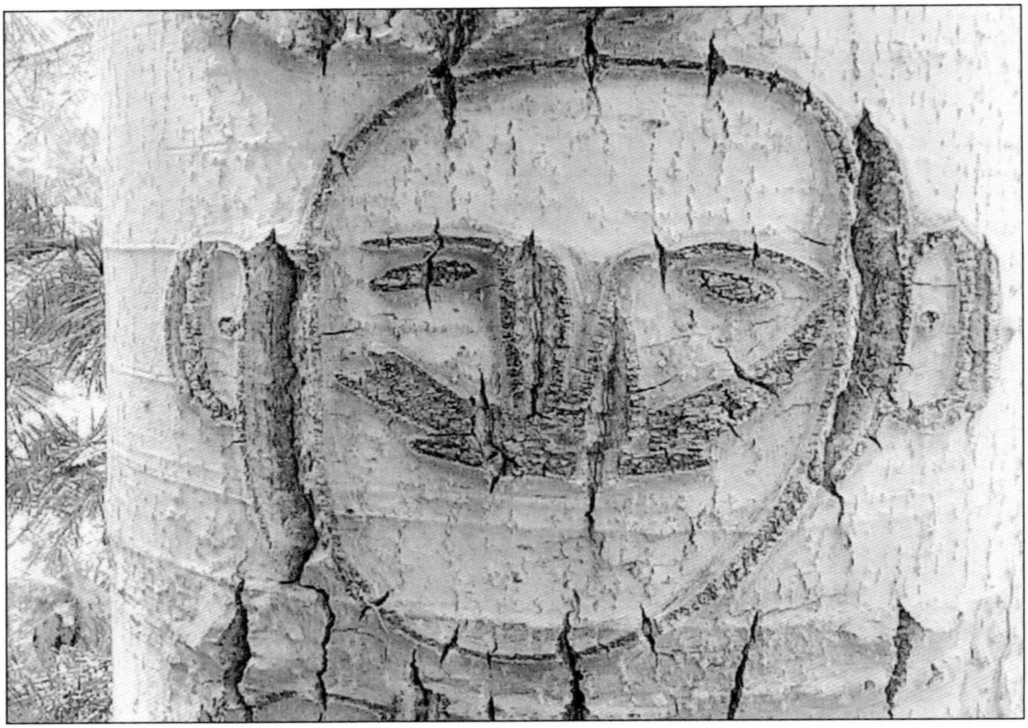

Summers in the high country are great with the right frame of mind. The very intelligent dogs were the sheepherder's constant companions with whom they held conversations, though it appears donkeys were better listeners. Carving figures of women and self-portraits—this fellow here is Salbador Larrañeta, dated 1929—made the long summer days more bearable.

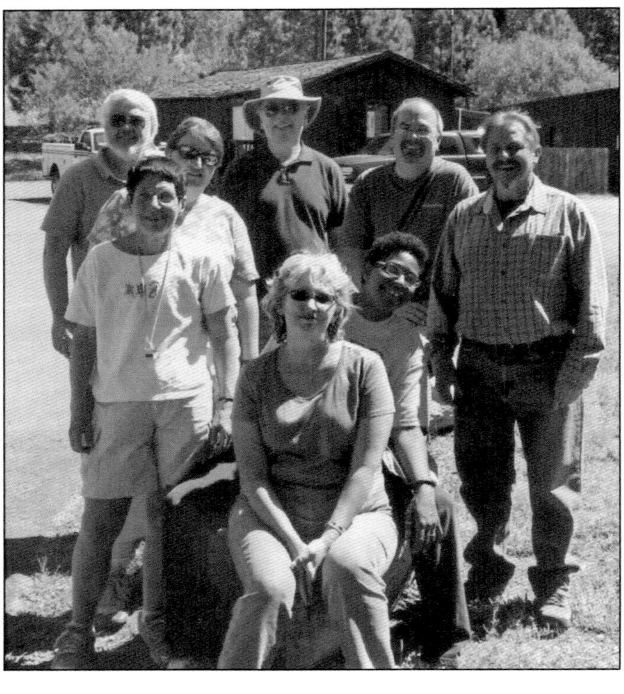

In September 2007, fifteen environmental journalists—half of the group could not wait for the photographer—from all over the country hiked above Lake Tahoe to take a closer look at the aspen carvings. They were so impressed that several of them wrote articles for magazines.

Most aspen carvings are abbreviated records, but this one is fairly complete. It begins with a cross (not photographed) on top, followed by the message, "Alberto Viteri, 30–8–1967, Vizcaya Marquina, 1250 sheep." He added a realistic self-portrait, sporting a Basque profile with beret and pipe. Markina was his hometown in Bizkaia.

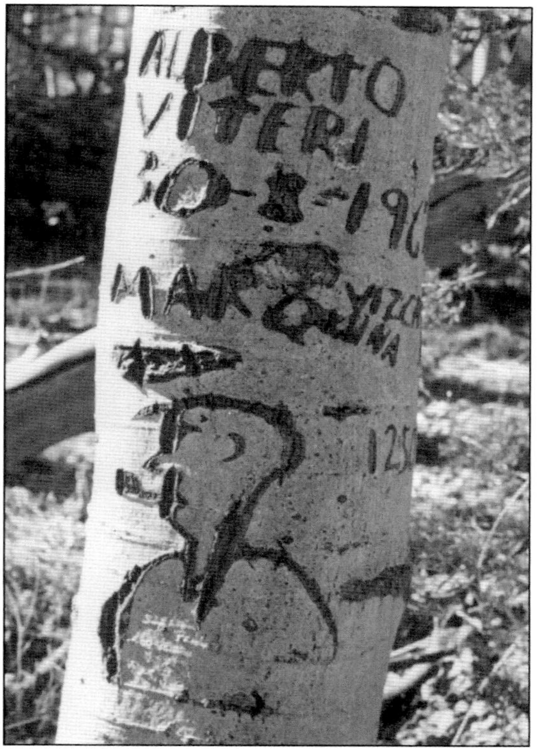

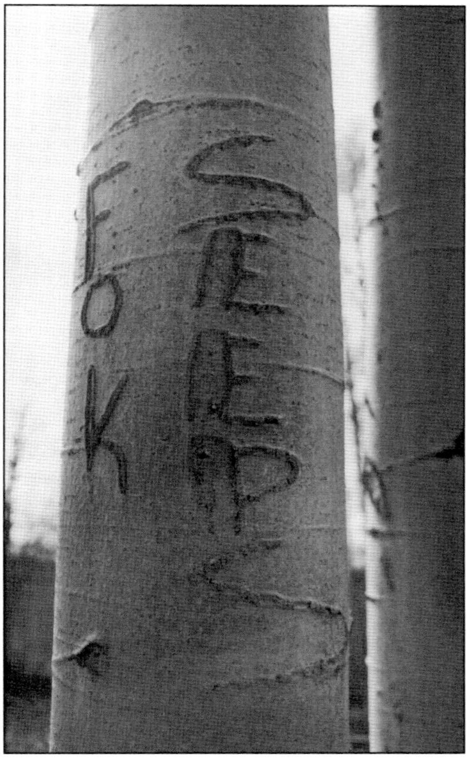

One thing the sheepherder had was absolute freedom to carve anything. There were no censors and no editors to worry about, nobody looking over his shoulder. "*Fok Seeps*"—you guessed it—is an expletive hurled at the woolies. Variations of this message were found in several groves, which were cut, and are now exhibited in local bars of northern Nevada.

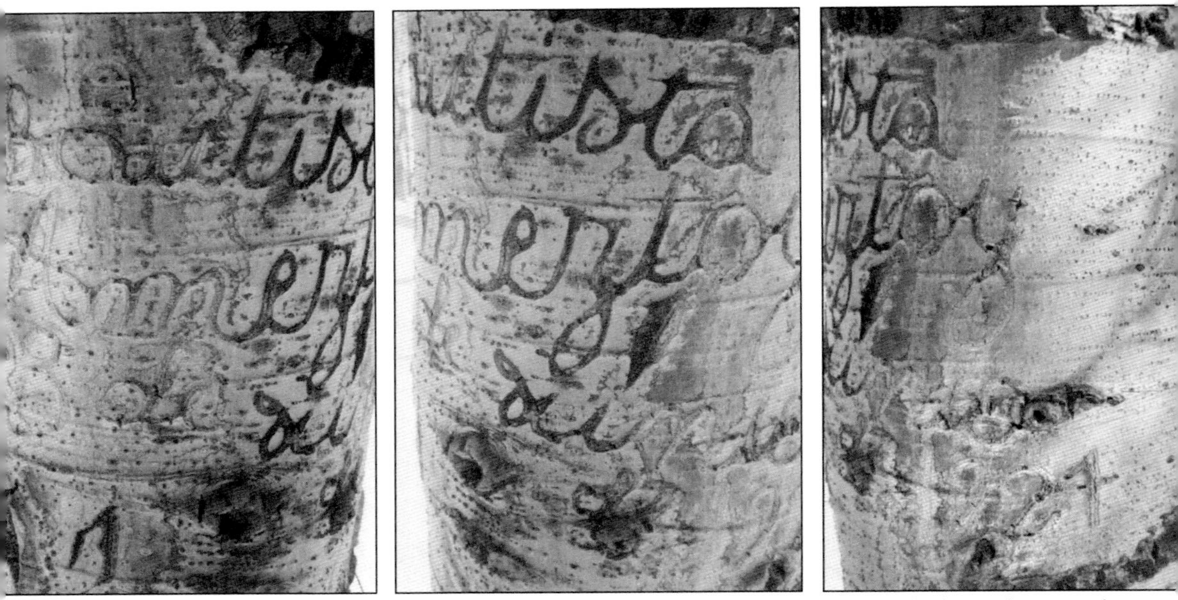

Though the message, "*Bautista Amestoy 23 de Junio de 1927,*" is not long, it took three photographs to record it because of the unusually large script letters. To carve it, Amestoy must have used for a knife something like a nail. This tree stood above Lake Tahoe but stands no longer. Amestoy, on a nearby tree, tells that he worked for the Bordas.

Here is a different rendition of a well-accessorized female with a grand necklace and belt, but without the more common high heels and garters. Women, especially naked ones, were depicted without arms, and this author's interpretation is that the arms obscured the curves, the sheepherders' focus of attention. Also, many could not carve arms and hands very well.

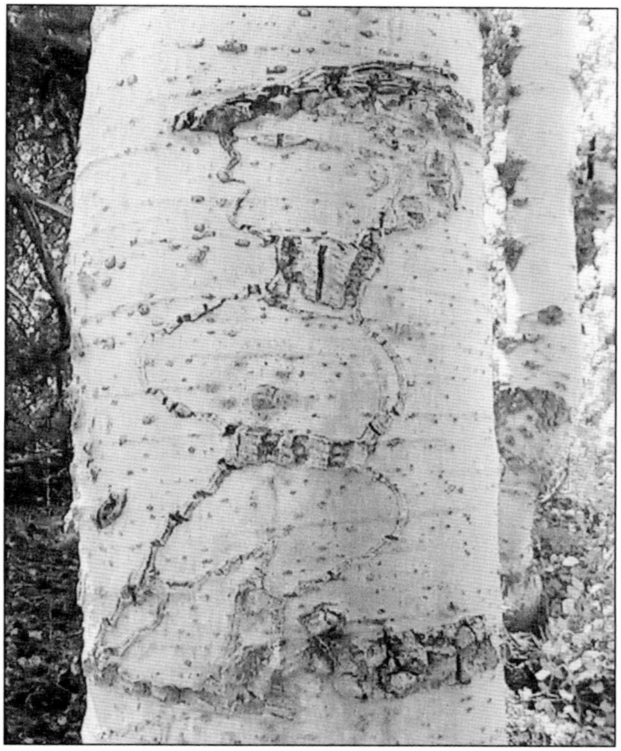

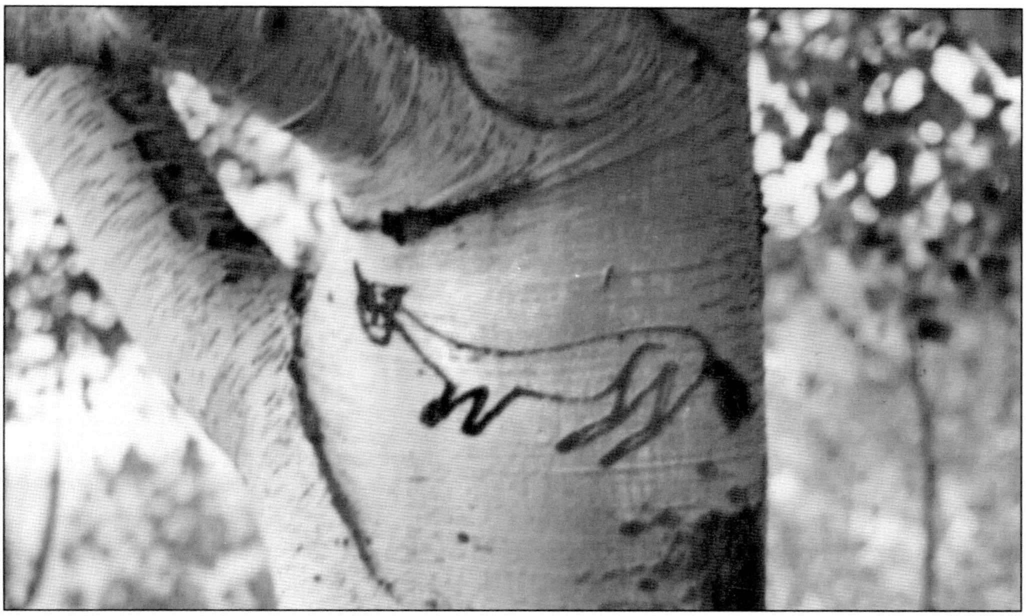

The sheepherders lived around the clock in the great outdoors and had a keen sense of nature around them. They were particularly skillful at carving realistic animals, such as the elusive cougar here, near Reno. There is no name or date associated with it, but it is probably dated around 1960. Cougars were less of a problem for the sheepherder than coyotes, except that one cat could kill dozens of sheep in a single night.

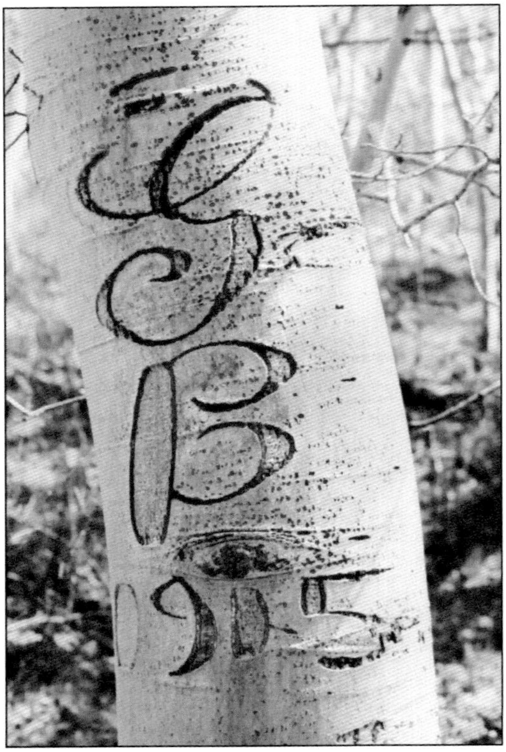

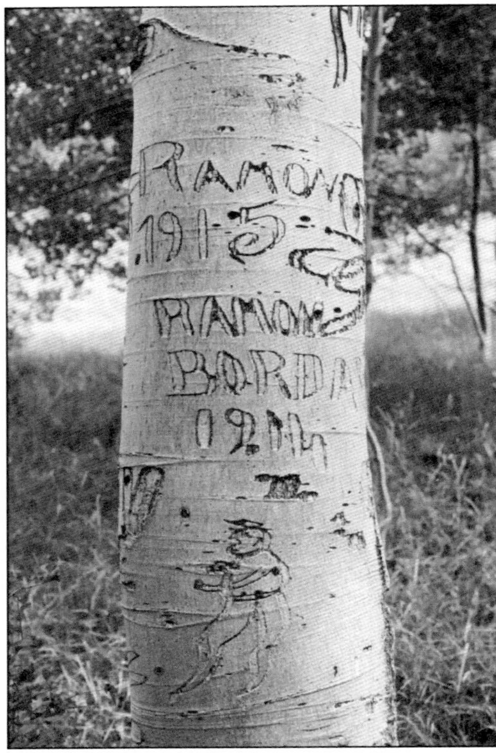

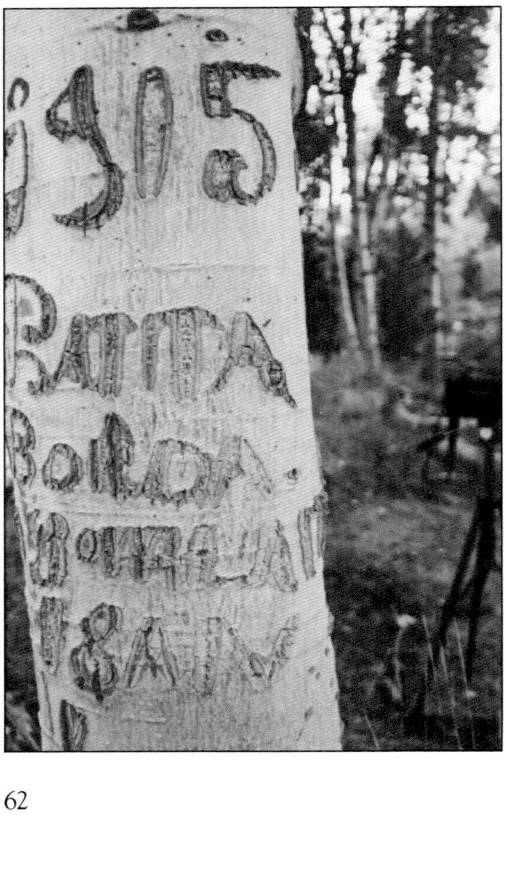

The large Borda clan in western Nevada originated in Bidarray (Iparralde), but the parents were Argentine-born repatriates. There were 10 in the family, and five brothers came to the United States in the 1910s. Three of them—Gilen, Ramon, and Batita—herded sheep together in the Sierra south of Gardnerville, Nevada. In these photographs is Batita Borda's 1915 carving dated in Basque: "*Agorrilaren 18n*" (August 18). This is highly unusual as most dates were written in either Spanish or English. The Bordas soon became sheep owners and eventually bought ranches and Basque hotels.

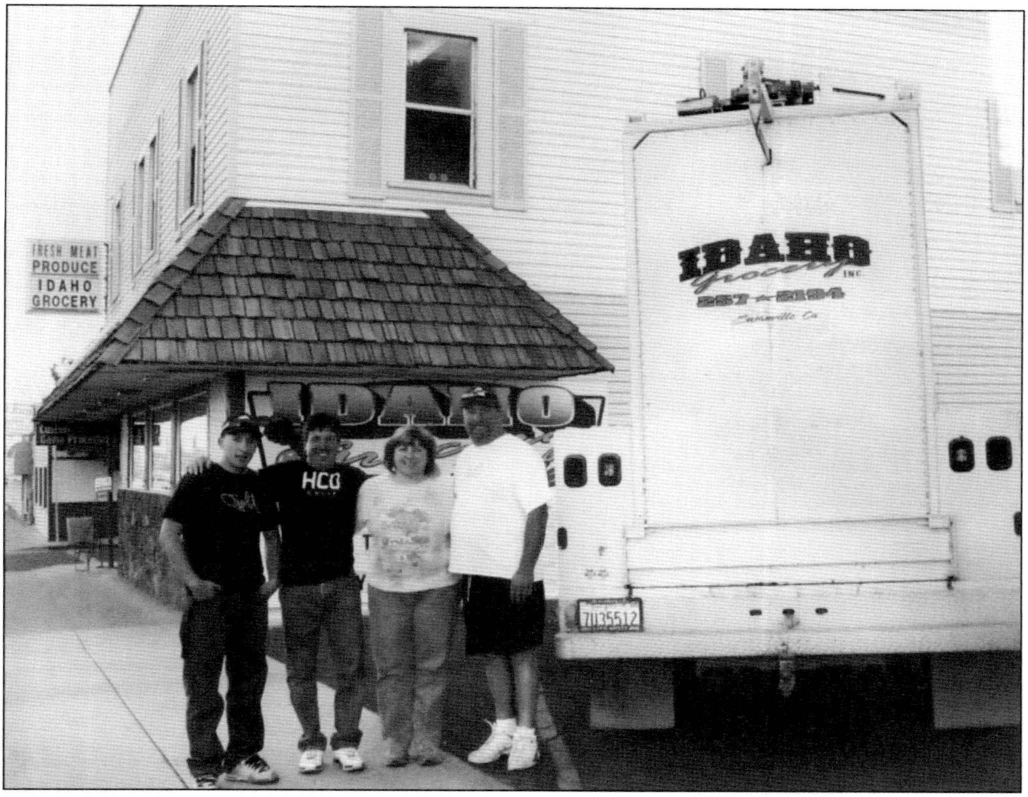

The Urrutias stand in front of their newly remodeled grocery store in Susanville, California, bought by their immigrant parents in 1968. From left to right are Jesse, his father Robert Urrutia, Renee, and Joey, who drives the butcher truck to ranches to butcher beef, hogs, and other animals on-site. Idaho Grocery specializes in custom meats, which amounts to the greater part of the business.

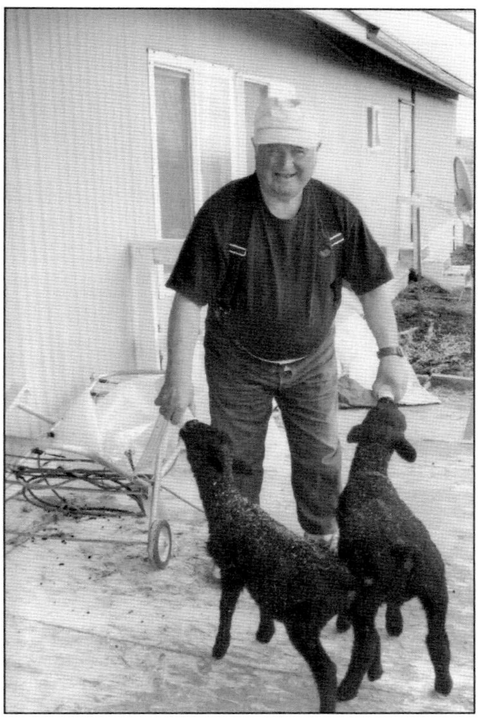

Today, throughout the West, there are a number of sheep companies owned by Basques, but the few who still work directly with sheep are managers or camp tenders. The photograph shows Inazio Ajuria, a small-acreage sheep owner, bottle-feeding his pet lambs. Black sheep were used—50 to 1—for counting purposes.

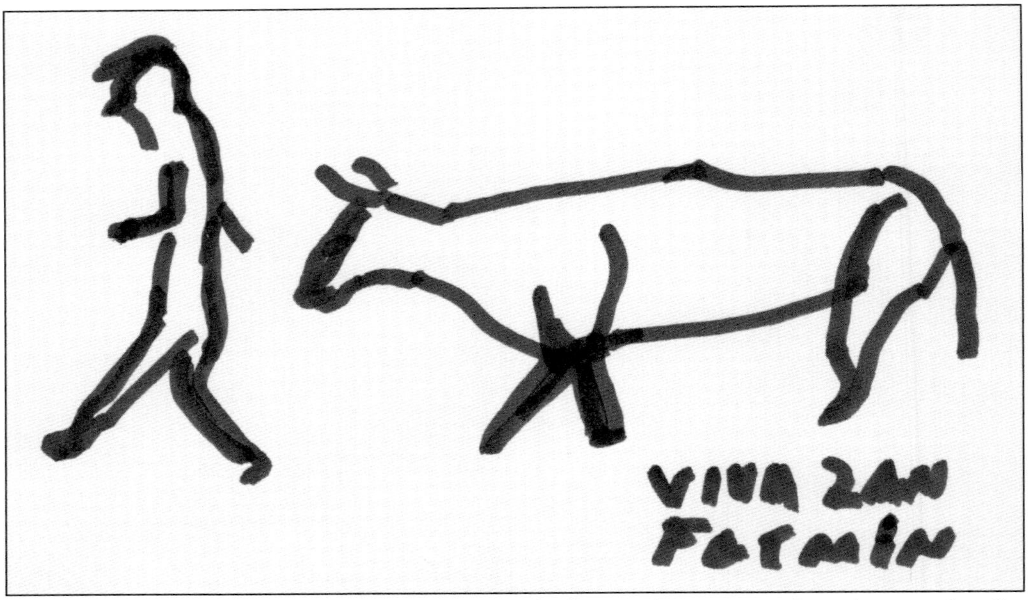

This is an accurate drawing of an actual carving, which is too faint to reproduce photographically. Also, it wraps around the tree, so at least two shots were needed to capture the scene that happens every year in July in the streets of Iruñea (Pamplona). This is, of course, the running of the bulls, and the carver was very probably from Navarre.

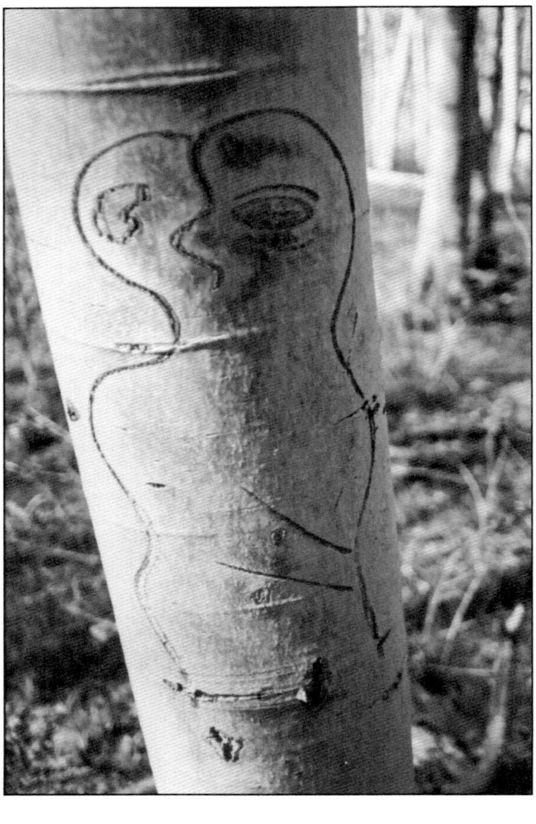

It is a real pity that the carver of this unique figure did not leave a signature, but it is without a doubt the epitome of sheepherder art that conveys an idea with few yet powerful lines. It is so simple that some people look at the figure and fail to see an embracing couple. Picasso himself would have been proud to sign this arborglyph.

This figure of a female dated in the 1920s is a good example of sheepherder art, which frequently consists of naked women or ladies in fine dresses with belts, like this one. Simple and tasteful, it faithfully represents someone's fantasy. It is good to remember that the heavy lines are the result of the tree's growth, not the original sheepherder's incision.

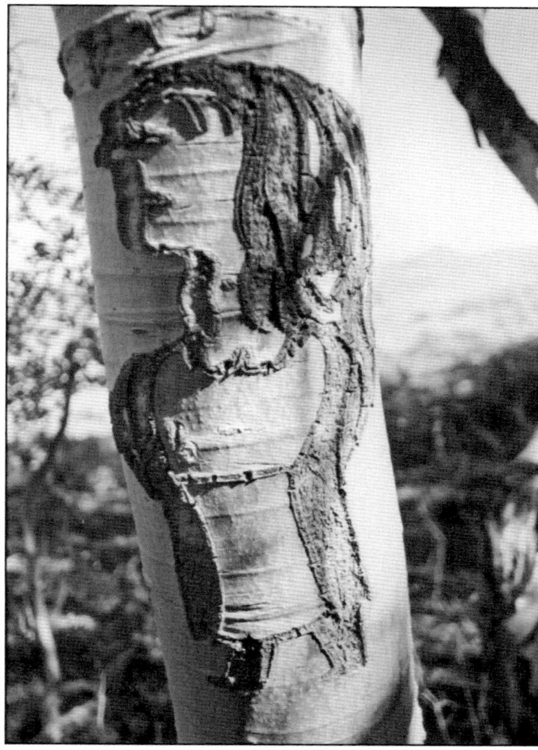

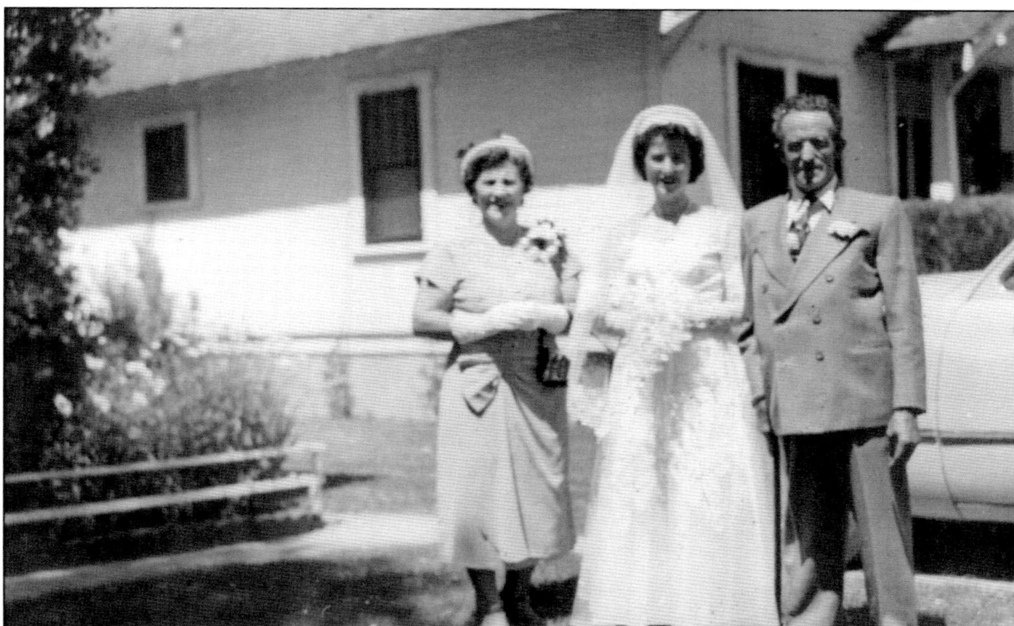

Anacleto Goñi (right) carved many trees in what today is the marine base near Bridgeport, California, where he worked in 1916–1917. Ramona Gaston (left), his wife, stands with their daughter Lorraine on July 8, 1951, the day of her wedding to Don Taylor of Ely, Nevada. They are standing in front of their house, located on 449 East Ninth Street in Reno. (Courtesy Irene Arbeloa.)

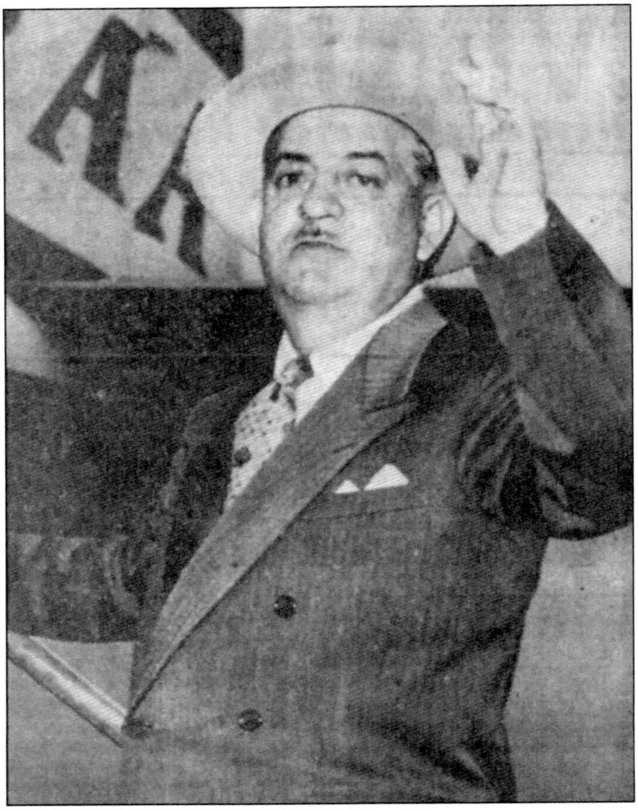

In the 1940s and 1950s, sheep owners in the West organized to press Congress to pass special laws to import Basque herders. In the photograph, John Bidegaray of Fresno, California, president of the California Range Association, boards a plane in New York. The association could afford to send him to Europe for three months to recruit 500 sheepherders. (Courtesy Basque Library, UNR.)

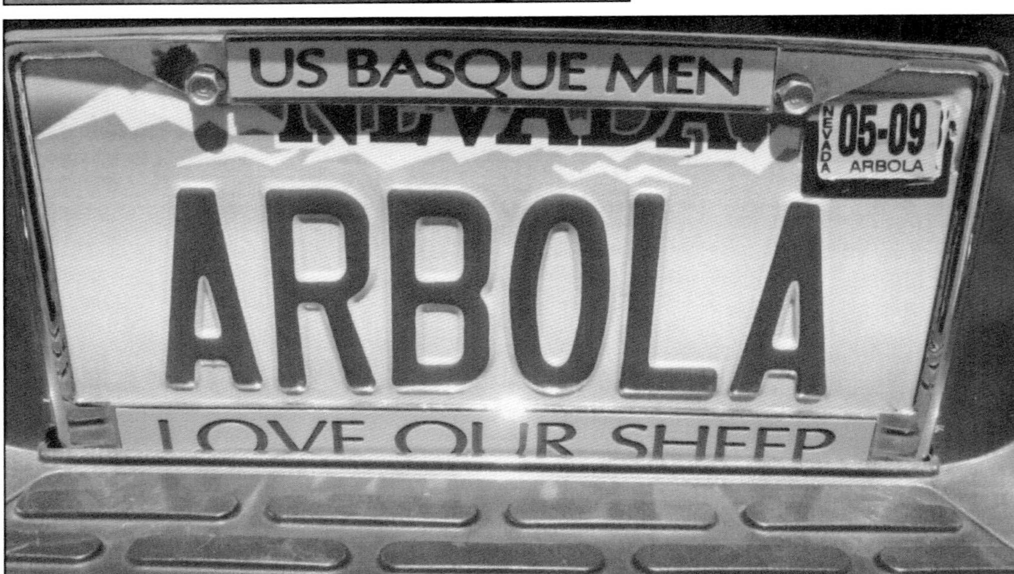

This license plate seen on a truck was photographed in Gardnerville, Nevada. "*Arbola*," one of the words Basques use for tree, is a clear reference to *Gernikako Arbola*, the Oak Tree of Gernika and the rallying symbol of Basque liberties. The owner of the truck is obviously one who loves and probably owns sheep.

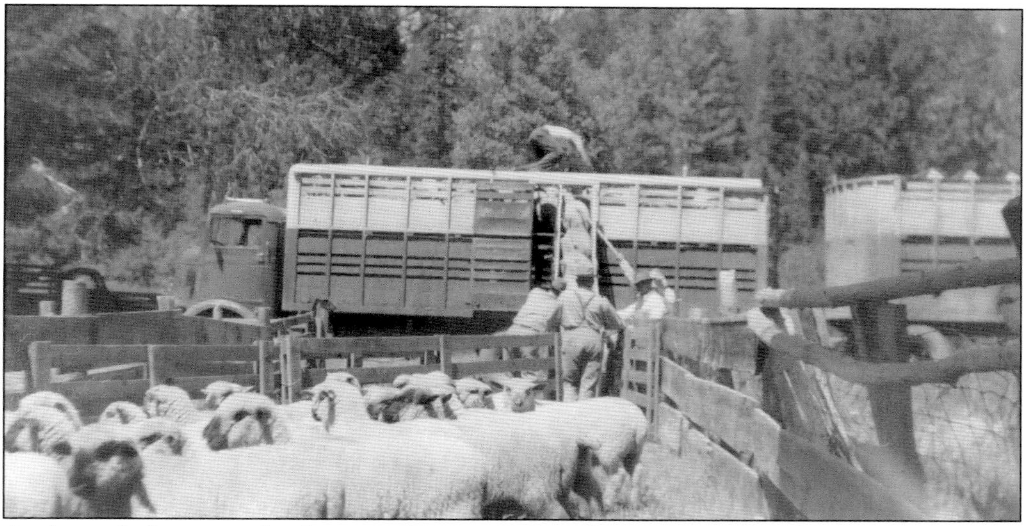

At the end of summer, lambs were always trailed to the nearest railhead for shipping, but in the early 1940s trailer trucks started to drive into sheep corrals, revolutionizing some itinerant aspects of sheepherding. The 1944 photographer captured the first truck, owned by M&M Livestock Transportation of Madera, California, in Blackwood Canyon, Lake Tahoe. (Courtesy Anastasio Landa.)

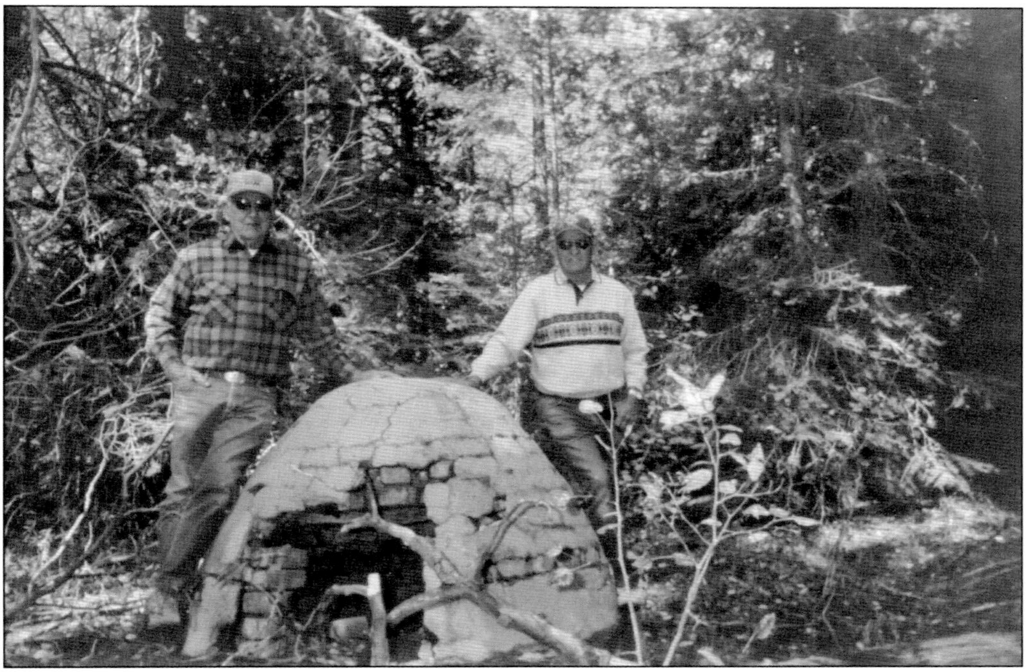

Long after they sold off their sheep company, brothers Anastasio (right) and John Landa of Reno still visited their old sheep camp at Blackwood Canyon, California. In this recent photograph (Anastasio died in 2008), they investigate the damage by the elements to the bread oven at the camp, built by their brother Steve Landa in the 1930s. (Courtesy Landa family.)

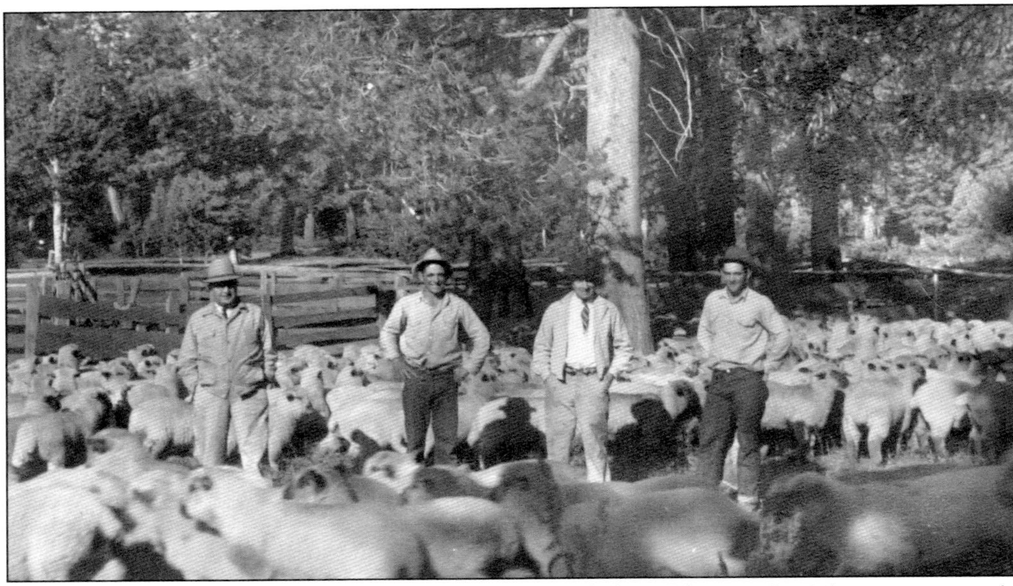

The two fellows with clean clothes and ties look out of place. They are lamb buyers visiting the Landa Sheep Camp to look over the stock and settle on a price. This late-1930s photograph captured the big moment sheepmen waited for all year. The price decided the profit of margin, if any. (Courtesy Anas Landa family.)

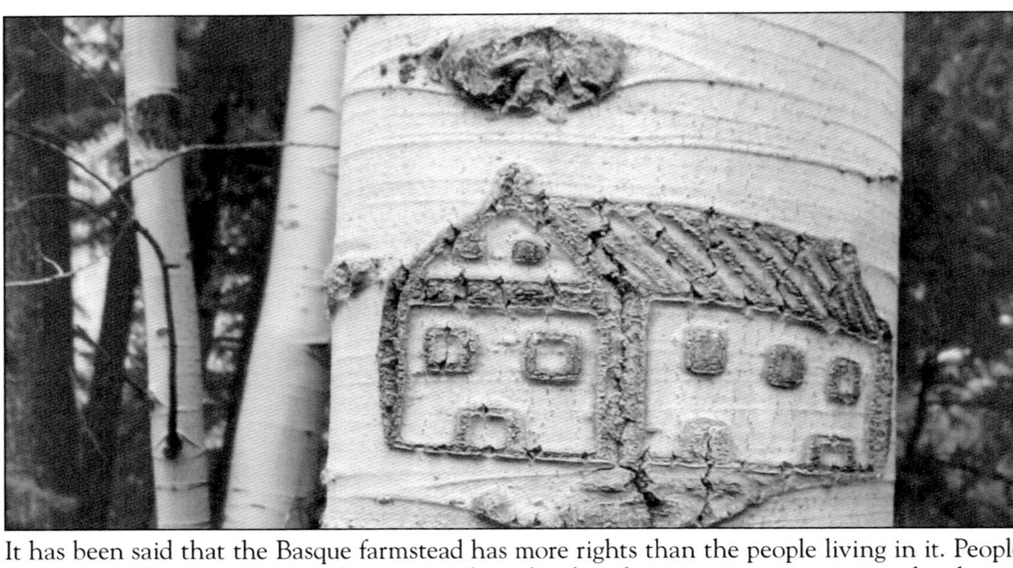

It has been said that the Basque farmstead has more rights than the people living in it. People were known by their farmstead's name and not by their last name, so it is no wonder that in America the displaced sheepherders carved many figures of their homes back in Europe. This version, though architecturally correct, has too many doors and windows.

A classic female figure of the aspens was nude, with garters, high heels, necklace, and one arm (most carvings had none). It probably represents a prostitute, the type of woman sheepherders passing near a town could hope to meet. She is facing a nearby tree that in Spanish and English states, "Let us see if she/he wants it. Bye boy." The answer, carved on her arm, is "no."

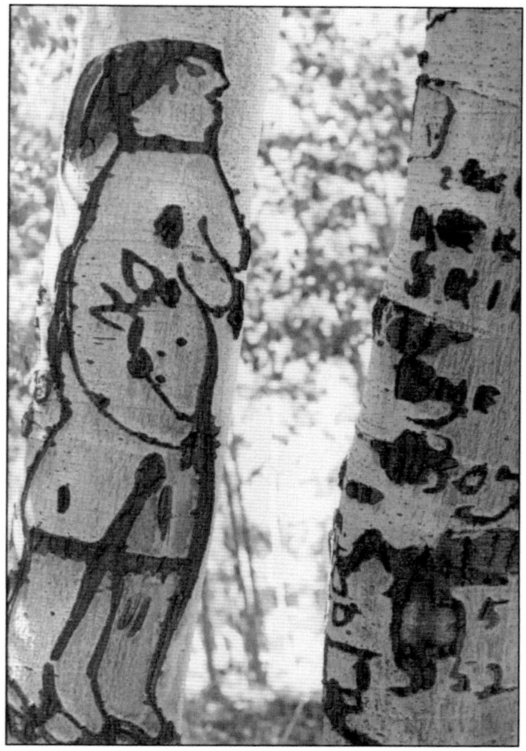

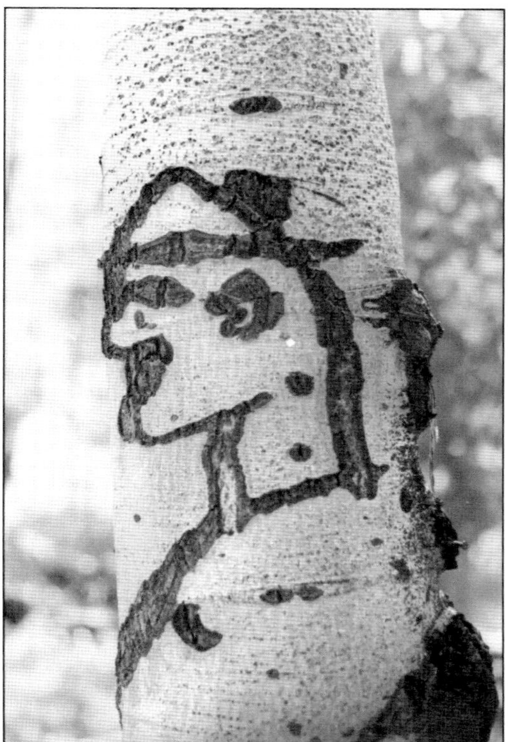

Here is a crude but powerful self-portrait of an unidentified herder with a prominent jaw and neck. The great majority of the herders wore hats, as this one does, but the anomaly here is that he is not smoking. Herders preferred to go hungry than be without tobacco. In the rare occasions it happened, they found some "dried mule's ears," rolled it up, and smoked it. In Nevada, "mule's ears" refers to asteraceae since the flower looks like a sunflower with large green leaves that grows in the high country.

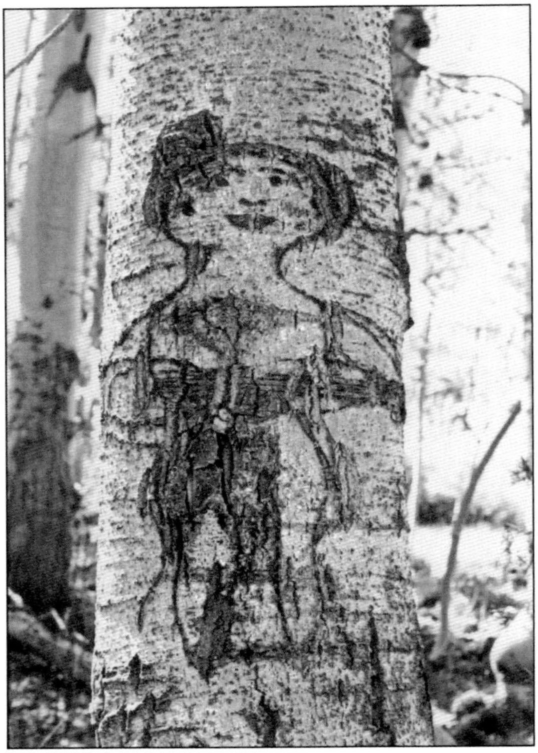

Some sheepherders paid attention to details. Observers cannot miss the rose in her hair, but the carving is old and time has disfigured it. Is she wearing a short skirt or none at all? She appears to have a top, but the garters are more problematic; the feet, less important, are missing. However, there is no doubt that this guitar-playing lady has eyes only for the sheepherder.

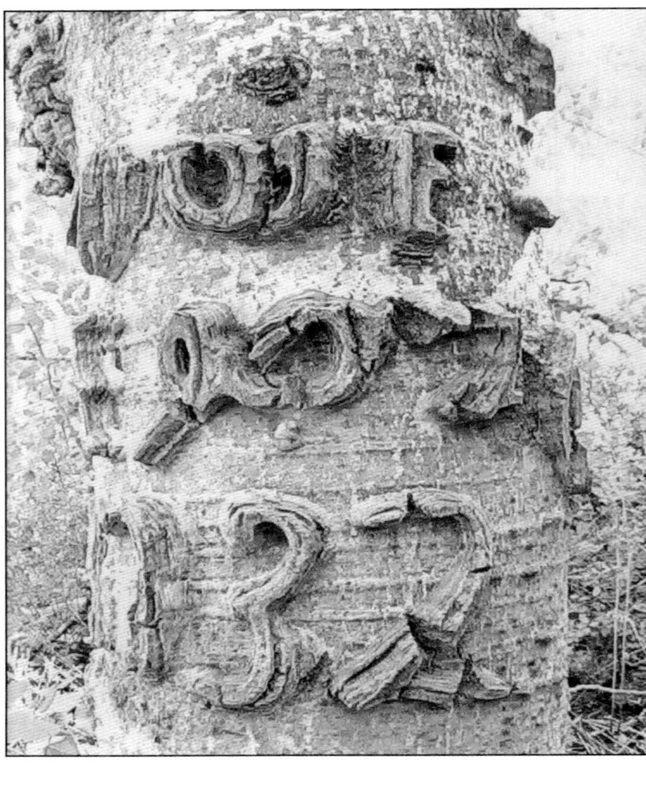

Aspens near water grow large and straight, while those at high elevations away from water stay smaller and more gnarled. The same thing can be said about their response to the carver's knife; some scarred more easily than others. This photograph illustrates a glyph that exhibits extreme protuberance; "Jose Egoscue 1932" sticks out about an inch.

This is drawing by Frances Wallace and Hans Reiss of E. M.'s carving petting his dog. Most herders had two or three dogs, and without them it would have been extremely difficult to herd sheep in the Sierra. Sheepdogs were greatly appreciated, and the herders fought for them. (Courtesy Special Collections, UNR.)

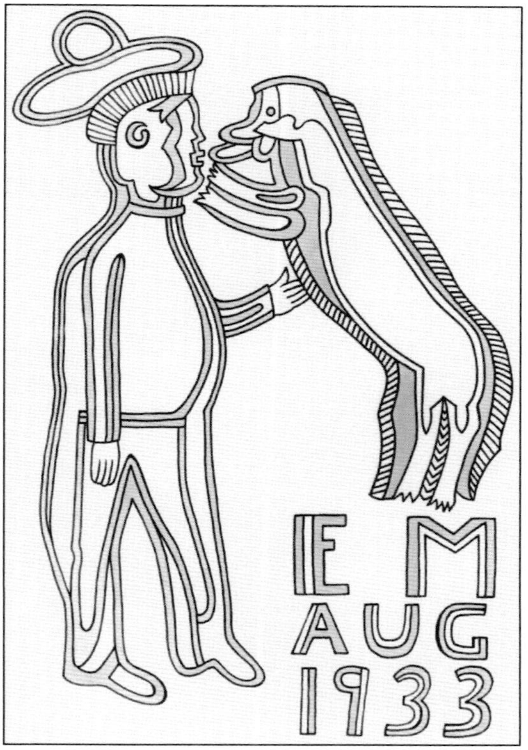

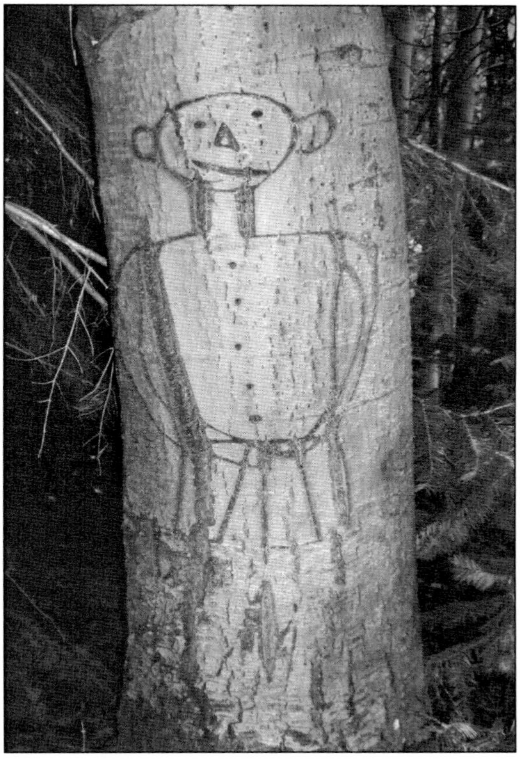

This certainly is a cute self-portrait, reminiscent of naïve art, even the work of a child, buttons and all. It dates from the 1920s, and on the side it states, "*Domingo Tomasena gizon fina*," a rhyming statement meaning, "Domingo Tomasena is a hard-working man." All male figures appear with feet firmly planted on the ground, but Domingo forgot all about it.

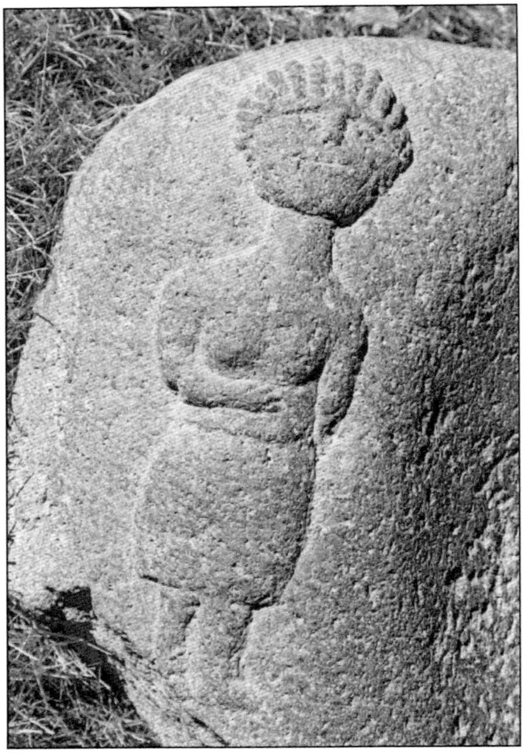

Sheepherders fashioned petroglyphs when trees were lacking—not many, because petroglyphs were harder and took much longer to carve, but herders experienced in stonework obviously enjoyed the practice. This photograph was sent to the author by Mr. Trujillo of Mono County, California.

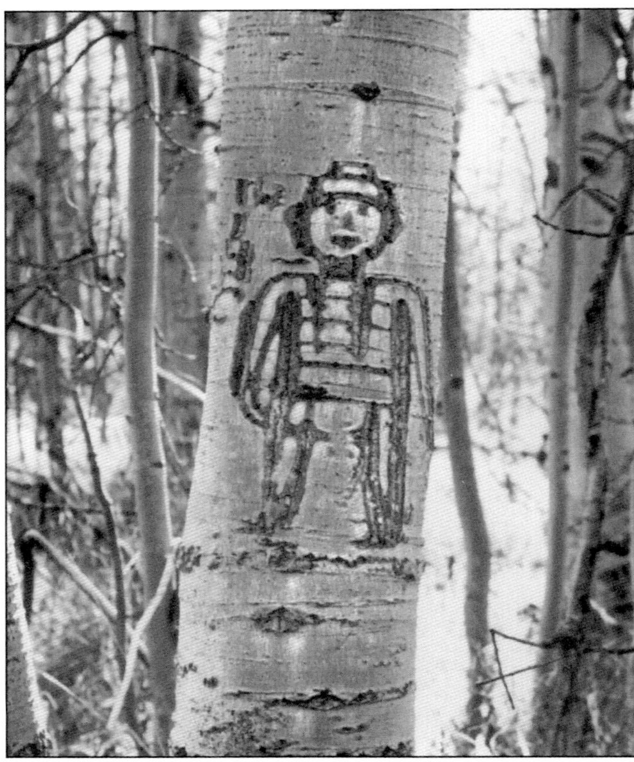

People who saw this tree or the photograph could not help but wonder what it represented. Some thought it to be an astronaut, as sheepherders in the high country had good views of space vehicles in the sky and in fact carved about Sputniks. More likely, though, the figure is a *dantzari* (folk dancer) from Zuberoa, and it underscores the importance of dancing in Basque culture.

Four

OSTATUAK AND RESTAURANTS

After sheep camps, Basque hotels and boardinghouses comprised the social center of the Basque colony, and hundreds of men met their future wives in these establishments, where the women worked. The larger buildings were a combination hotel/bar/restaurant, often located near the railroad station so the arriving immigrant could find them easily. This business started in California and was later replicated in many Western towns. Some private homes with a room or two to spare also rented out to herders. Both types were known as *ostatu*.

According to Jeronima Echeverria, Reno, which is a regional hub, had over a dozen recorded *ostatu*, but today two remain—the Santa Fe and Louis' Basque Corner, which operate as restaurants. Gardnerville had at least six, and one survives as a restaurant. Fallon, Carson City, Susanville, and other towns had them as well, but no longer.

When Basque immigration stopped, there was no reason for the boardinghouses to exist. However, the bar/restaurant part of the business endured to become an icon. Today Basques are not known primarily for their sheepherding abilities, but for the food, which is served "family style." The emphasis is on quantity and protein, as if calories and cholesterol never existed. The favorites are lamb and steaks with the everyday soup, red beans, bread, and red wine.

Of course, while waiting for a seat at the long dinner tables, visitors might as well try picon punch, a drink that almost guarantees one will make new friends soon.

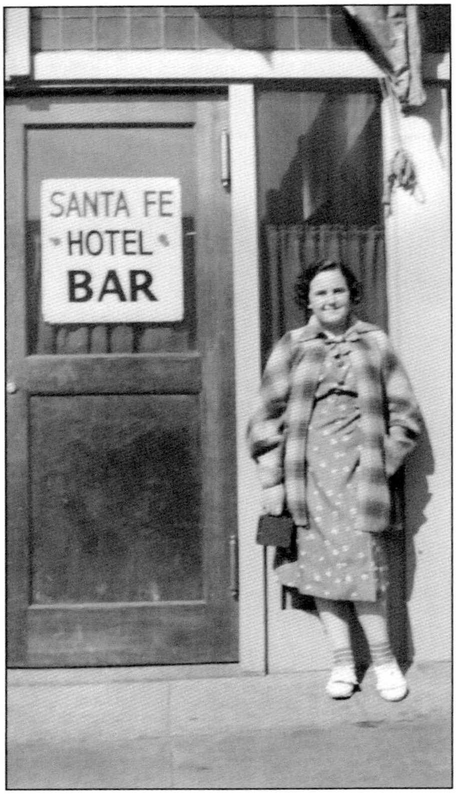

This photograph of Lucy Orriaga/Ghiglieri standing in front of the old Santa Fe Basque Hotel, Reno, is dated 1937. Her parents, Martin Orriaga and Josephine Gaston, owned it with partners John and Louise Etcheberry. The Orriagas were Reno's Basque hotelkeepers: they owned or managed several of them from 1927 to 1948. (Courtesy Irene Arbeloa.)

A charming 1937 photograph includes, from left to right, Mary Erquiaga, Lorraine Goñi, Marie Arrua, and Trini Erquiaga. The Erquiaga sisters were from Fallon, and Arrua was from Maule (Zuberoa); she worked at the Toscano Hotel in Reno. The Toscano had a special entrance for women only—to avoid the bar. In 1950, the Orriagas bought the Toscano from Joe Elcano and Dominique Lartey. (Courtesy Irene Arbeloa.)

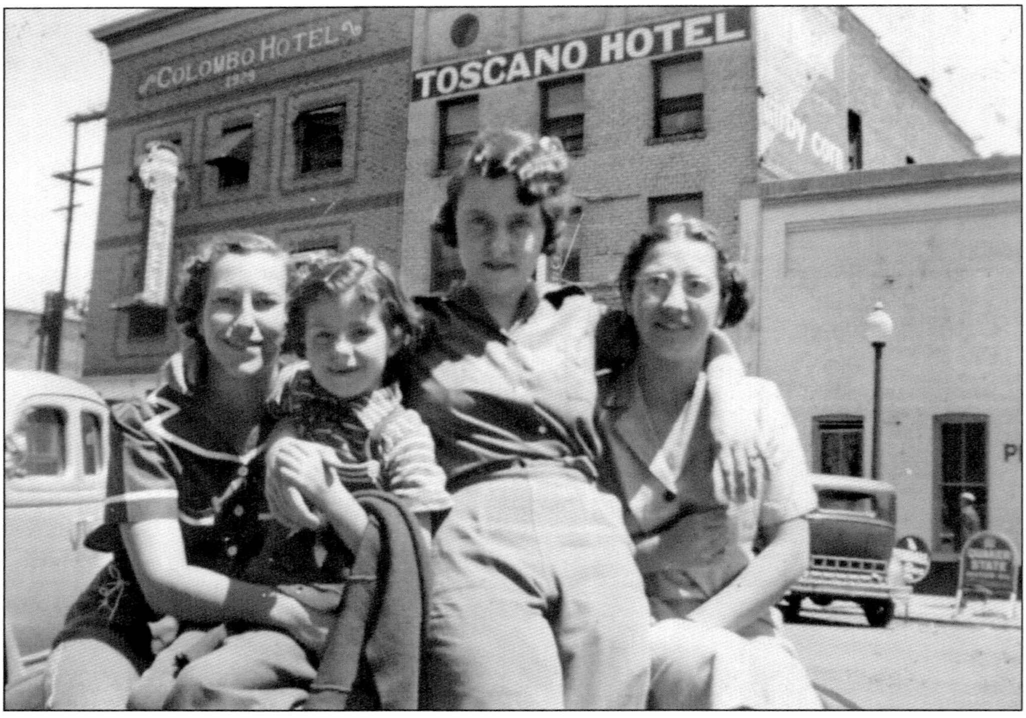

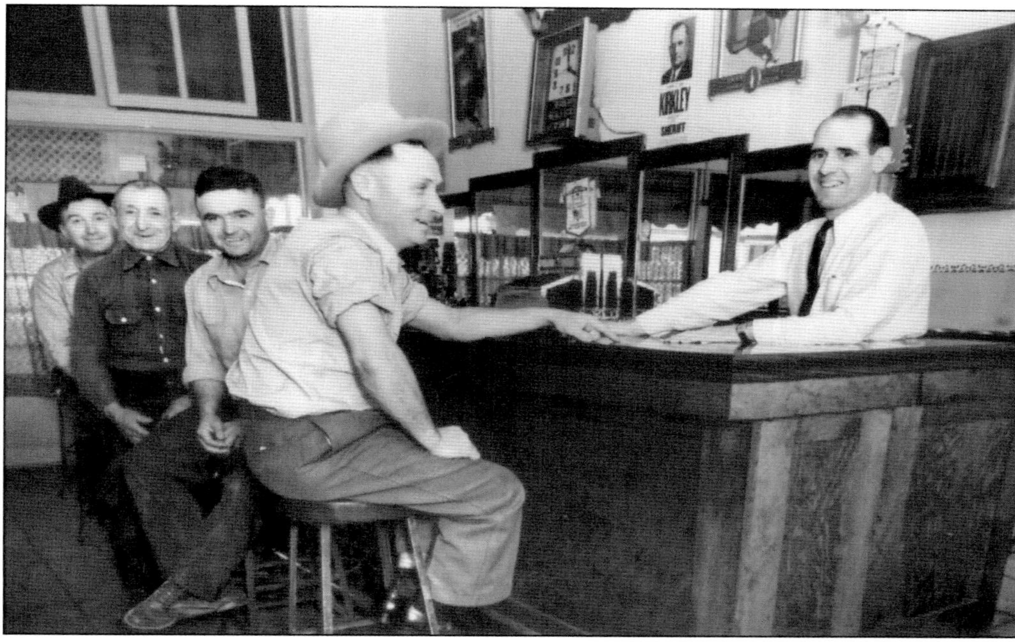

The Santa Fe Basque Hotel of Reno burned down in 1948. This photograph shows Martin Esain, the owner, at the bar with unidentified Basque patrons sometime in the 1940s. The hotel was rebuilt in 1949 and today is one of the two Basque hotel/restaurants surviving in Reno. Esain sold it to his relatives, Aurelia, Anita, and Joe Zubillaga. (Courtesy Philip Zubillaga.)

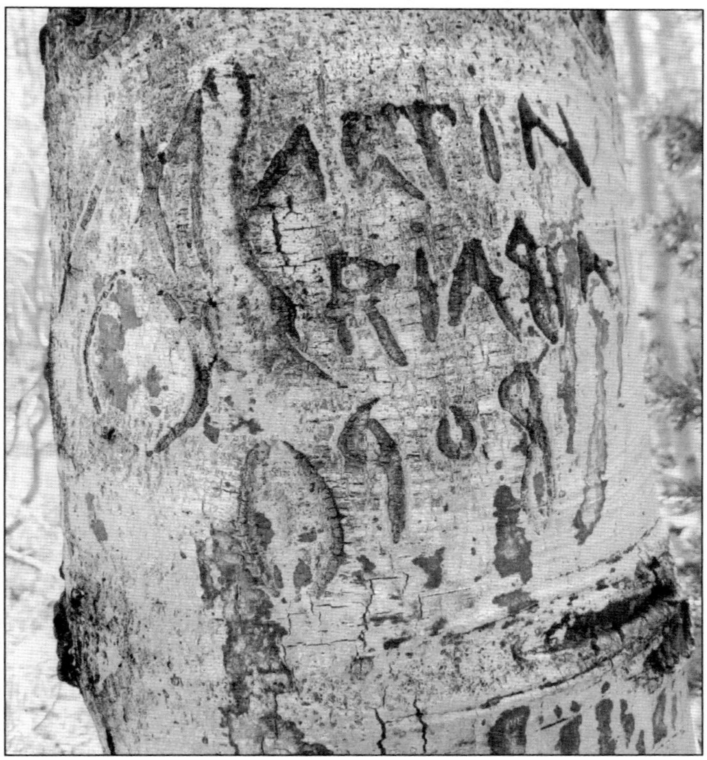

Sheepherder Martin Orriaga left his marks in the Sierra in the early 1900s. He followed in his older brother Jose's footsteps, and both worked for the same company. Obviously Martin put to good use the money he earned as a sheepherder, first to buy an ice cream parlor in Wellington, Nevada, and later hotels in Reno.

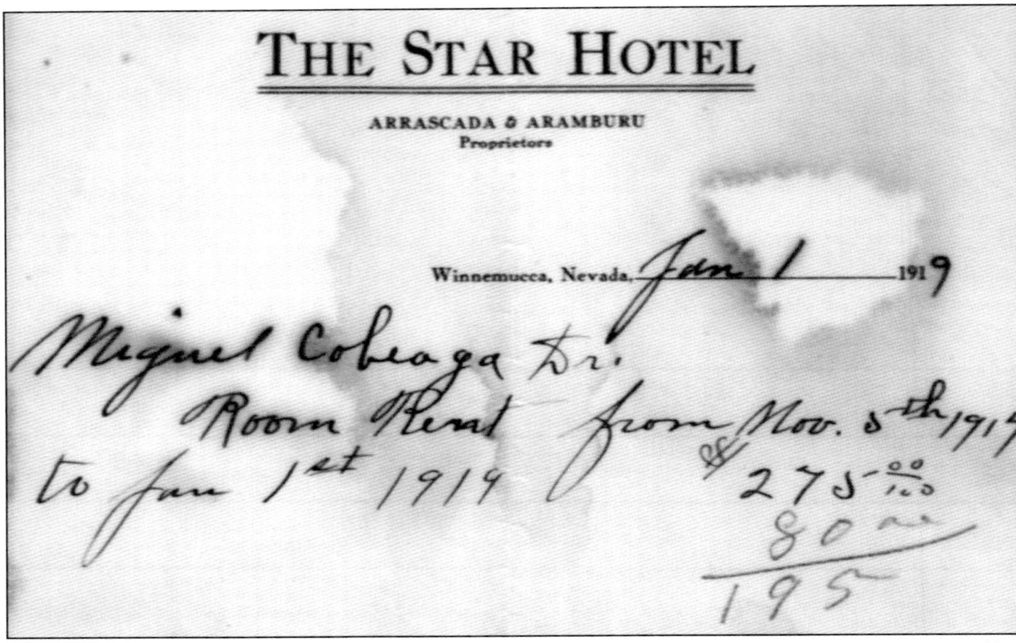

THE STAR HOTEL

ARRASCADA & ARAMBURU
Proprietors

Winnemucca, Nevada, Jan 1 1919

Miguel Cobeaga Dr.
Room Rent from Nov. 5th 1917 to Jan 1st 1919 $275.00/100
80.00
195

LeRoy Arrascada of Reno keeps this 1919 hotel bill in his office. His grandfather Ignacio and his partner, E. Aramburu, owned the Star Hotel in Winnemucca, Nevada, where Miguel Cobeaga was a guest for almost 14 months. There is no explanation for the $80 deduction, after which the bill came to $195, or 46–47¢ a day. (Courtesy LeRoy Arrascada.)

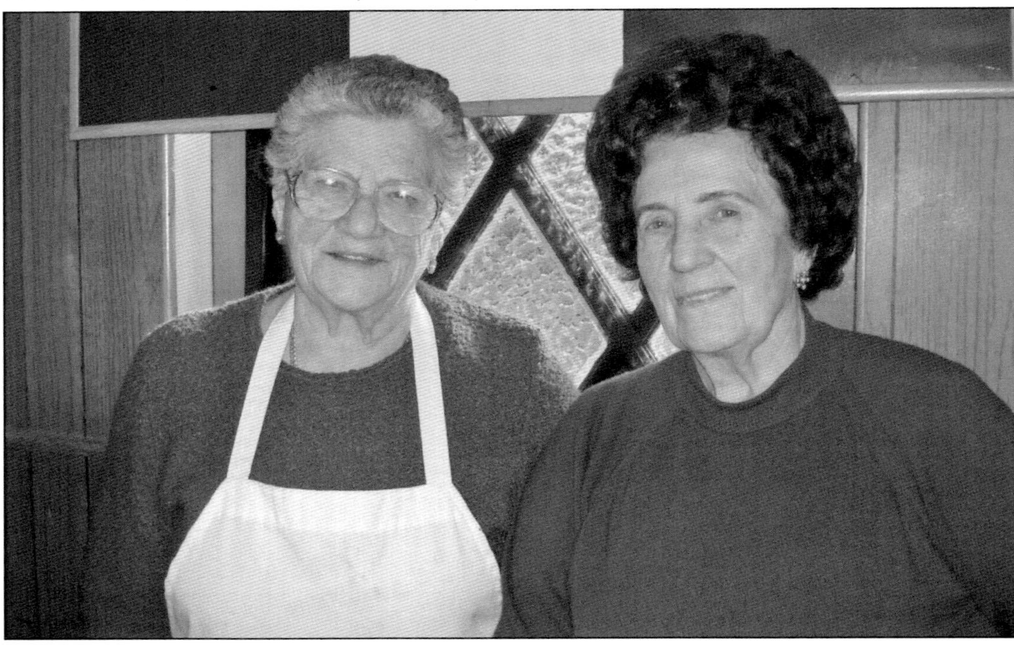

Elvira Cenoz (right) and her sister Josephine Larrañeta are pictured on Easter Sunday in Gardnerville, Nevada, in 2008. Elvira owns the Overland Hotel-Restaurant in Gardnerville, and Josephine owns the Brass Rail Basque Restaurant in Alturas, California. Elvira serves a special brunch on Easter Sunday, which is Aberri Eguna for the Basques, a national holiday.

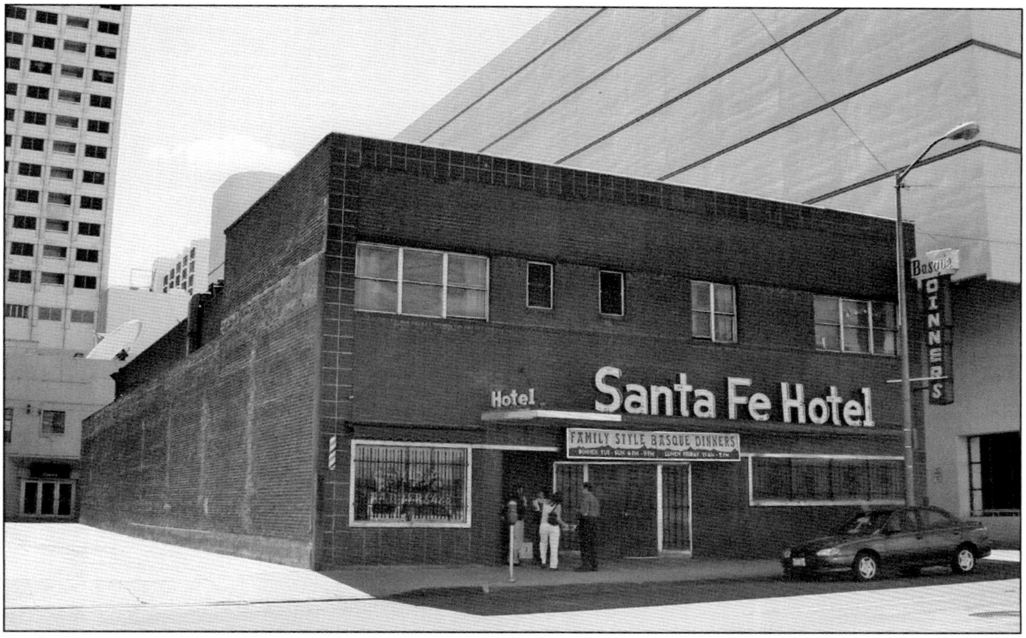

Today's Santa Fe Basque Hotel Restaurant in downtown Reno, butting against giant casinos, marches on impervious to time. Harrah's Casino tried to buy the place several times, but the Zubillagas declined the offers. The Santa Fe is a large building, serving excellent and plentiful food, and is currently owned and operated by Philip, son of Joe Zubillaga, who died in 2008.

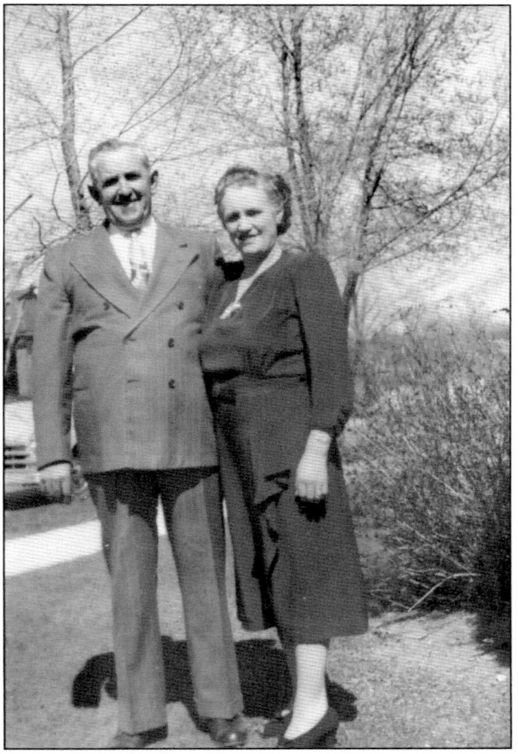

In this 1944 photograph, Martin Orriaga and his wife, Josephine Gaston, appear in front of their home at the of Taylor and Gordon Streets in Reno. The couple was one of the most successful Basque hotel owners/operators in Reno. At the time, they owned the Martin Hotel. (Courtesy Irene Arbeloa.)

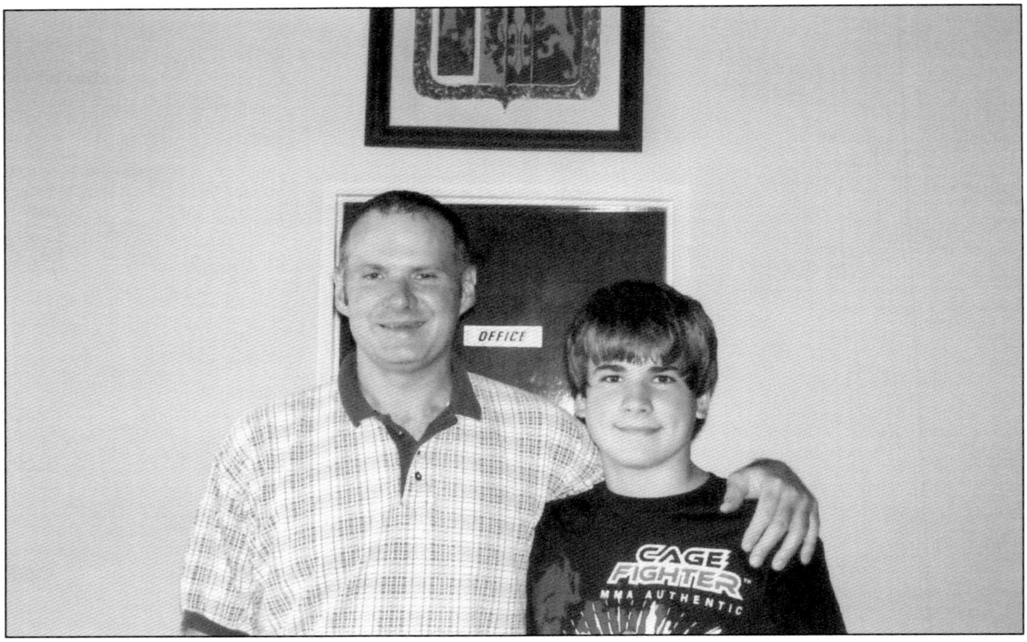

Philip Zubillaga and his son Patrick stand in their Santa Fe Hotel Restaurant in Reno. It must be heartening for dad to see his young son "hanging around" and helping in a line of work that requires long hours and few off days. There are fringe benefits that come with working in a Basque hotel: people are more tuned to diversity issues and more likely to speak Euskara.

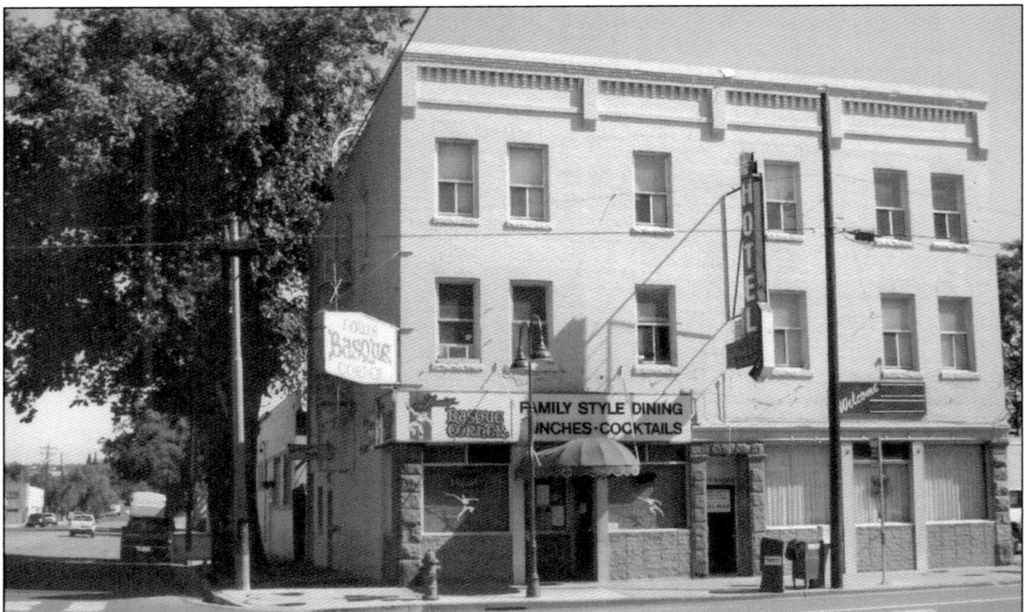

Since 1968, Louis' Basque Corner stands on the busy corner of Fourth and Evans Streets. Newcomers to Reno may not know that until I-80 was built, Fourth Street handled all the east-west traffic, which passed right by the front door of Louis and Lorraine Erreguible's place. It is a very popular corner in Reno, earning several awards for the best ethnic restaurant.

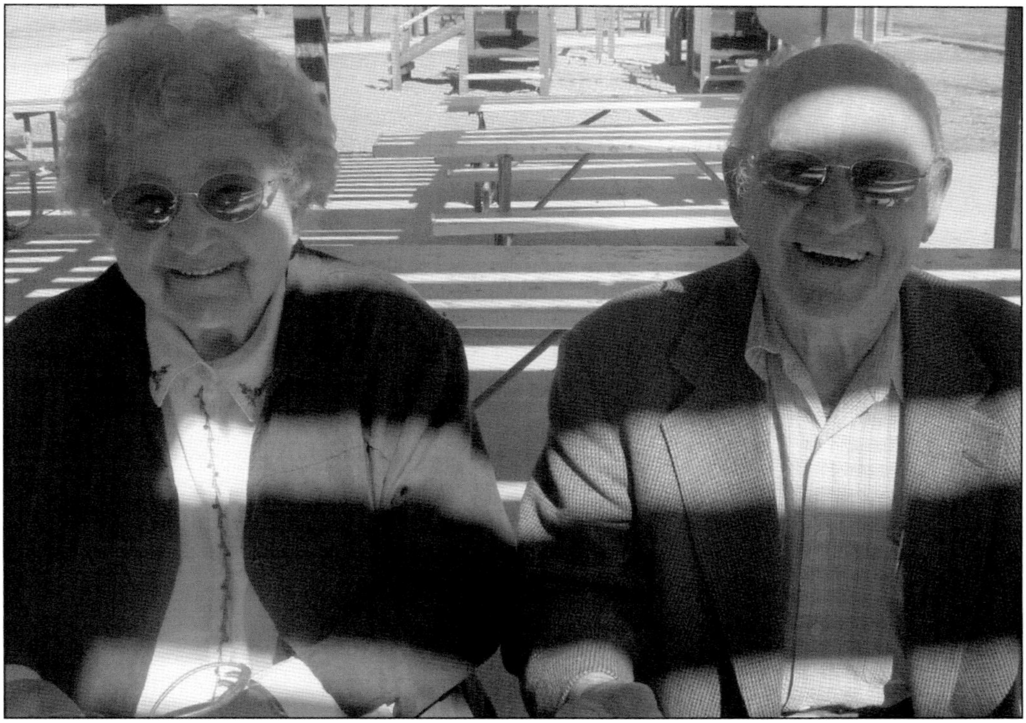

Lorraine and Louie Erreguible, owners of Louis' Basque Corner and longtime supporters of the Reno Basque Club, enjoy a club-sponsored get-together in Sparks, Nevada, in 2007. Though semiretired, they, along with their son Mark, still keep an eye on the business and on their many patrons and friends who frequent the establishment near downtown Reno.

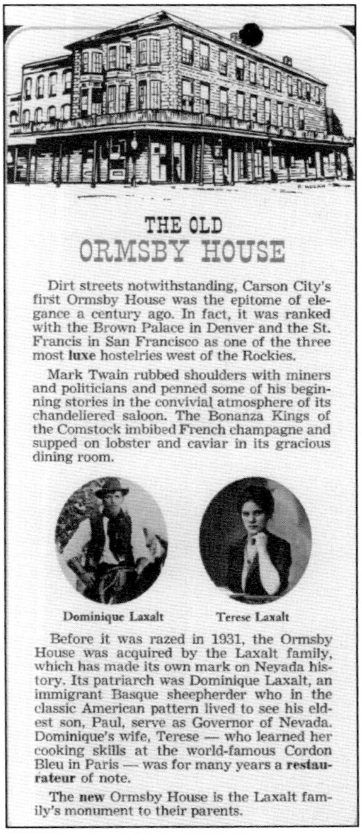

THE OLD
ORMSBY HOUSE

Dirt streets notwithstanding, Carson City's first Ormsby House was the epitome of elegance a century ago. In fact, it was ranked with the Brown Palace in Denver and the St. Francis in San Francisco as one of the three most **luxe** hostelries west of the Rockies.

Mark Twain rubbed shoulders with miners and politicians and penned some of his beginning stories in the convivial atmosphere of its chandeliered saloon. The Bonanza Kings of the Comstock imbibed French champagne and supped on lobster and caviar in its gracious dining room.

Dominique Laxalt   Terese Laxalt

Before it was razed in 1931, the Ormsby House was acquired by the Laxalt family, which has made its own mark on Nevada history. Its patriarch was Dominique Laxalt, an immigrant Basque sheepherder who in the classic American pattern lived to see his eldest son, Paul, serve as Governor of Nevada. Dominique's wife, Terese — who learned her cooking skills at the world-famous Cordon Bleu in Paris — was for many years a **restaurateur** of note.

The **new** Ormsby House is the Laxalt family's monument to their parents.

The Ormsby House was built in the capital city of Nevada, Carson City, in 1860 by Major William Ormsby, who was killed soon after in Nevada's first war between American Indians and whites. After the famed hotel started to show its age, it was bought by none other than an immigrant Basque sheepherder and his wife who owned a boardinghouse in Carson City. (Courtesy Ormsby House brochure.)

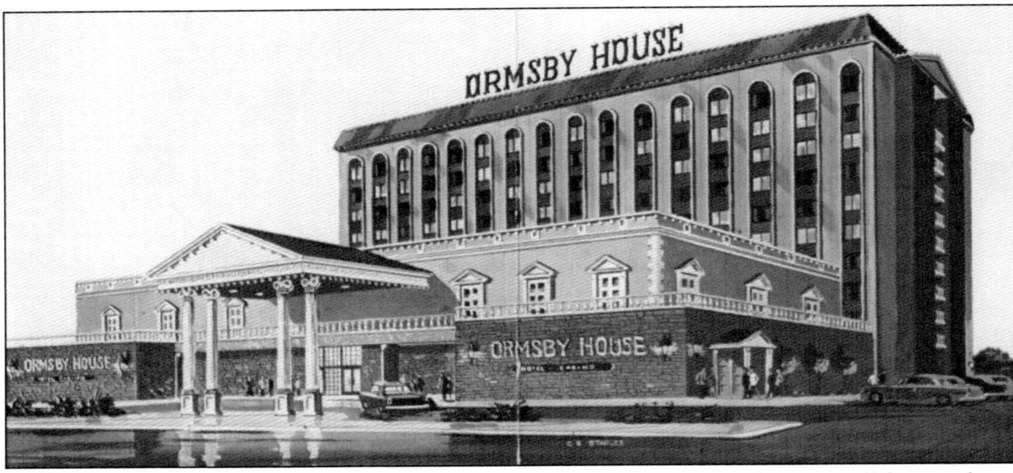

The Laxalts rebuilt the new Ormsby House in 1972 during Paul Laxalt's time off from politics, after he ended his tenure as governor of Nevada and before he became a U.S. senator. According to Paul Laxalt's *Memoir* (2000), the new hotel-casino ran into hard economic times as soon as it was finished, and it was disposed of in 1975. (Courtesy Ormsby House brochure.)

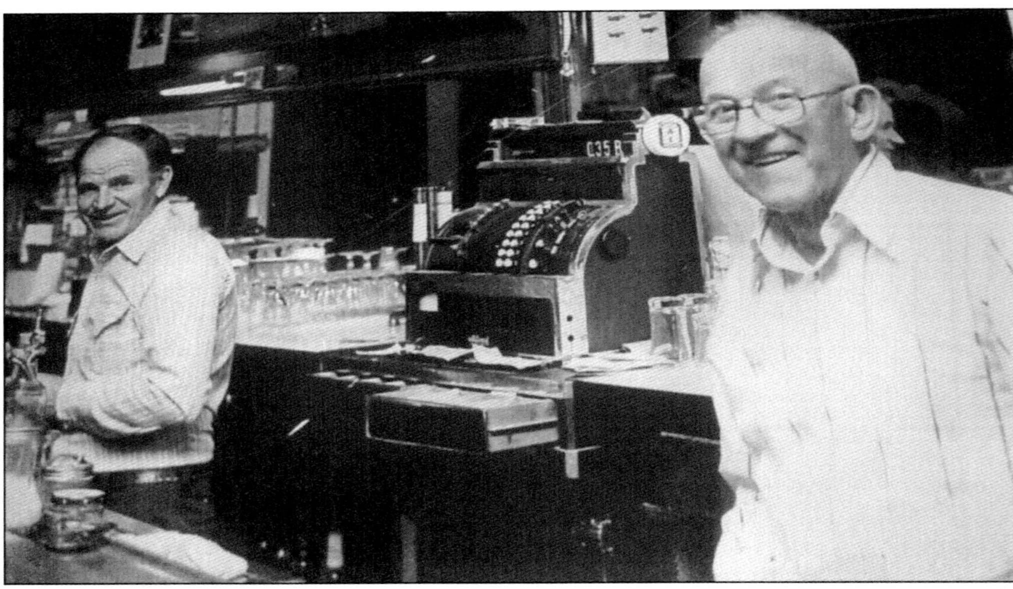

Jean Lekumberry (left) and John Jaunsaras are tending bar at the JT Bar-Restaurant in Gardnerville, Nevada. Lekumberry, often with a cigar in his mouth, was a fixture in the Basque community of the area. Jaunsaras and his brother Joe, while sheepherding in the High Sierra, went down in history for saving from extinction the pure strain of the Paiute trout. (Courtesy Helen Jaunsaras/Chappell.)

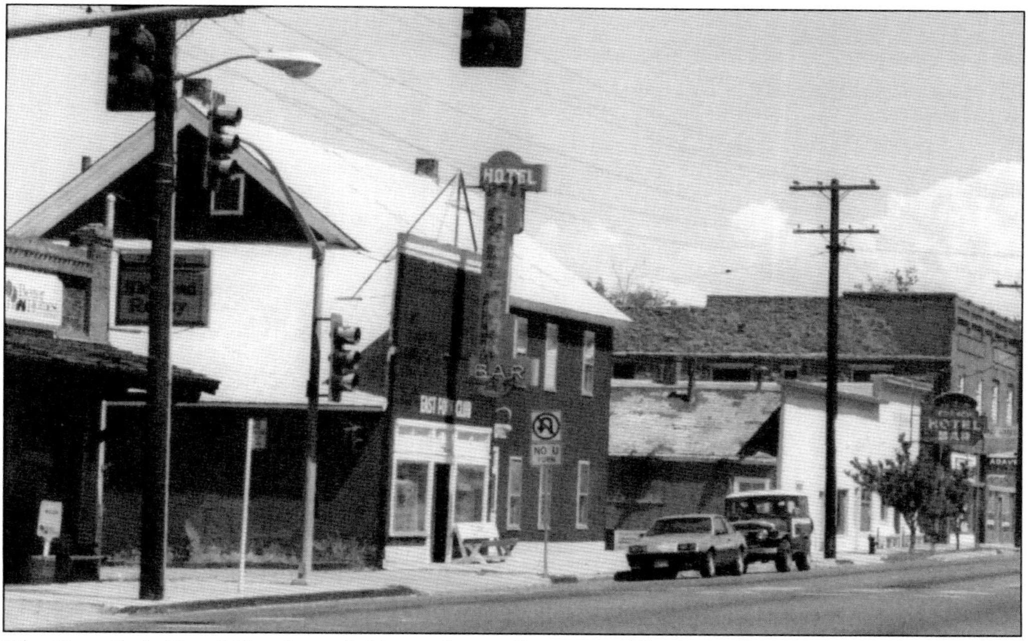

The East Fork Hotel Bar (near left) saw heavy Basque traffic from the 1900s to July 18, 1986, when it burned down. According to *From the Basque Country to the Sheep Camps of the Carson Valley—Eskual Herritik Carson Valley'ko Artzain Kanpamendurat* (2001), Raymond Borda and his wife, Gorgonia Martinez, bought the East Fork in 1921. (Courtesy Shirley Yvonne Fraser.)

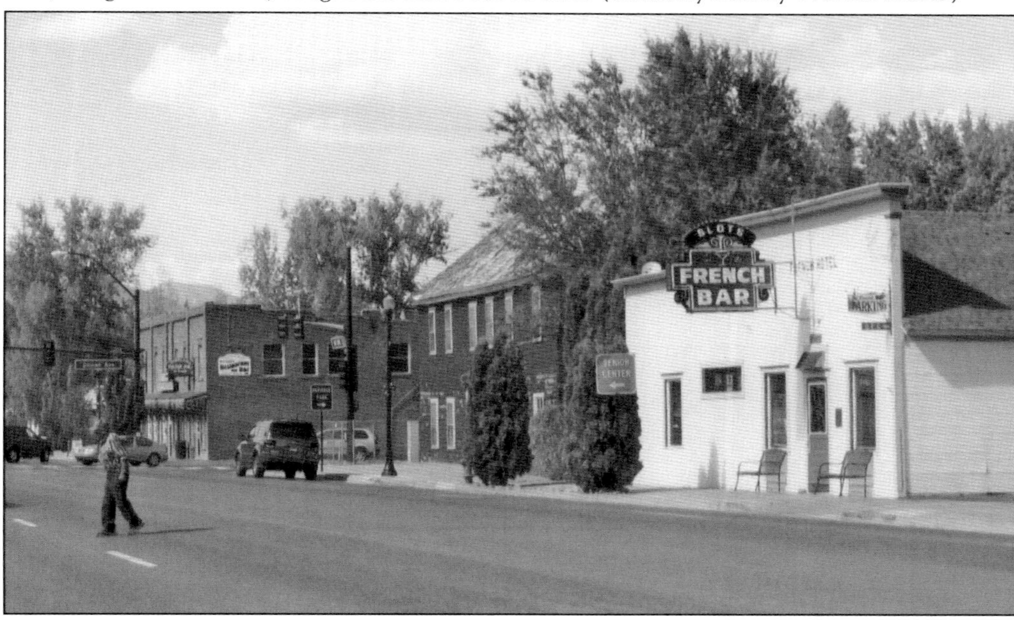

The French Bar and Hotel of Gardnerville, Nevada, is located next to East Fork Hotel. There are, or were, a lot of "French" businesses and place names all over the West, but many of them are undoubtedly Basque. Many people who called themselves "French Basques" could not speak French, but in school they were indoctrinated that being French was chic, while being Basque was not.

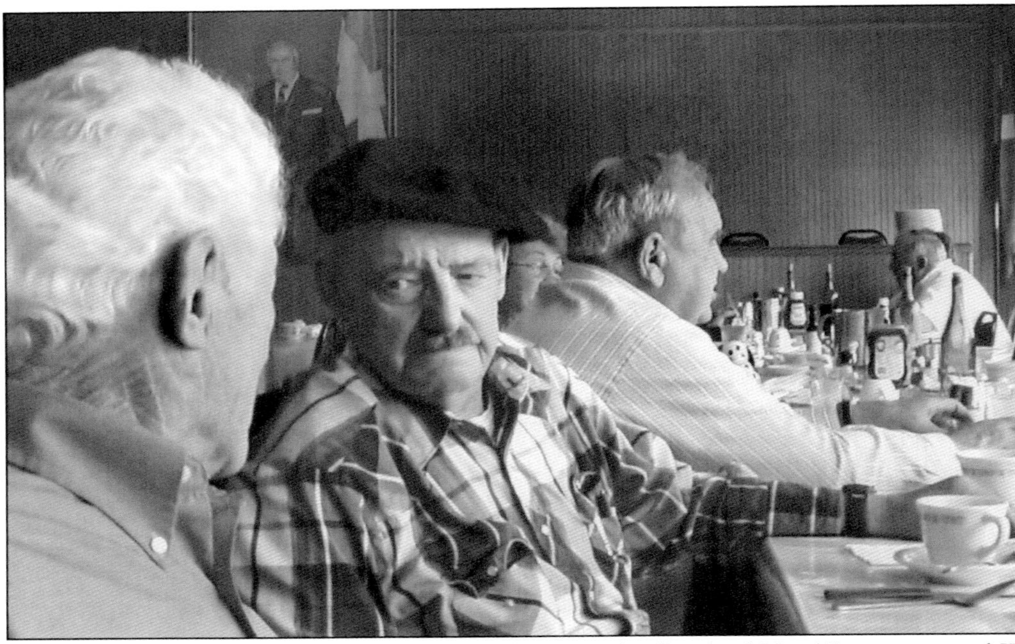

The Basque neighborhood in Gardnerville lay between the Overland Hotel-Restaurant and JT Bar-Restaurant. In the photograph, from left to right, Jean Jaureguy, J. P. Gezanburu, and Mike Inda enjoy the annual Easter Sunday dinner at the Overland. Special dishes like prawns, salami, asparagus, and dry-cured hams are served with all the lamb one can eat, topped off with café royale and singing.

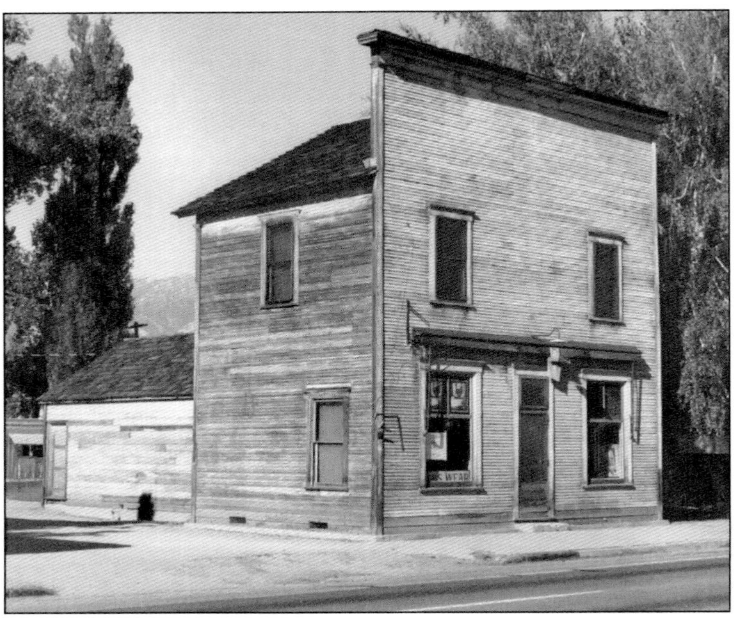

Frank Yparraguirre had a long surname, and when in 1945 he bought Olly Hogner's store in Gardnerville, he called it Perry's Dry Goods. The unusual building was moved down from Virginia City in 1893. The Yparraguirres now lease the place, and there are stories about the ghost of a nice old man still living in the building—Frank died a centenarian.

At the back of this 1925–1926 photograph, a handball court with the spectators' sitting area is visible. It was attached to the Hotel Español, a classy Basque hotel in Reno, owned by Eusebio and Francisca Barcos; it had a big bar, and from the large dining area patrons could see the players. Photographed is Josephine Orriaga with her two daughters, Irene and Lucy, and an unidentified third little girl. (Courtesy Irene Arbeloa.)

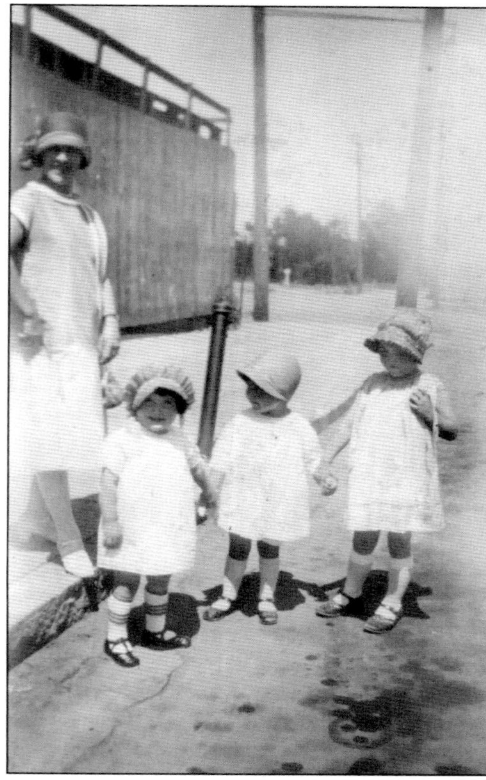

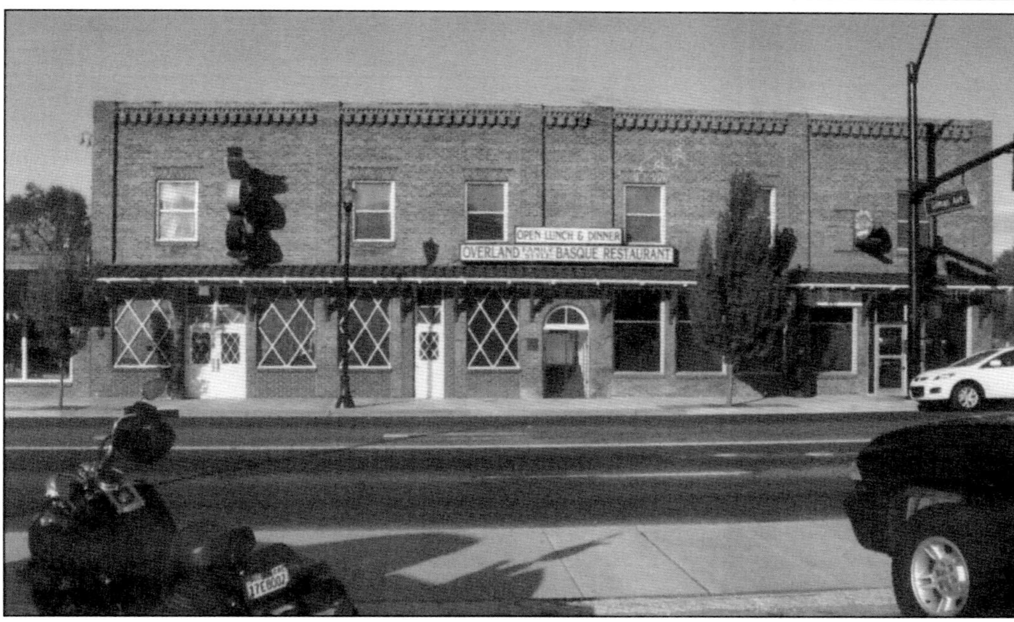

In the afternoon sun, the Overland Hotel-Restaurant in Gardnerville has that solid look of a brick building even though it is over 100 years old. Its present owner, Elvira Cenoz, keeps it in tiptop shape inside and outside. She is willing to sell the place to a good buyer, but until then, she will continue cooking Basque food.

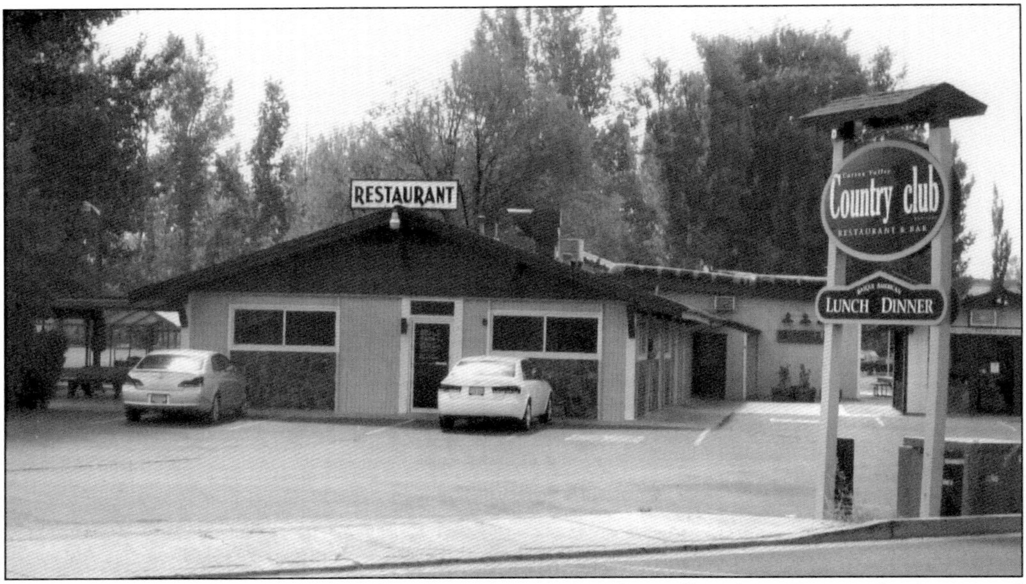

The Country Club Restaurant is the third place in Gardnerville where Basque food is served today. The shady setting under the big trees at the edge of the golf course differs dramatically from the typical Basque restaurant surrounded by concrete. Dick Chapell and Helen Jaunsaras owned it before Jesus Rey and Carlos Iribarren bought it in 1974.

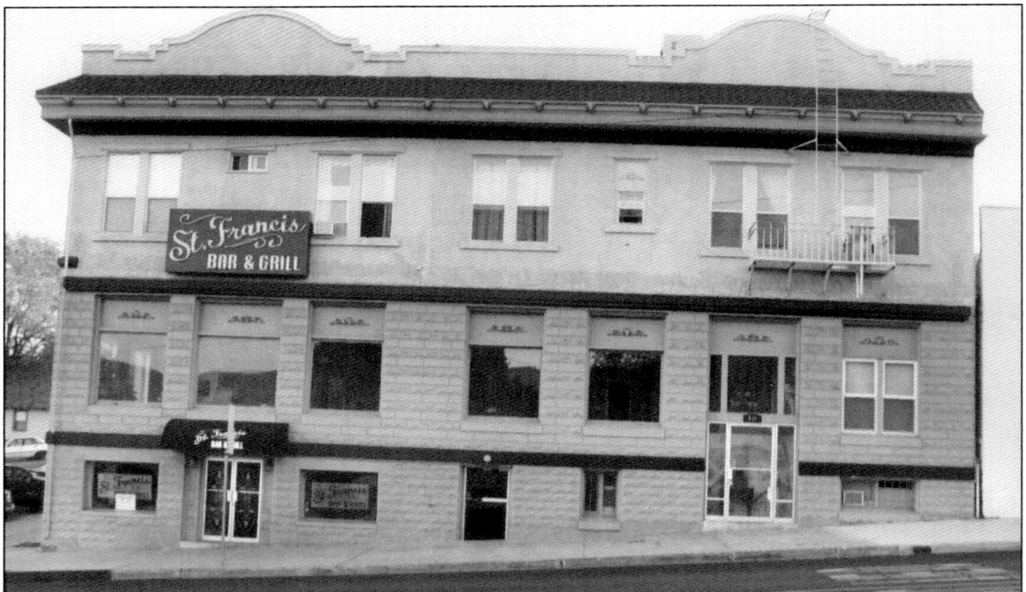

Susanville, California, had sawmill jobs and attracted many Basques and a few hotels, among which the St. Francis, built of stone, excelled. In 1989, the author met the elderly Marie Jeanne Goñi, the owner, with whom she spoke in Basque before they had dinner. No one could forget the 2-inch-thick prime ribs they served. The Goñis sold the place in 2000.

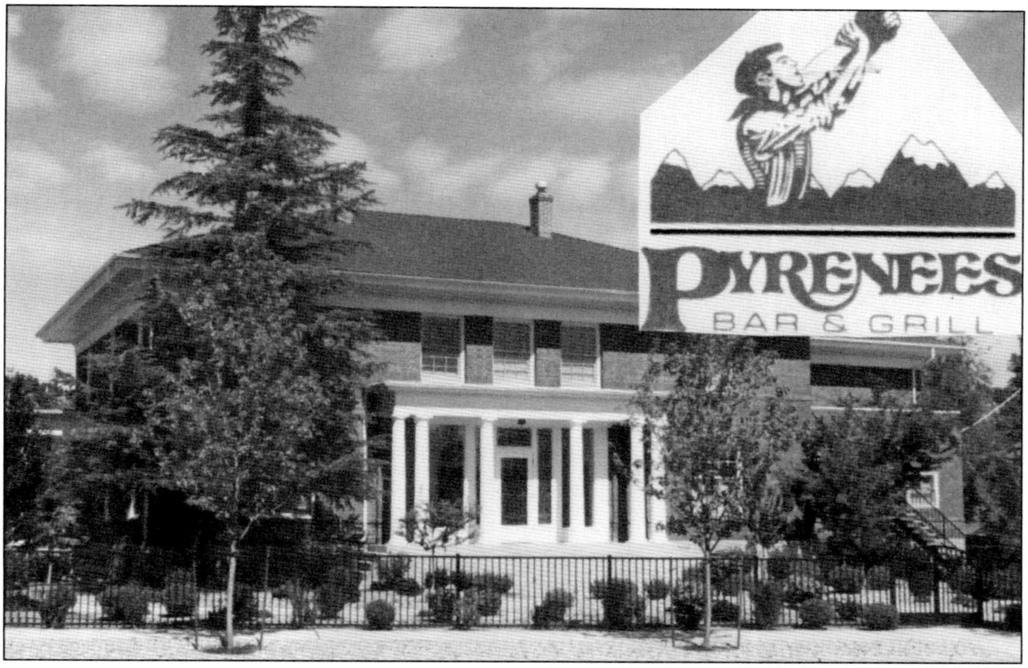

During the few years the Pyrenees Basque Restaurant was open in the early 1990s, it caused a stir for its upscale setting (see picture), location (California and Flint Streets in Reno), and food. The manager, G. Kent Mowry of Winnemucca, Nevada, tried to offer a different Basque cuisine, but the nudes in the men's restroom certainly gave the patrons something to talk about.

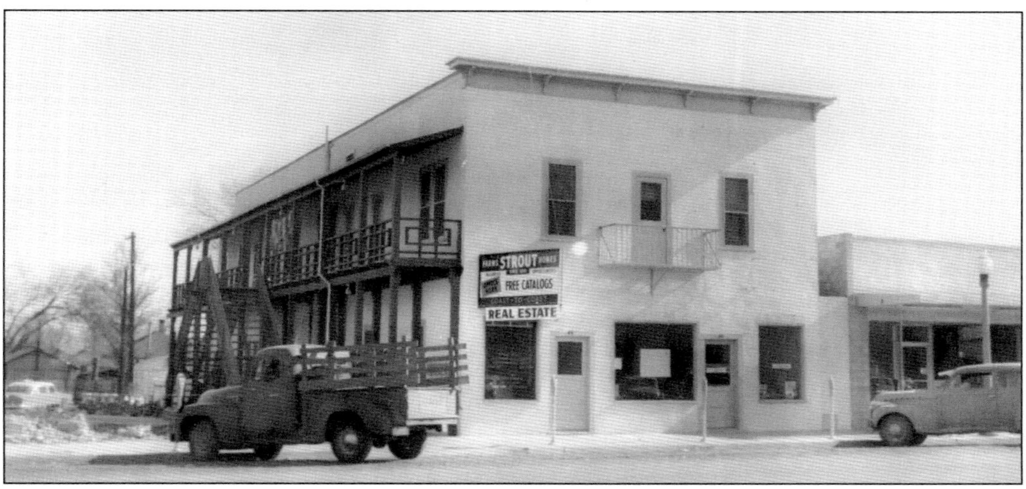

Ramon Arrizabalaga and his wife, Tomasa Erquiaga, bought the Grand Hotel in Fallon in 1929 from Pete and Juanita Hauret. This is a 1954 photograph after they sold it to their son Ramon Jr. and Louie Moiola and had been converted into apartments. Arrizabalaga came from Araba to the United States in 1909 and herded sheep near Austin, Nevada. (Courtesy Joan Arrizabalaga.)

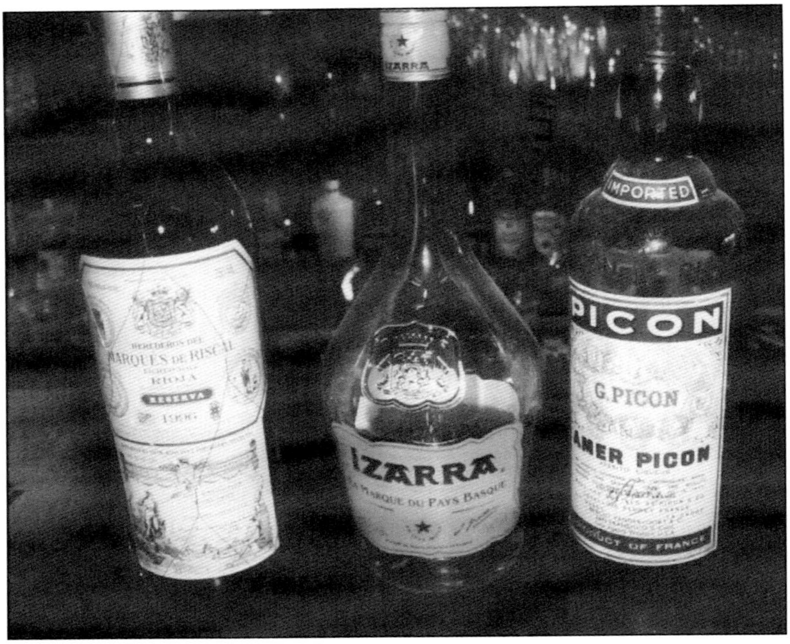

Picon is a French drink, but here in the United States, the Basques have made it their own. One reason for eating at a Basque restaurant is to have a picon before dinner. The bottle on the left contains red wine from the world-famous wine region of Rioja. Izarra (meaning "the Star" in Basque) is a sweet-tasting green liqueur made with Pyrenean herbs.

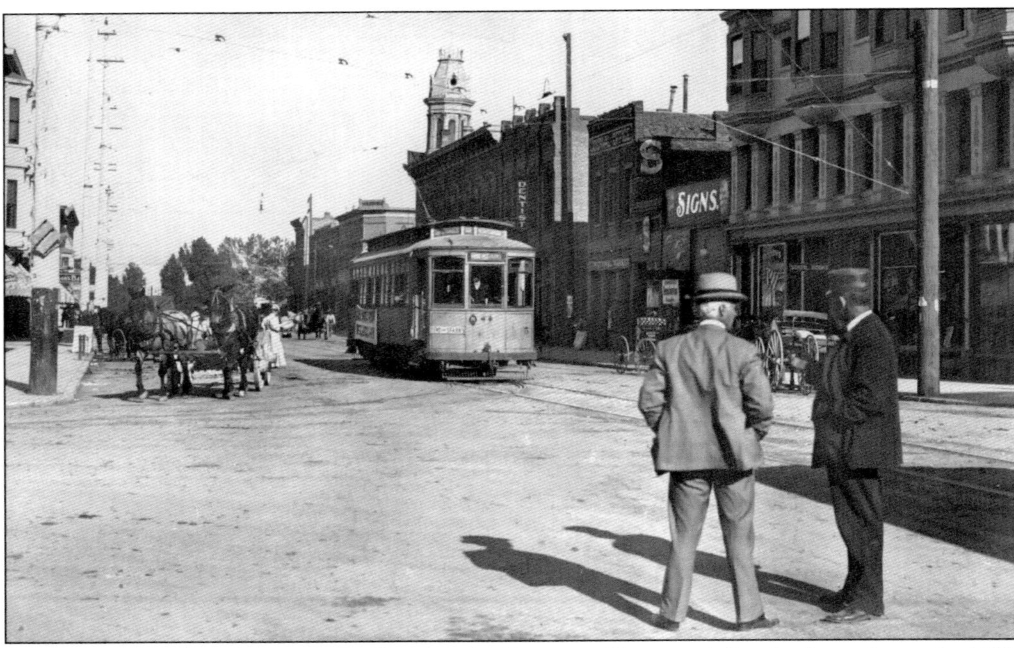

Neil Cobb says that the Reno Trolley shuttled between Reno and Sparks from the early 1900s until the 1920s. The trolley was slow but fare was cheap. The photograph was taken on Second Street looking east. The tallest building on the right was the Washoe County Bank. (Courtesy Nevada Historical Society.)

Five

Getting Exposure through Festivals and Clubs

For nearly a century, the Basques were almost invisible to mainstream America. Besides being hardworking and law-abiding, sheepherding was no ticket to receive media attention. Thanks in part to Hollywood, cattle are better known than the cute lambs, and steaks are more popular than lamb chops. But lamb is actually healthier.

The Basques had no civic organizations, and they did not really have much of a chance, but they hardly missed occasions such as weddings to get together to eat, drink, sing, and dance. However, the first ethnic jolt that the Basques across northern Nevada and California experienced took place in Reno in 1931 when Paulino Uzkudun fought Max Baer. Under the blazing sun, a huge crowd attended the bout, among them 3,000 Basques. It was the largest concentration of Basques ever seen in the West, and the best part was that Uzkudun won the match. His victory influenced the way Basques perceived themselves vis-à-vis the American society. Local Basque hotels not only made a healthy profit on that day, but the pumped-up Basques were singing a different song. The downside was that, with the sheepherders in town, the coyotes got fat.

Almost two decades later, the conditions were right to organize the 1959 Western Basque Festival in Sparks, which turned out to be a landmark of its own. It attracted thousands of Basques as well as Americans, and it laid the format for future festivals still celebrated today.

Reno Basques formed their Zazpiak Bat Club in 1966, and it is still going strong, claiming a membership of 200 families and individuals. Gardnerville's Mendiko Euskaldun Kluba, initiated in 1981, became very active and has been hosting Kantari ta Bertsolari Eguna (Sing and Improvise Poetry Day). Susanville has an annual *mus* tournament, and Carson City has the best-attended festival but without the benefit of a club.

Today most Basque organizations in the West are undergoing cultural adjustments and even survival pains, as the immigrants who were the backbone of the clubs in the past are aging and passing the baton to the next generation. One thing seems certain: The younger Basques still love most of the things their parents did and will carry on eating, drinking, and dancing.

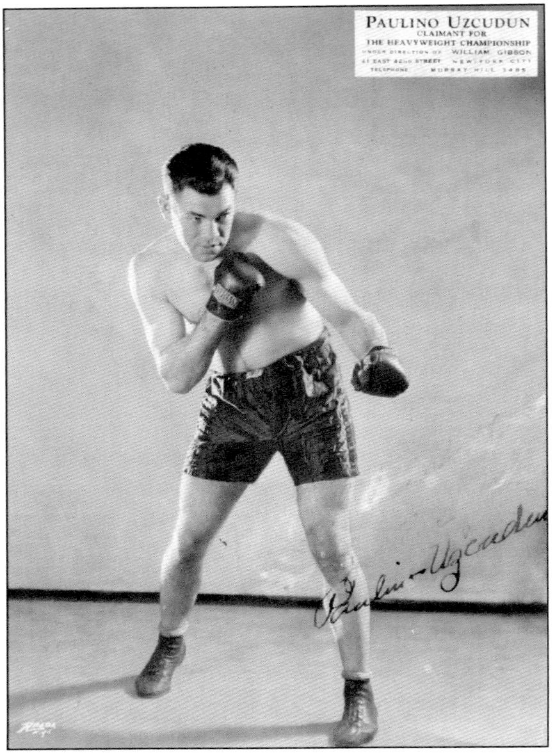

Paulino Uzkudun, Europe's heavyweight boxing champion, came to Reno because Nevada sponsored boxing. He wanted to fight the American champion, but he was told he would have to become a citizen first, which he refused. Uzkudun began his career as an *aizkolari* (Basque woodchopper), later migrating to boxing. (Courtesy Special Collections, UNR.)

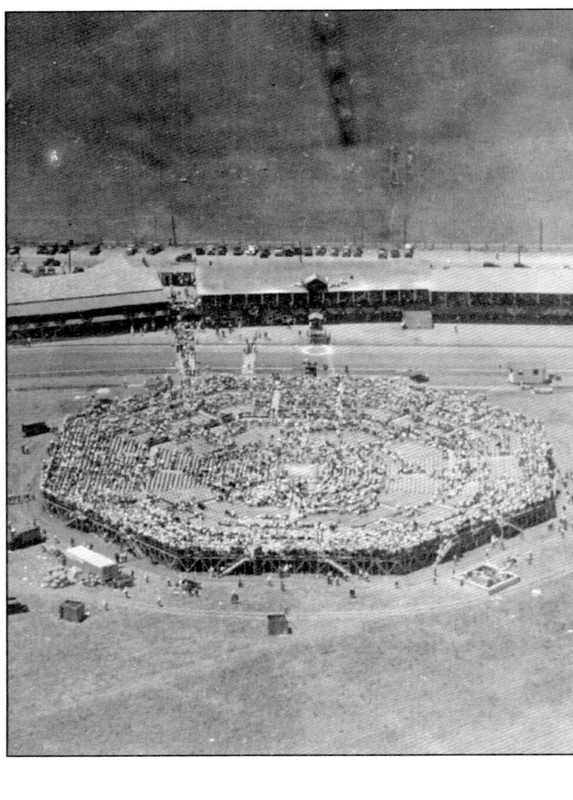

According to the local media, more than 18,000 people came to Reno to watch the match between Max Baer and Paulino Uzkudun, the "Bounding Basque." It was the Fourth of July 1931, and the weather was hot and sunny, but the fighters went at each other for 20 rounds. In the end, the Basque "Woodchopper" won. (Courtesy Special Collections, UNR.)

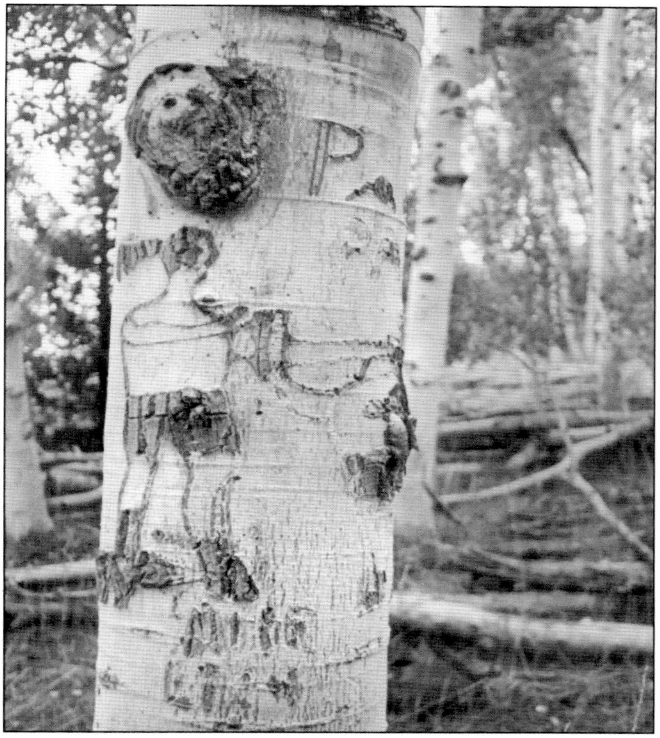

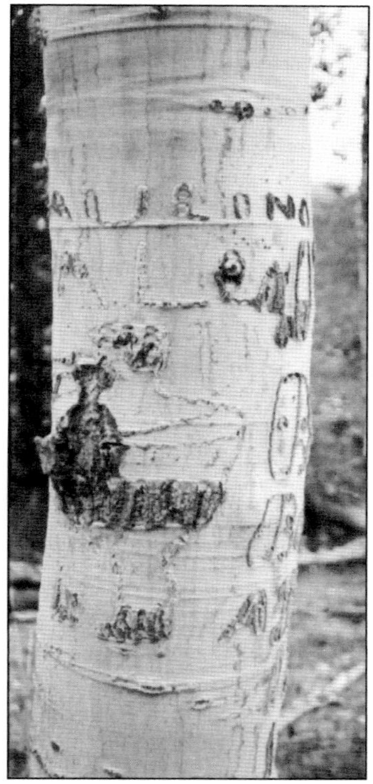

According to local historian C. Elizabeth Raymond, thousands of Basques cheered Uzkudun in his win against Max Baer in Reno. When many of them returned to the sheep camps, they could not wait to carve figures of boxers on aspens. Here is Paulino Uzkudun looking much bigger than his challenger, so anyone can guess who is going to win the fight.

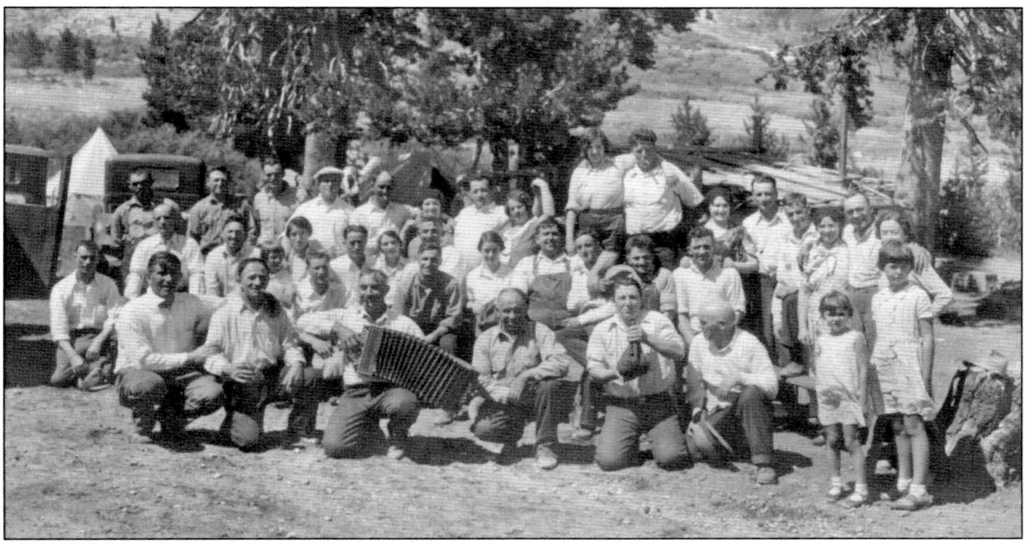

Thirty-nine happy Basques celebrate their way of life in the Sierra (a detail of this photograph is on the cover). Such picnics took place every year but became larger after Uzkudun's 1931 victory, which galvanized his compatriots. At far right is Nicolas Larena with his arm around his wife, Gabina; in front are their two daughters, Candida (left) and Grace. (Courtesy Irene Arbeloa.)

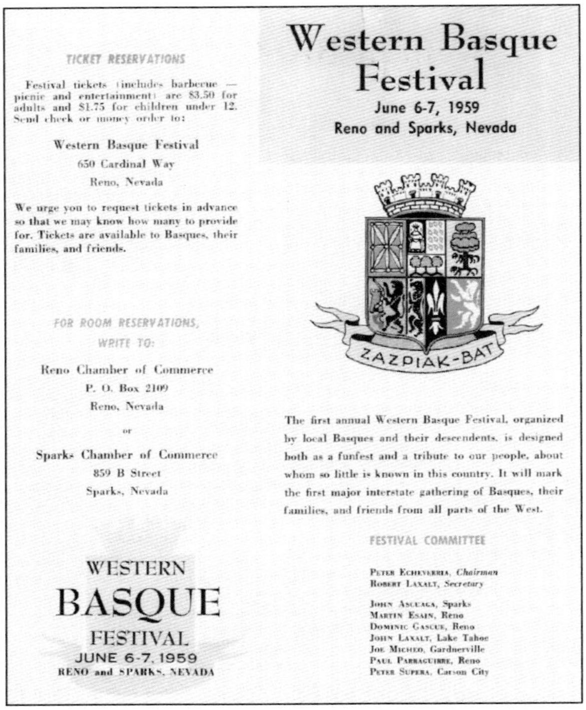

TICKET RESERVATIONS

Festival tickets (includes barbecue — picnic and entertainment) are $3.50 for adults and $1.75 for children under 12. Send check or money order to:

Western Basque Festival
650 Cardinal Way
Reno, Nevada

We urge you to request tickets in advance so that we may know how many to provide for. Tickets are available to Basques, their families, and friends.

FOR ROOM RESERVATIONS, WRITE TO:

Reno Chamber of Commerce
P. O. Box 2109
Reno, Nevada

or

Sparks Chamber of Commerce
859 B Street
Sparks, Nevada

WESTERN
BASQUE
FESTIVAL
JUNE 6-7, 1959
RENO and SPARKS, NEVADA

Western Basque Festival
June 6-7, 1959
Reno and Sparks, Nevada

ZAZPIAK-BAT

The first annual Western Basque Festival, organized by local Basques and their descendents, is designed both as a funfest and a tribute to our people, about whom so little is known in this country. It will mark the first major interstate gathering of Basques, their families, and friends from all parts of the West.

FESTIVAL COMMITTEE

Peter Echeverria, *Chairman*
Robert Laxalt, *Secretary*

John Ascuaga, Sparks
Martin Esain, Reno
Dominic Gascue, Reno
John Laxalt, Lake Tahoe
Joe Micheo, Gardnerville
Paul Parraguirre, Reno
Peter Supera, Carson City

Cultural clubs arose as more Basques retired from the sheep industry and settled in towns. In 1959, nine men from Reno-Sparks set up a committee for an ambitious event of Basque festivities, and by all accounts the success surpassed expectations. According to the local paper, more than 5,000 people attended, not all of them Basques. (Courtesy Basque Library, UNR.)

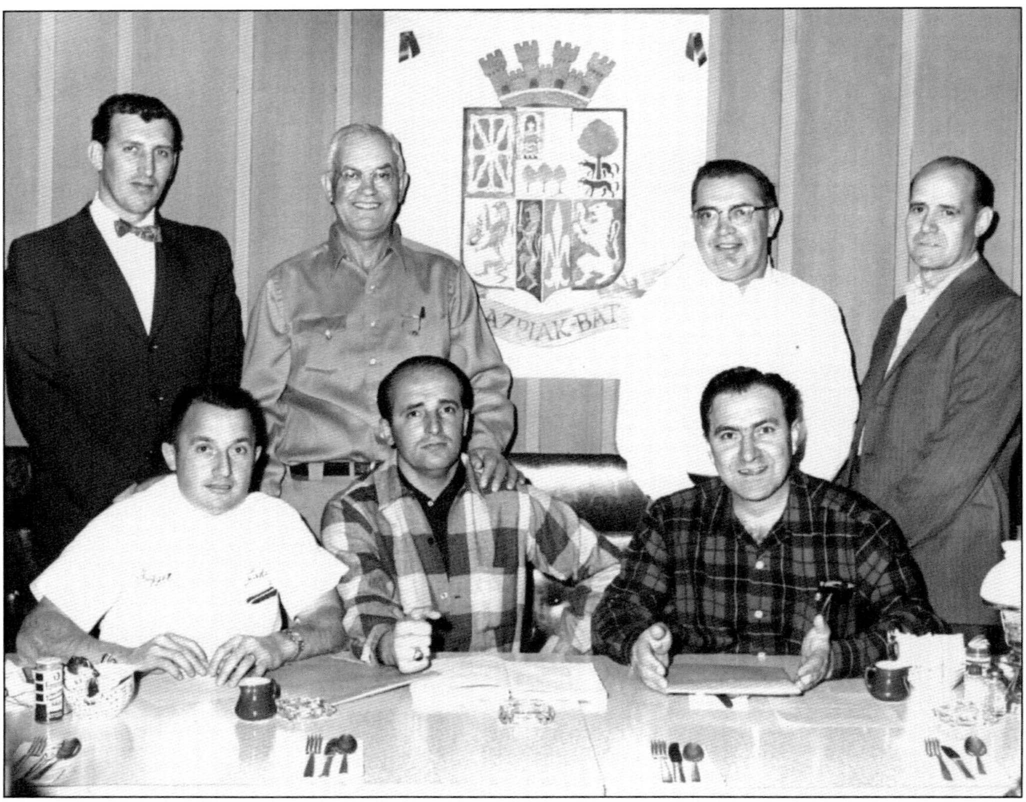

Seven of the nine committee members in charge of the Western Basque Festival appear in this picture. From left to right are (seated) John Ascuaga, Robert Laxalt, and Peter Echeverria; (standing) John Laxalt, Joe Micheo, Pete Supera, and Martin Esain. Even though the festival was promoted as the "first major interstate gathering of Basques," there had been an antecedent in 1931. (Courtesy Basque Library, UNR.)

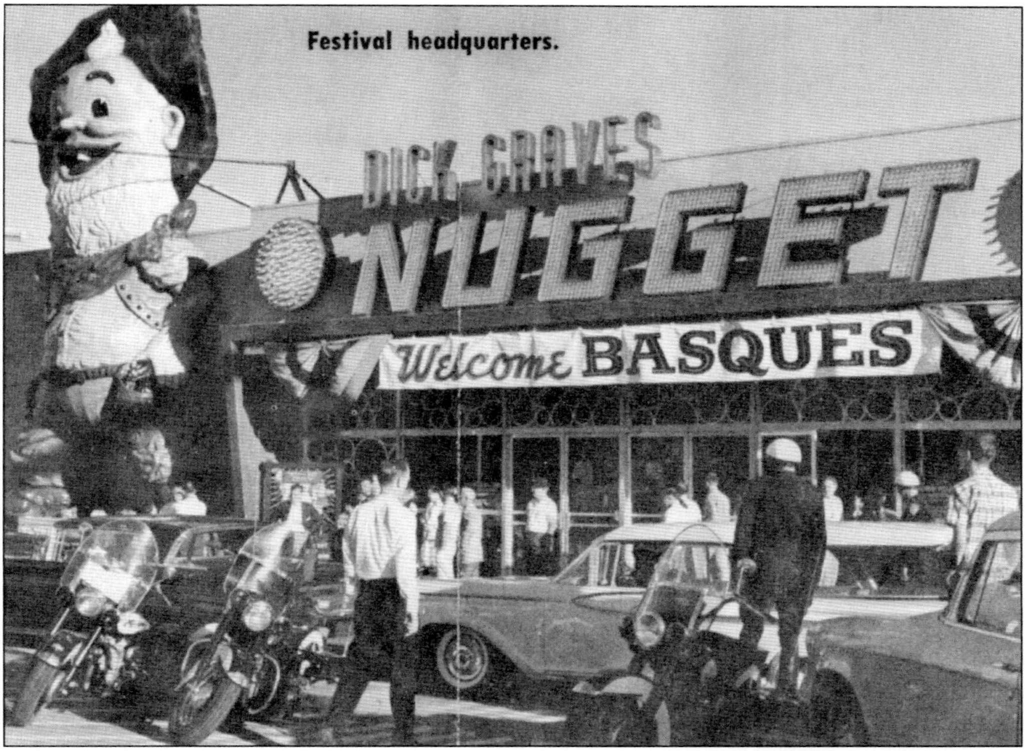

Dick Graves of Idaho, owner of the Nugget Hotel Casino in Sparks, Nevada, was married to a Basque, and his casino manager, John Ascuaga, was also Basque American. The two were probably the main reasons why Graves became the major sponsor of the 1959 festival, which turned out to be a great weekend financially and culturally. (Courtesy Basque Library, UNR.)

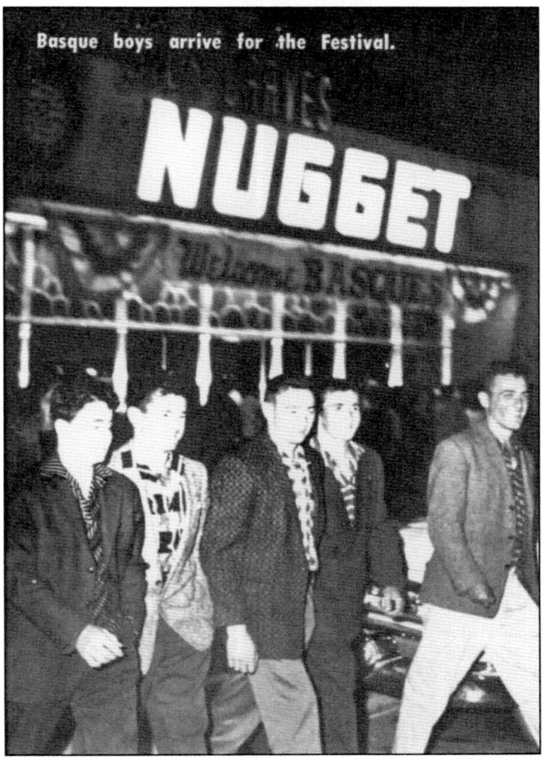

Under the "Welcome Basques" sign that hung over the entrance to the Nugget, a group of smartly dressed young Basque men look ready for fun and action. Though most of the visitors came from the contiguous states, some no doubt came from as far away as New York, Florida, and perhaps Mexico, too. (Courtesy Basque Library, UNR.)

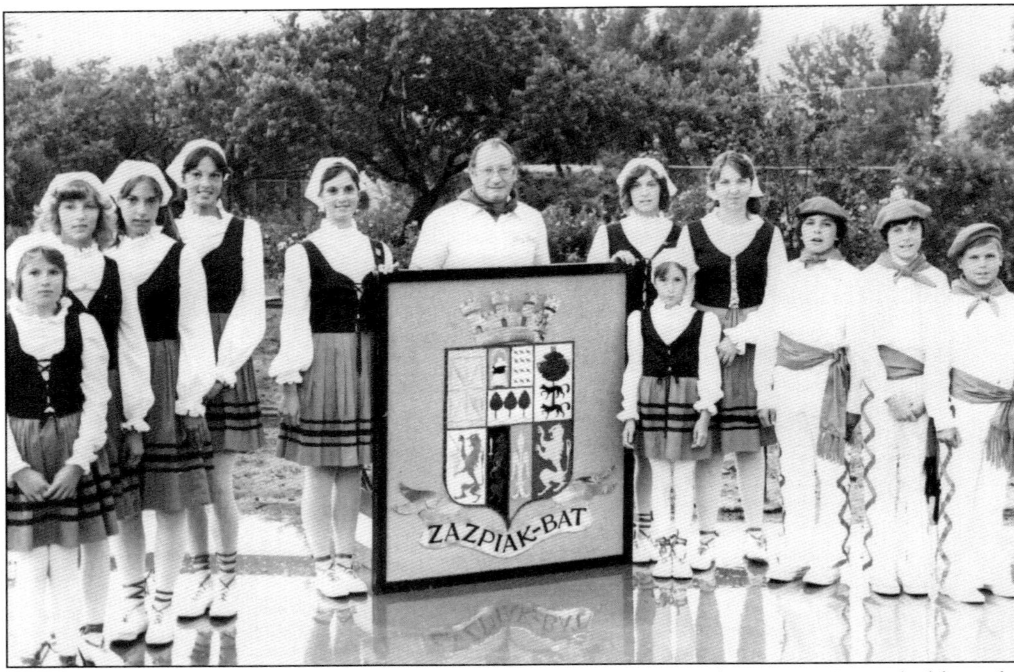

The Zazpiak Bat Reno Basque Dancers pose with the club's president, Tony Laca, holding the Basque coat of arms. The year is 1976, when the club had 317 paid members. (Courtesy Zazpiak Bat, Reno, Basque Club Archive.)

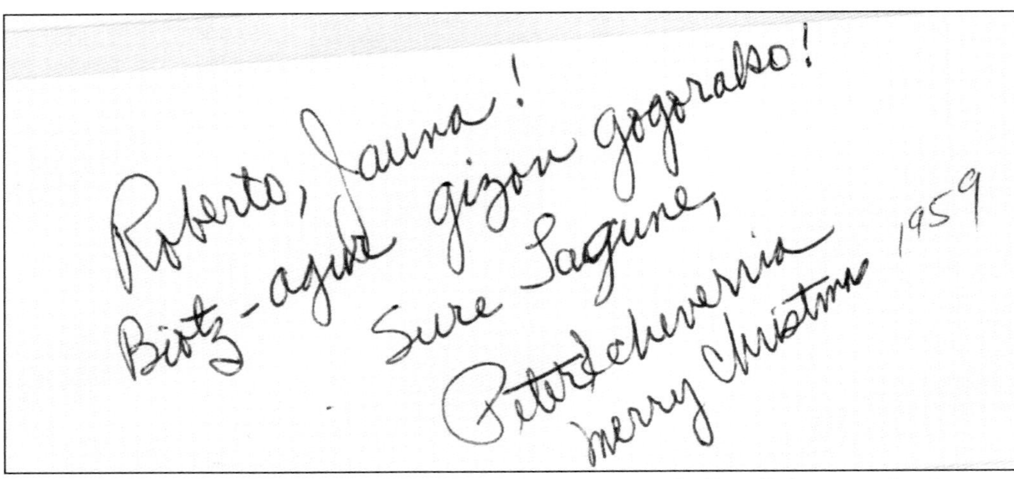

A memorable handwritten Christmas greeting in Basque was sent by Peter Echeverria, the chairman of the 1959 festival, to secretary Robert Laxalt. With the ethnic flames obviously still burning, this was an honorable effort by Echeverria, who wrote, "Mister Roberto, a cordial greeting to a man I remember; your friend Peter Echeverria." (Courtesy Basque Library, UNR.)

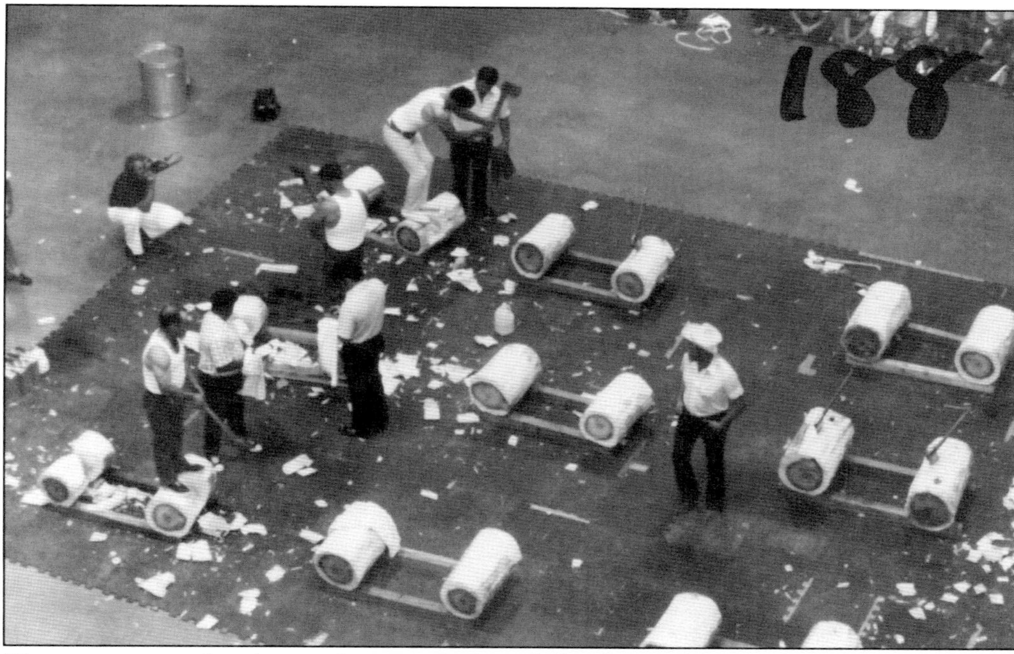

Three neat rows of six logs each are ready for *aizkolariak* (woodchoppers), and while they wait for the signal to start, their handlers offer the final instructions. The woodchoppers are almost always from the mountains of Navarre, as in this 1980s photograph of the Reno Festival. (Courtesy Zazpiak Bat, Reno, Basque Club Archive.)

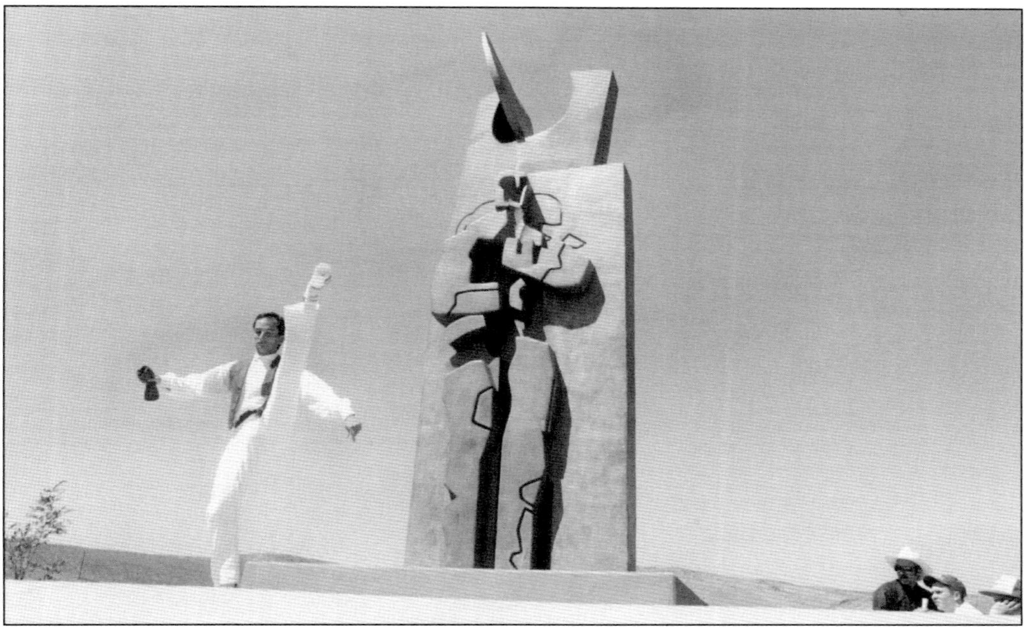

On August 27, 1989, the Basque Sheepherder Monument at the Rancho San Rafael Park in Reno was inaugurated. The abstract bronze sculpture is 23 feet tall, the work of Nestor Basterretxea. Representatives of the Basque regions joined local officials at the microphone, while the European dancer's stylistic high kick puts some life into the sculpture. (Courtesy Basque Library, UNR.)

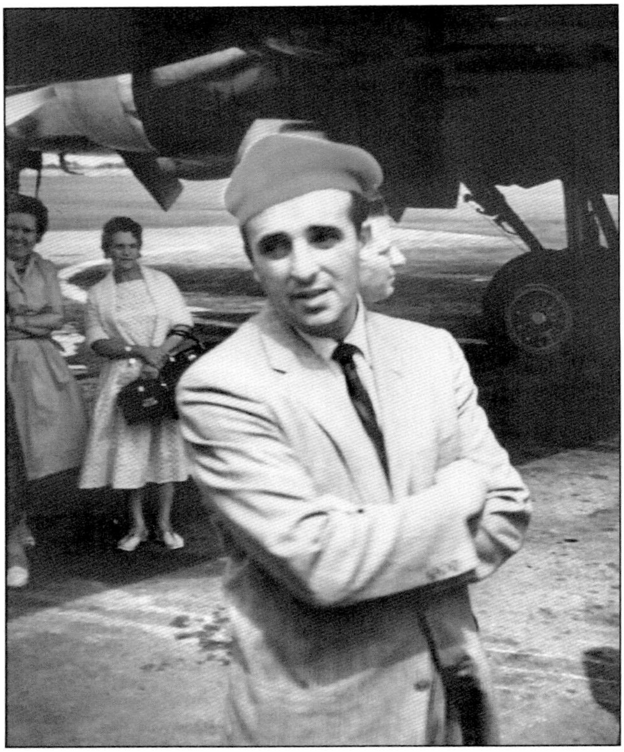

Robert Laxalt, here seen at the Reno airport, sports a red beret in 1959. Two years earlier, he had published *Sweet Promised Land*, the watershed story of his immigrant sheepherder father whose "home was the hills." As the number one book about Basque Americans, it was pivotal to the very idea of the 1959 festival and other subsequent developments. (Courtesy Basque Library, UNR.)

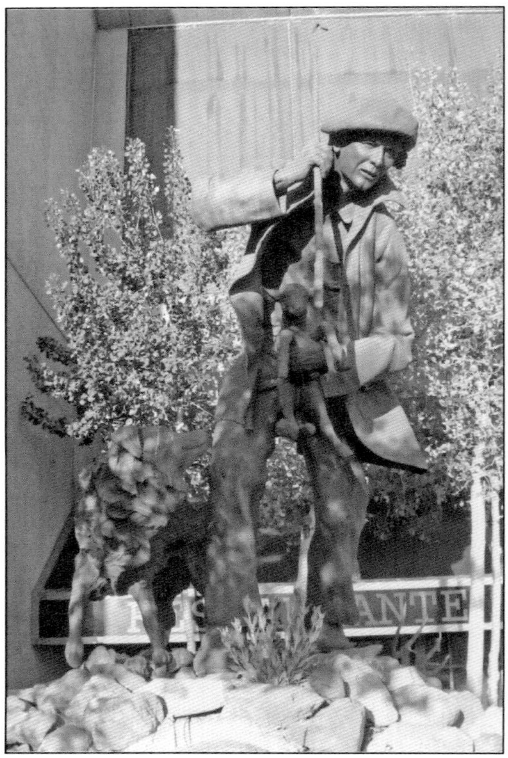

Many Basques, especially the sheepherders, did not like the abstract sculpture raised in Reno to honor them. They said there was "nothing sheepherder" about it—by the way, the lamb had been added to the statue to appease such critics. John Ascuaga, owner of the Nugget Hotel Casino in Sparks, erected this more "natural" sheepherder monument outside the west wing of the casino.

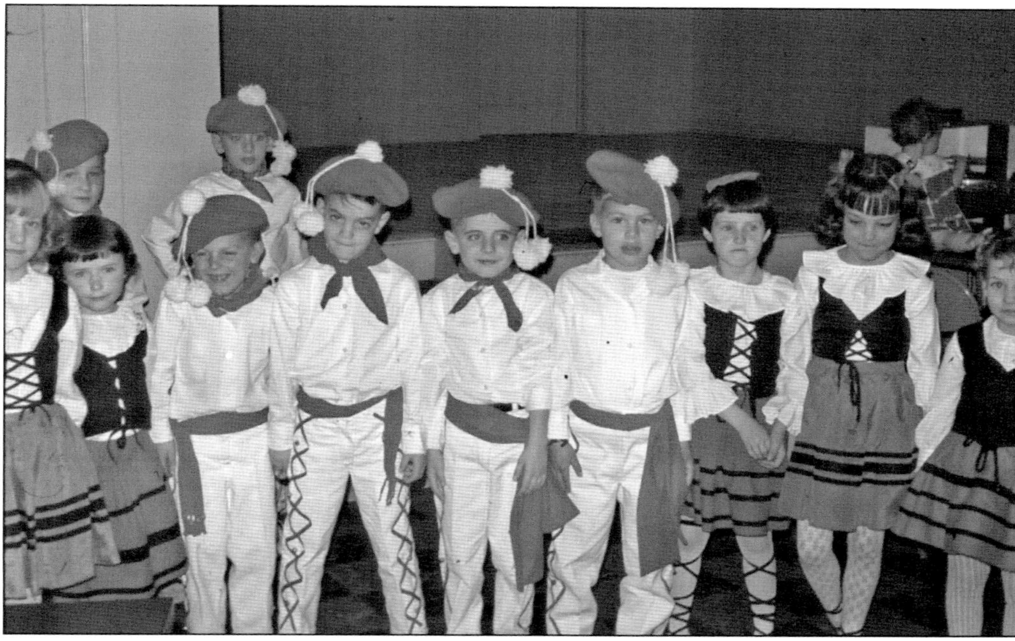

Voltaire identified the Basques as "the people who dance in the Pyrenees," and hundreds of young and old dancers in dozens of Western cities can vouch for that. Here is one such group in Reno dated 1969. One can tell in their faces that kids love to put on the colorful costumes and the red berets and dance. (Courtesy LeRoy Arrascada.)

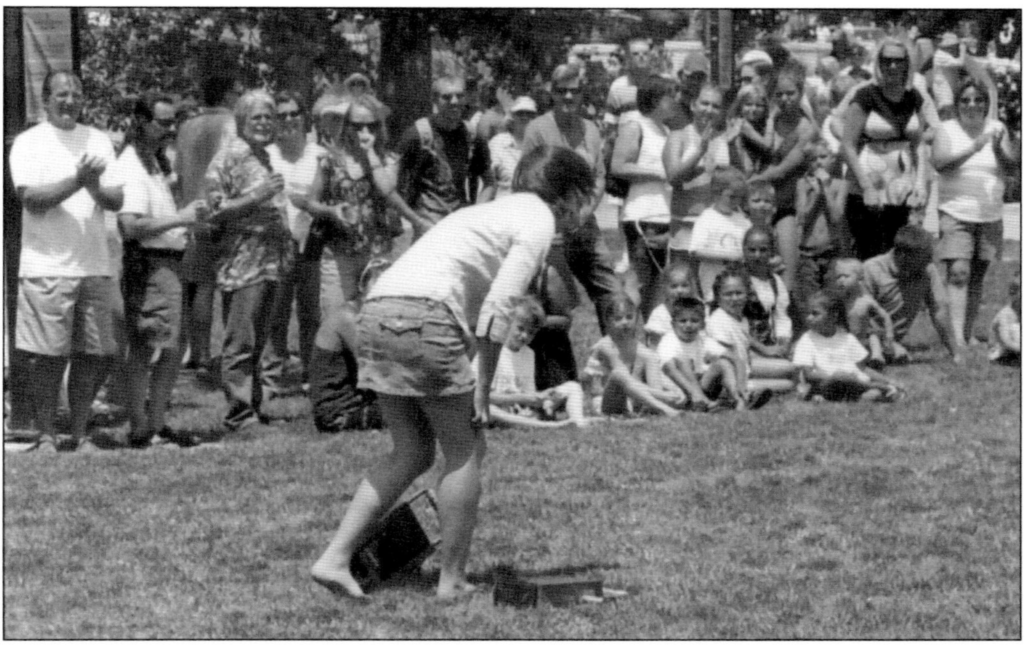

Basque sports are so popular that non-Basques come to watch and take part in the tug-of-war and *txingak*, and gender is not an issue. Participants carry txingak in their hands as far as they can (men's weigh 105 pounds and women's 75). Here a young lady reaches her limit and drops them. People cheer her just the same.

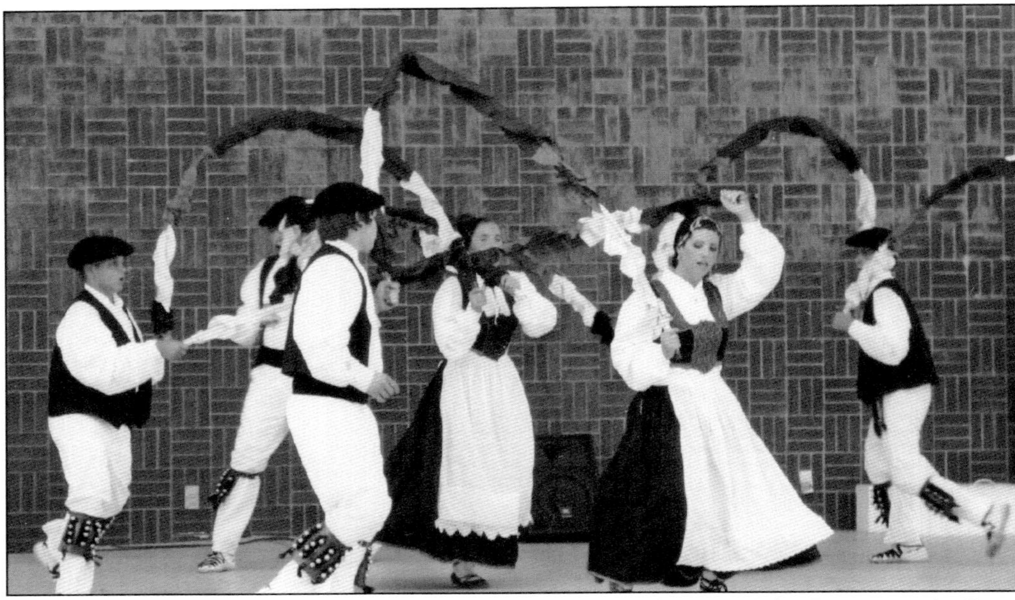

These are the Chino, California, Gauden Bat Dancers performing Arku Dantza at the Reno Basque Festival. It takes dedication to teach folk dancing, and then it takes discipline to practice and a little more sacrifice and money to travel almost 400 miles from Southern California to Nevada. *Aupa!* (Bravo!)

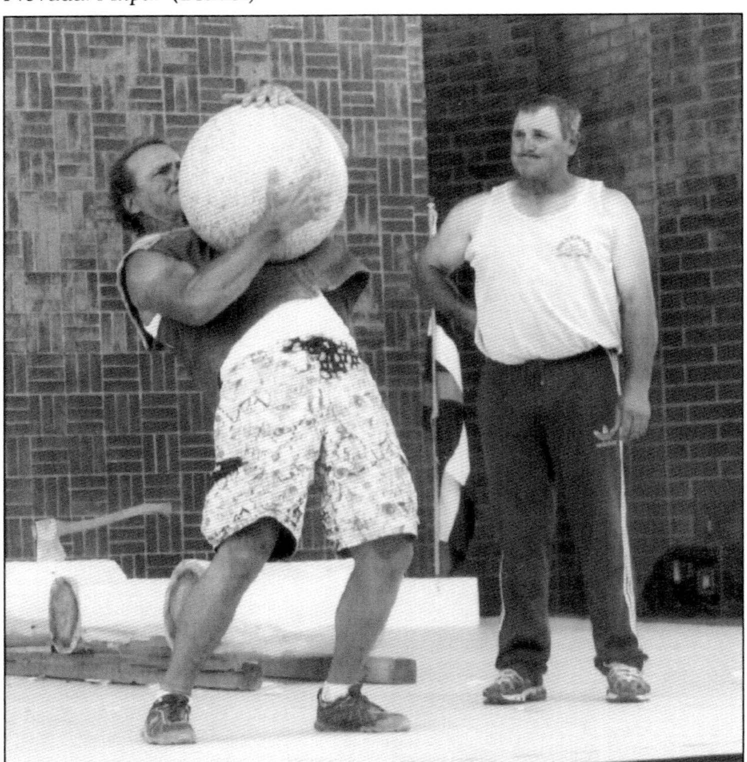

Tom Davison "plays" with the granite round ball weighing 100 kilos (220 pounds); he picks it up and then maneuvers it around his neck a few times before he sets it down. Here he performs at Wingfield Park during the 2008 Reno Basque Festival. The biggest stone lifted by the European Basque champion, Miel Saralegi, weighed about 740 pounds.

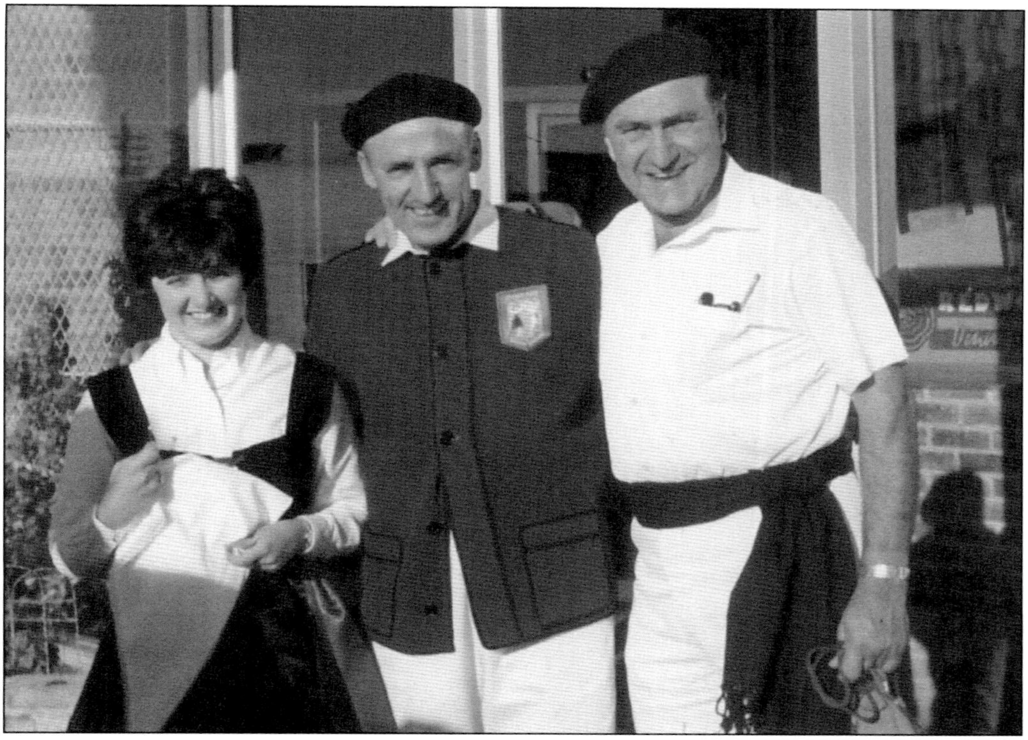

Music and dancing—with a little help from food and drink—put the spin into every Basque festival. Jimmy Jausoro of Idaho (1920–2004) and his accordion were the stars of hundreds of festivals. Always smiling, here he stands between Peter Echeverria and an unidentified lady in Reno in 1969. (Courtesy LeRoy Arrascada.)

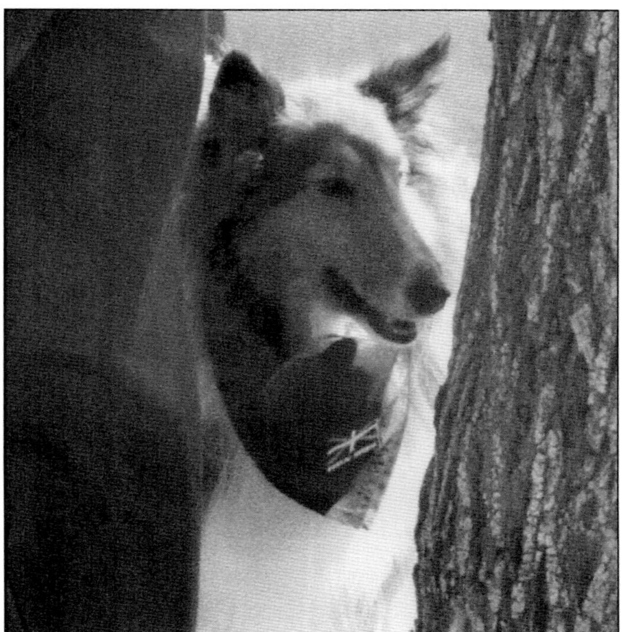

Nowadays even dogs—sheepdogs, that is—dress up for work. The Carson City, Nevada, Basque Festival features a sheepdog competition, and in 2008, there were about a dozen dogs—trainees and experienced—competing, all sporting Basque bandannas around their necks.

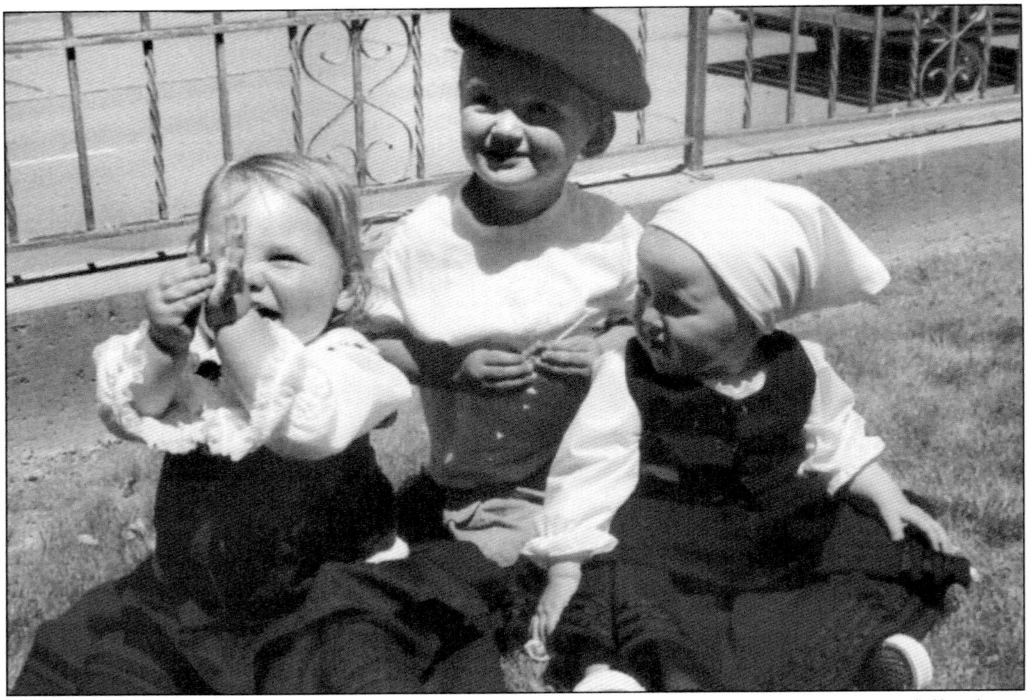

What photographer could resist these three charming little Basque Americans in full ethnic regalia? The picture was taken at a 2007 Basque Festival.

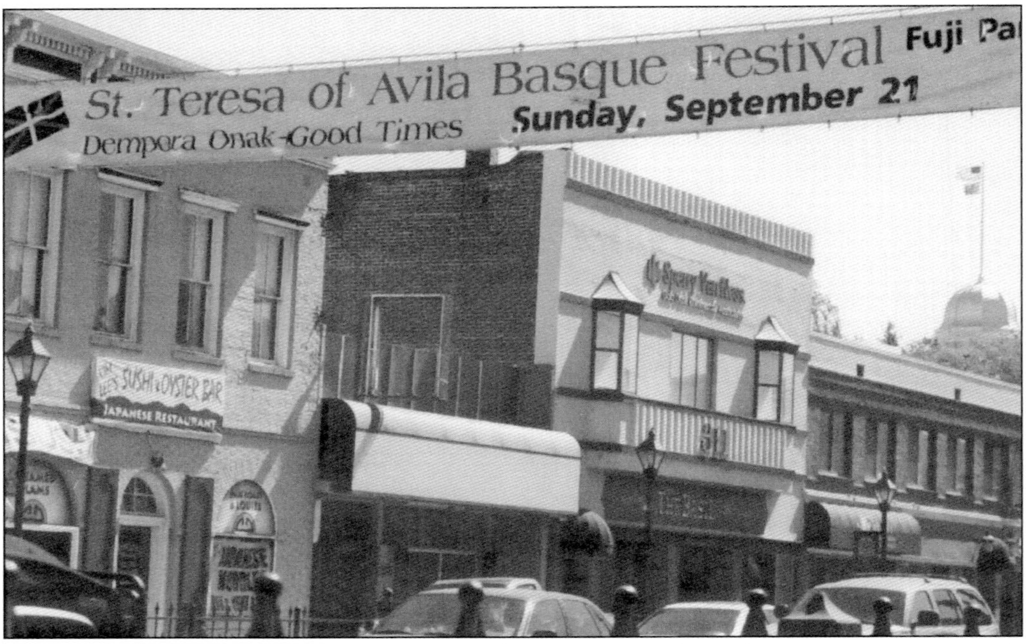

Against the background of the silvery dome of the state capitol and the American and Nevada flags flying in the afternoon sun, the banner announcing the 2008 Basque Festival was strung across the main street of Carson City, Nevada. The translation of *Dempora Onak* as "Good Times" is strictly literal, not the best, but everyone had a good time and the weather was great, too.

Six

Center for Basque Studies

The Basque-language weeklies *Escualdun Gazeta* (1885–1886) and *Californiako Eskual Herria* (1893–1898) of Los Angeles, California, pioneered news-reporting efforts to describe and document the Basques in the West. Among a few other short-lived publications, the *Voice of the Basques* of Boise, Idaho, was the most prominent, but alas nobody matched the Californians in their use of the language.

Uzkudun had awakened his countrymen in 1931, and the 1959 Sparks festival had introduced Basque culture to mainstream America. Just as significantly, in 1962, Paul Laxalt, son of a sheepherder, became lieutenant governor of Nevada, governor in 1966, and senator in 1974. His brother Robert Laxalt, a writer and founder of the University of Nevada Press, supported the idea of a Basque Studies Program (BSP), which had been proposed in 1961 by a University of Colorado consultant. Finally, in 1967, the BSP got off the ground, and for the next three decades, it ushered Basque scholarly work into the English-speaking world.

BSP came into being at the right time, when Basque culture was under attack by the Spanish dictatorship of Francisco Franco. In those circumstances, to have an American university initiate a program of Basque studies seemed like manna from heaven to Basque scholars. BSP received support from the Basques in the United States and after Franco's death from the Basque government of Euskadi as well. But officially at least, BSP remained distant from the Basque American community. However, through William A. Douglass, the coordinator for three decades, BSP published successfully the Basque Series and occasional papers on Basque topics.

In 1999, Basque anthropologist Joseba Zulaika, as BPS's new director, quickly established an advisory board that included leading Basques and Basque supporters. Profound changes followed; BSP's name was changed to the Center for Basque Studies (CBS), and fresh new initiatives were promoted; under Zulaika's leadership, the center was ushered into the digital age. CBS expanded with five full-time faculty positions, and it regained a prominence on the campus of the University of Nevada, Reno, and in the Basque Country. Aided by its extensive Basque Library, CBS has become a clearinghouse of Basque scholarship in the United States.

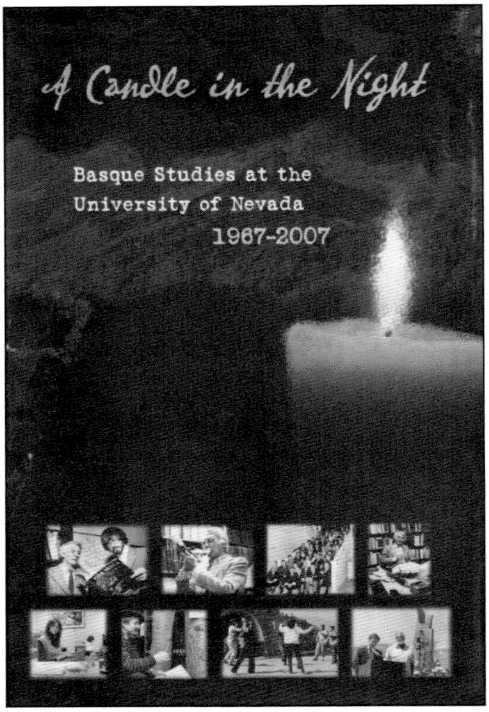

Basque president Jose Antonio Ardanza visited Reno in March 1988 and was moved by the University of Nevada's Basque studies. He said that considering the 35 years of dictatorship the Basques suffered under Franco, the Basque Studies Program was like a candle in the night. When in 2007 the history of the Center for Basque Studies was published, *A Candle in the Night* was an appropriate title.

This little-known 1968 photograph was taken in the governor's mansion in Carson City, Nevada. Seated at the far left at the bottom of the stairway is Robert Laxalt, followed by his brother Paul Laxalt, the governor. The occasion was a dinner to raise funds for the infant BSP at the University of Nevada, Reno. Such official support proved invaluable for the program. (Courtesy Basque Library, UNR.)

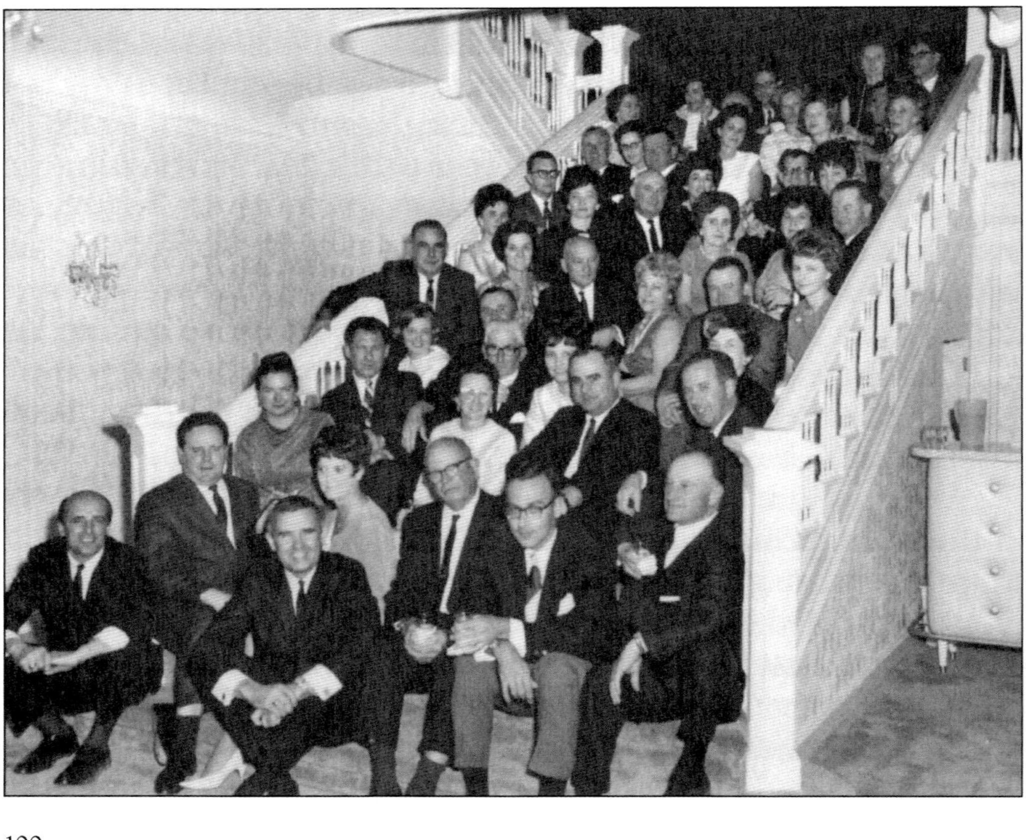

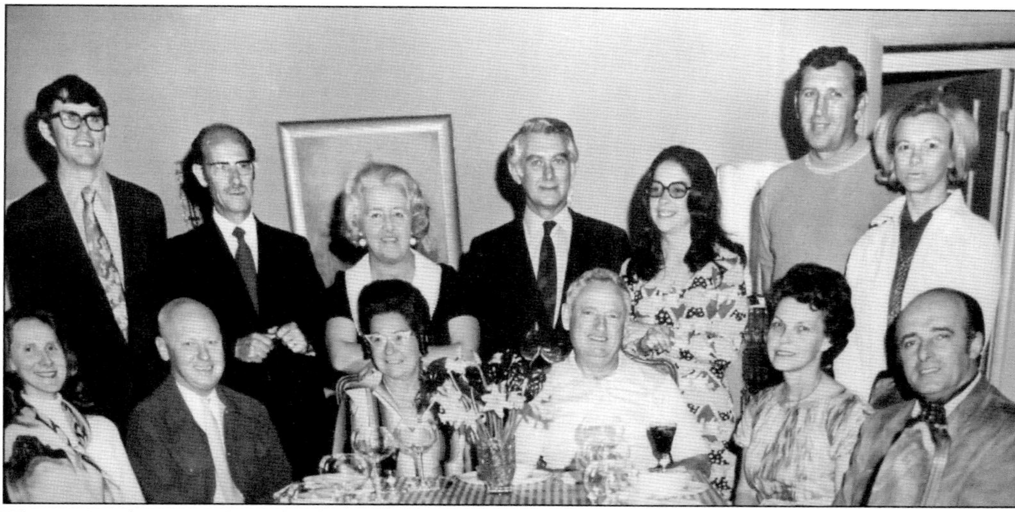

This 1971 photograph took place in the home of the Gastañagas of Reno. From left to right are (seated) Patricia Douglass, UNR president N. Edd Miller, Ellen and Eugene Gastañaga, Nena Miller, and Robert Laxalt; (standing) BSP coordinator William A. Douglass, Eloy and Amparo Placer, Jon Bilbao, Linda Gastañaga, John Laxalt, and Joyce Laxalt. (Courtesy Basque Library, UNR.)

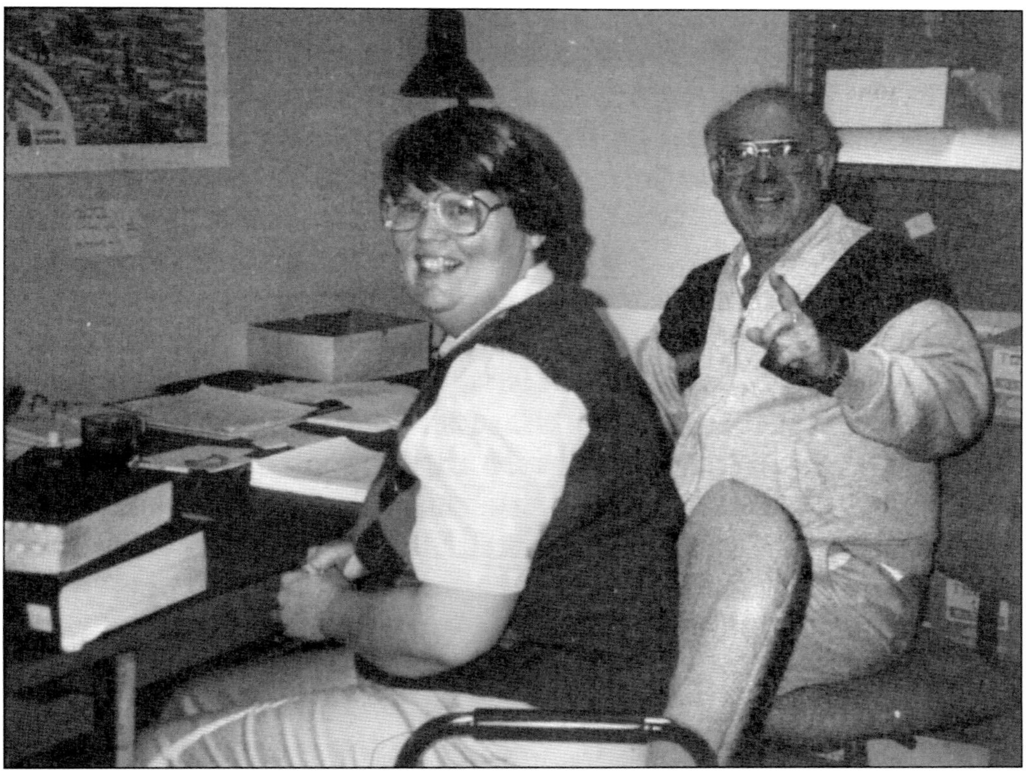

The Basque-English dictionary by Gorka Aulestia and Linda White—photographed here—is one of the signal accomplishments of CBS. Aulestia put together the Basque component and White the English part. It was published in Reno in 1989. (Courtesy Basque Library, UNR.)

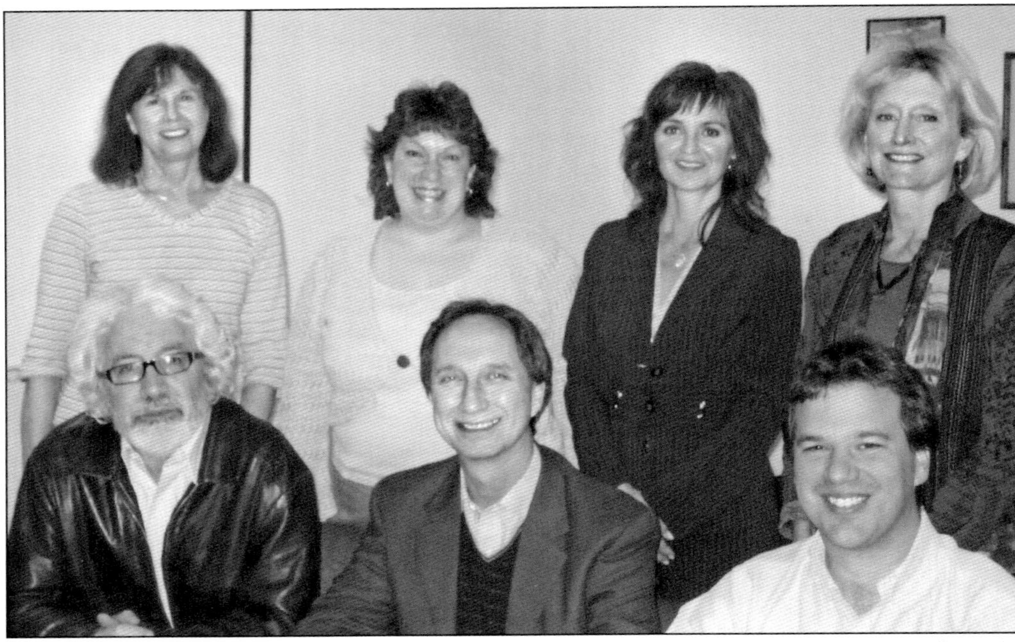

This is a *c.* 2005 photograph of the CBS faculty and staff. From left to right are (seated) Joseba Zulaika, Carmelo Urza, and Xabier Irujo; (standing) Jill Berner, Kate Camino, Gloria Totoricaguena, and Sandra Ott. Totoricaguena is no longer with CBS. (Courtesy Basque Library, UNR.)

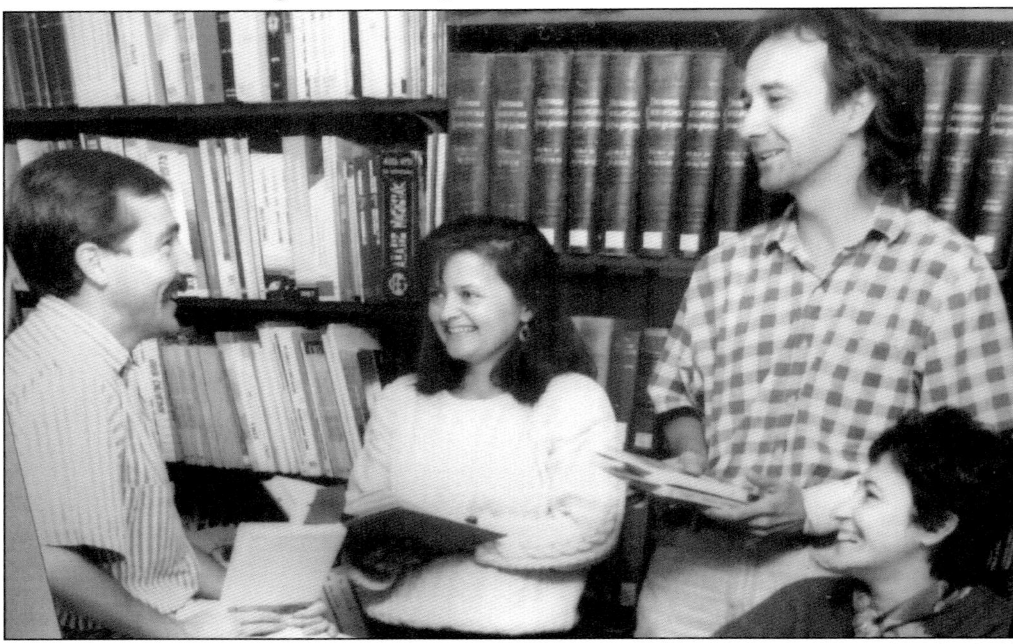

The Center for Basque Studies has become a must-visit school for scholars interested in the field. Every year, numerous individuals visit, stay, study, and conduct research. Taken in the Basque Library, this 1990s photograph shows, from left to right, Enrike Corocostegui, now an engineer; Estibaliz Amorrortu, who now has a Ph. D. in linguistics; Jabi Cillero, a European Union translator; and an unidentified woman.

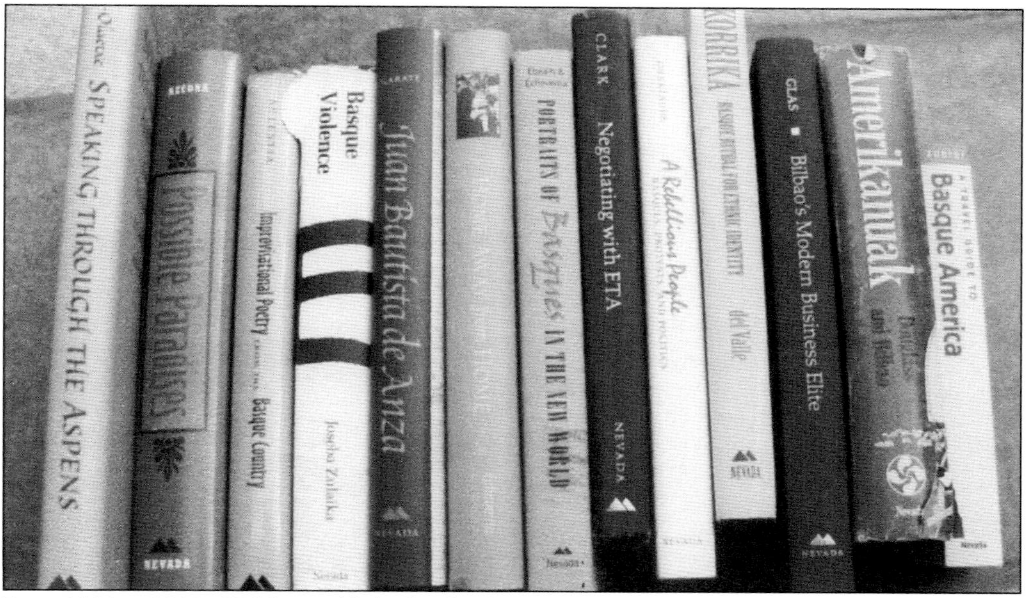

From 2000 to 2008, CBS has published 31 books. Under the auspices of the University of Nevada Press, the Basque Series, initiated by William Douglass, has published approximately 60 volumes on a number of Basque topics, but mainly history, anthropology, and literature.

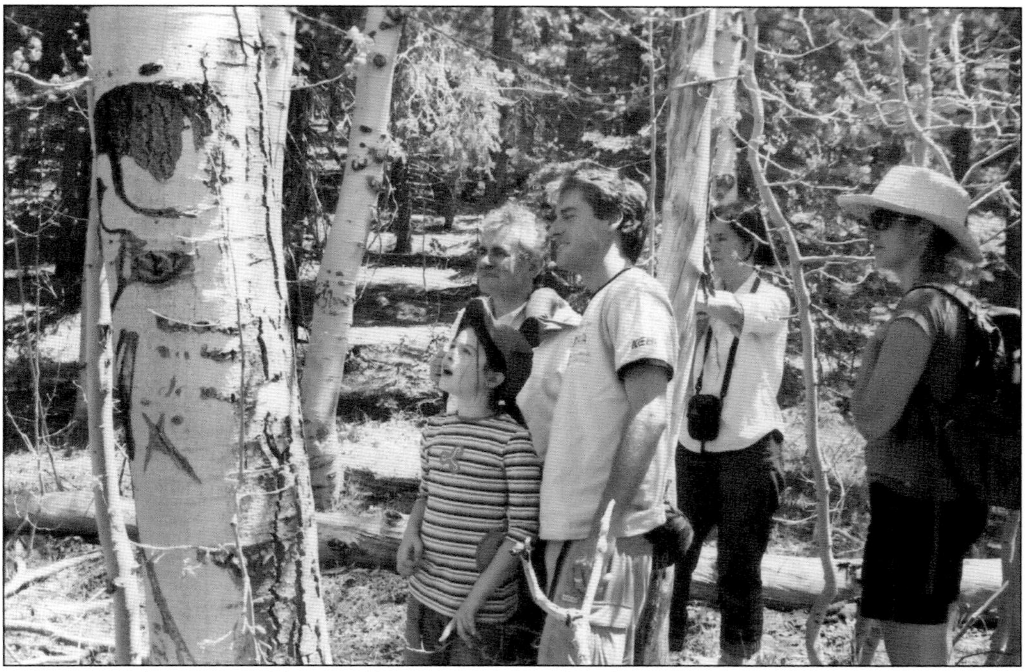

The Basque literary world is small, so it is no wonder that CBS attracts the most prominent individuals in the field, such as Bernardo Atxaga, whose books have been translated into several languages. Photographed while visiting a forest of arborglyphs in 2008 are, from left to right, Eli Atxaga, Bernardo Atxaga, a guest, Asun Garikano (Bernardo's wife), and Nora Arbelbide.

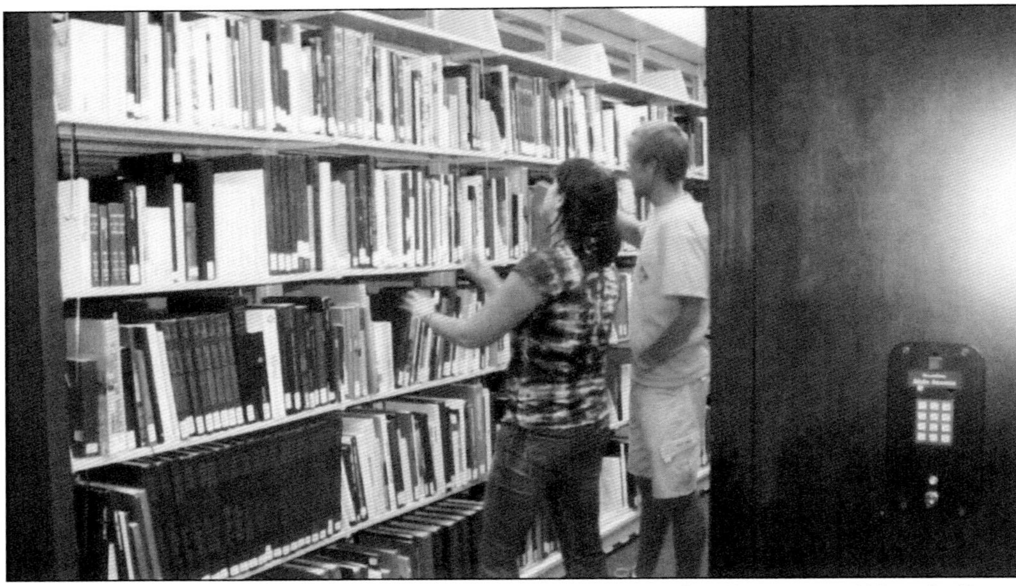

The new Basque Library opened officially in August 2008 at the University of Nevada, Reno, Mathewson-IGT Knowledge Center. In the photograph is librarian Marimar Ubeda explaining to a patron how the book stacks, mounted on tracks, open and close by punching numbers on the keypad. Thus, the books take up a much smaller space than in traditional shelves.

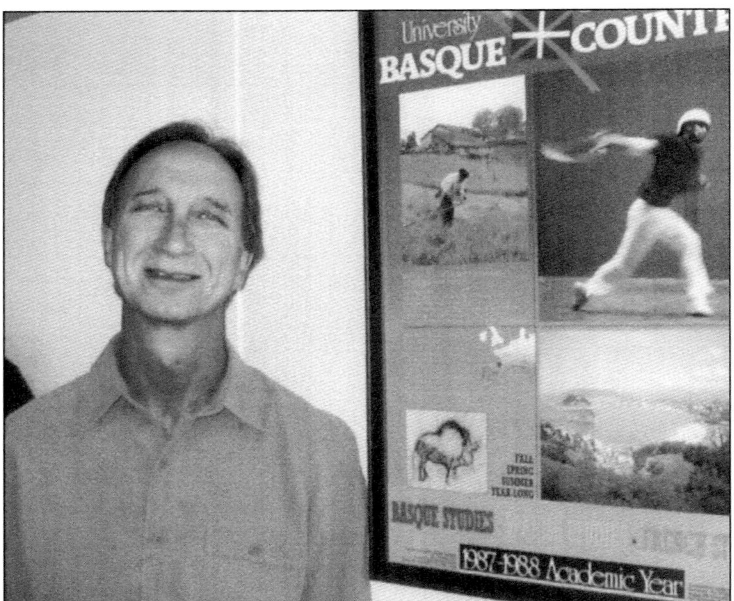

This is no place for a comprehensive summary of all the CBS's accomplishments, except to add that the University Studies Abroad Consortium (USAC), cofounded by UNR-CBS and Boise State University in 1982, has been always directed by Carmelo Urza, who is photographed here. USAC has 33 member universities with 25,000 students in 25 countries and 39 sites.

Seven

The Basques Today and Tomorrow

The Basques are gregarious and at the same time individualistic to the point that disagreements are preferably settled when the outcomes are clearly totally right and totally wrong. A compromise of 70/30 is not desirable, and yet Euskal Herria is full of associations, fraternities, and clubs of all kinds. In the United States and Canada is the North American Basque Organizations (NABO), founded in Sparks, Nevada, in 1973, which is an umbrella entity for 38 Basque clubs. This may seem like a lot, but the total club memberships are about 6,000.

NABO operates under the leadership of immigrant or American-born Basques, men and women with no particular preparation for the job except their dedication to the culture. This book is dedicated to them. The delegates that each club sends to the meetings constitute NABO's architecture. The proceedings are conducted in English by necessity because few delegates speak Basque fluently. NABO is nonprofit and apolitical, but the *ikurrina* (Basque flag) and its red, white, and green colors that blanket every picnic in the West might prompt the visitor to read too much nationalism in it. It is mostly a symbolism of colors. European Basques attending these festivals do indeed get a boost from the tricolor T-shirts and especially the cute little kids in dancing costumes and red berets.

The primary goal of NABO and its eight action committees is to coordinate the efforts of individual clubs, which are independent. In recent years, the small grants that clubs get from Eusko Jaurlaritza (Basque government) for their projects have energized the can-do Basques and indirectly NABO. Many believe the golden age of the Basque clubs is in the past, but NABO can be instrumental in repairing the generational gap between the waning immigrants and their children. Let the sons of the Pyrenees in America continue to jump and kick their feet to the haunting melodies of the *txistu* (Basque flute) and the gay sounds of the accordion.

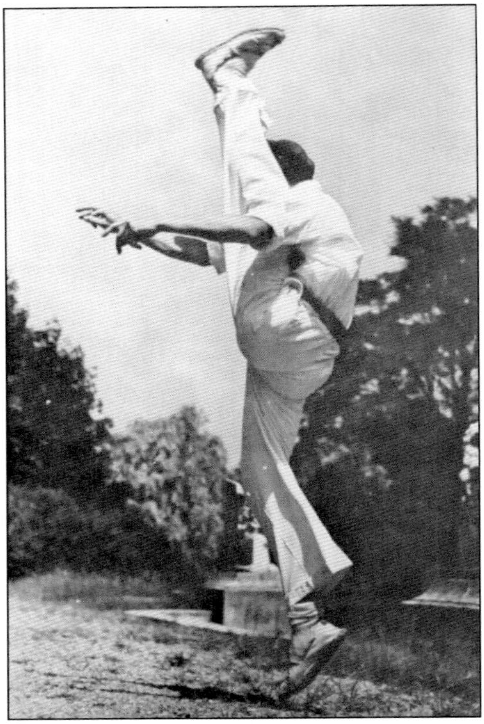

If traveling across the West in the summertime, one may catch a glimpse of Basque colors somewhere along the I-80 corridor, from Wyoming to San Francisco, California. If a person stops to look, he or she is likely to enjoy the agility of dancers in their costumes kicking up their feet. Basques worship physical prowess, and they often express it by *horrek bai ankak altza* (he can really kick up his feet).

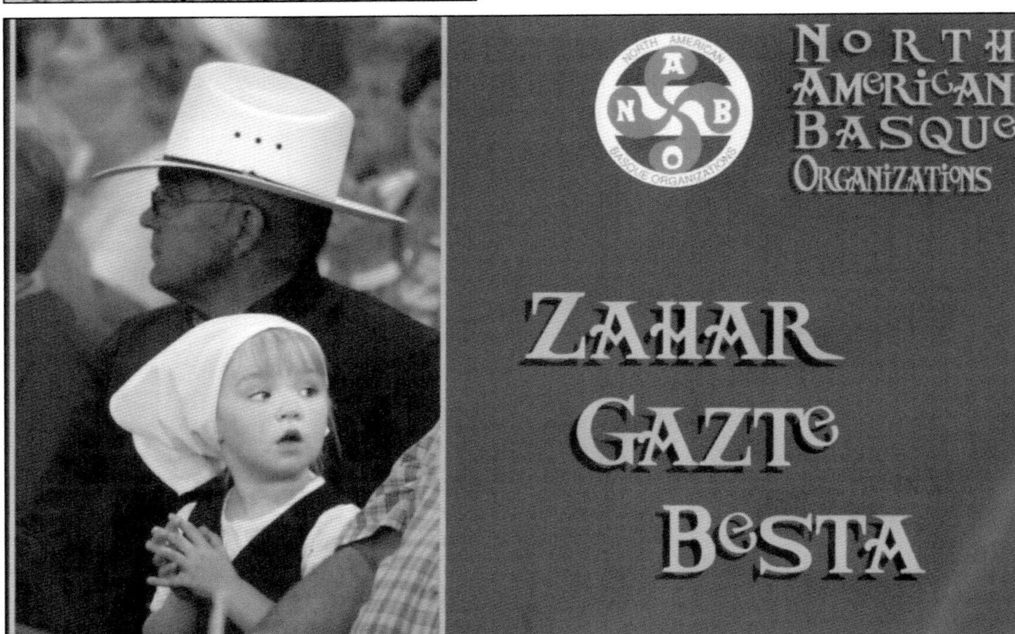

NABO makes itself visible among the Basques through its annual meetings, held in different states and sponsored by the local clubs on a rotational basis. Mary Lou Urrutia of Reno prints NABO's yearly calendar that keeps the community in touch and informed on festival schedules, while the appealing photographs contained in every issue capture the pulse of the Basque community. (Courtesy 2007 NABO calendar.)

The Reno Basque Festival may not be the largest or the best in the West, but the arena is unrivaled. Ever since it became part of the City of Reno's Artown, the festival takes place in Wingfield Park, which is an island of the Truckee River in downtown Reno. If weather is too hot, no problem; attendees can quickly cool off by wading into the cold river stream, where kayakers frolic.

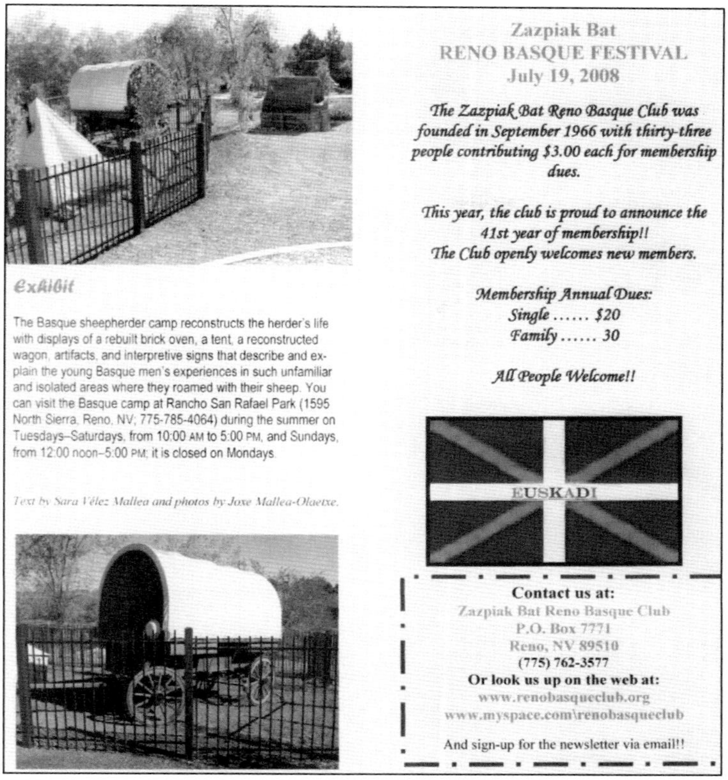

Zazpiak Bat
RENO BASQUE FESTIVAL
July 19, 2008

The Zazpiak Bat Reno Basque Club was founded in September 1966 with thirty-three people contributing $3.00 each for membership dues.

This year, the club is proud to announce the 41st year of membership!!
The Club openly welcomes new members.

Membership Annual Dues:
Single $20
Family 30

All People Welcome!!

EUSKADI

Contact us at:
Zazpiak Bat Reno Basque Club
P.O. Box 7771
Reno, NV 89510
(775) 762-3577
Or look us up on the web at:
www.renobasqueclub.org
www.myspace.com\renobasqueclub

And sign-up for the newsletter via email!!

Exhibit

The Basque sheepherder camp reconstructs the herder's life with displays of a rebuilt brick oven, a tent, a reconstructed wagon, artifacts, and interpretive signs that describe and explain the young Basque men's experiences in such unfamiliar and isolated areas where they roamed with their sheep. You can visit the Basque camp at Rancho San Rafael Park (1595 North Sierra, Reno, NV; 775-785-4064) during the summer on Tuesdays–Saturdays, from 10:00 AM to 5:00 PM, and Sundays, from 12:00 noon–5:00 PM; it is closed on Mondays.

Text by Sara Vélez Mallea and photos by Joxe Mallea-Olaetxe.

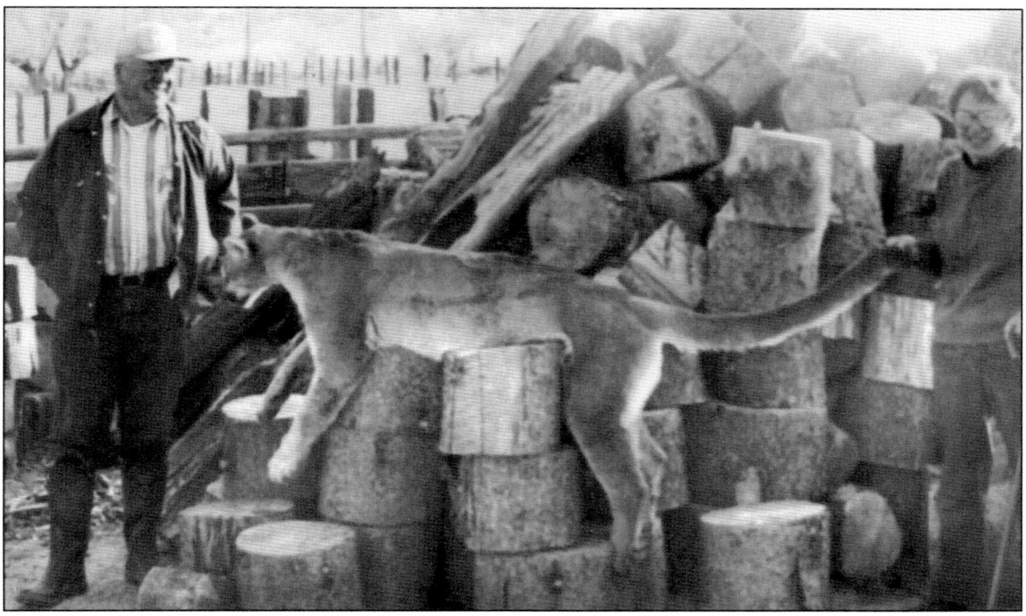

When people have cute fat lambs on their acreage in the wild country near Susanville, California, they are going to have unexpected guests show up for dinner. Photographed here are Juanito Mendiolea, who, alerted by the dogs, killed the large uninvited guest cougar, and Lola Ochotorena, Juanito's wife. (Courtesy Juanito and Lola Mendiolea.)

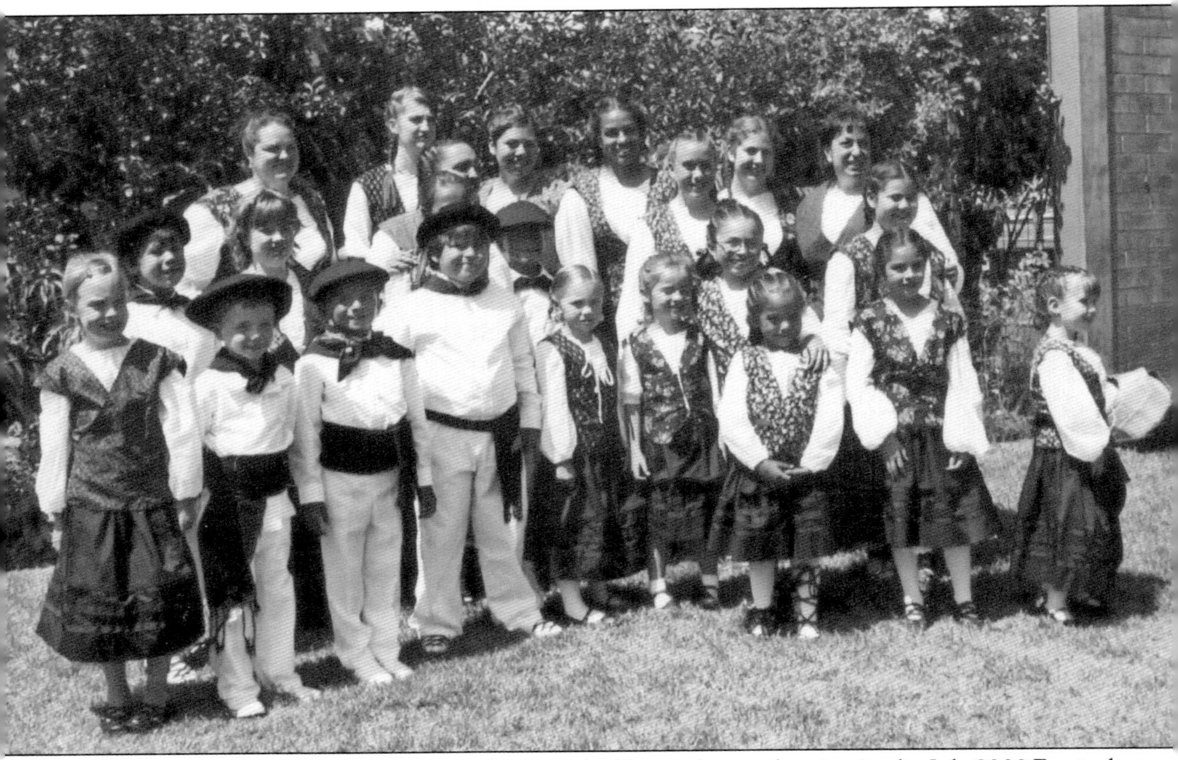

The Reno Zazpiak Bat Dancers are photographed here after performing in the July 2008 Festival. From left to right are (first row) Gracie Demars, Peter Bertolino, Angel Mendoza, Jacob Campos, Elena Aramini, Amaia Condon, Desyre Mendoza, Gailen Sendon, and Amaia Stanley; (second row) Jared Campos, Lexi La Bella, Emma Condon (hidden), Jennifer Etcheberry, Dominique Stallworth, Ezti Villanueva, Natalie Lara, and Jennae Campos; (third row) Mary Lou Etcheberry, Kathryn Aguirre, Jessica Campos, Danielle Stallworth, Jennifer Campos, and Kate Camino, the dance instructor.

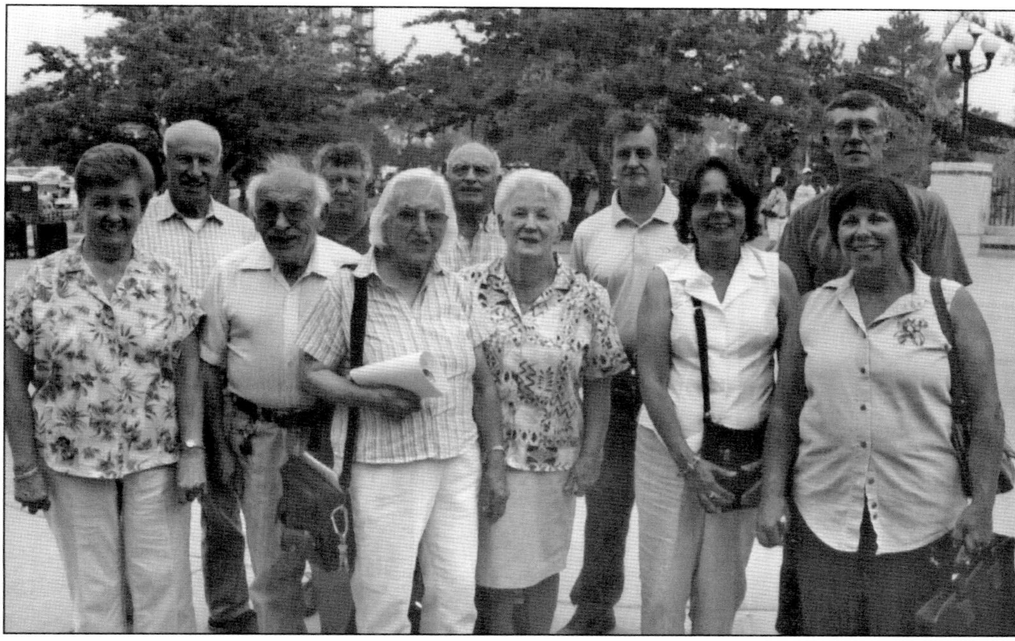

The 2008 Reno Zazpiak Bat board members and others who lend unwavering support to the club include, from left to right, Jeanne Mosho, Mike Mosho, John Castillo, Gerard Garra, Gloria Castillo, Pierre Calleja, Pierrette Calleja, Javier Narvarte (president), Sara Velez, Austin Wilson, and Marguerite Wilson.

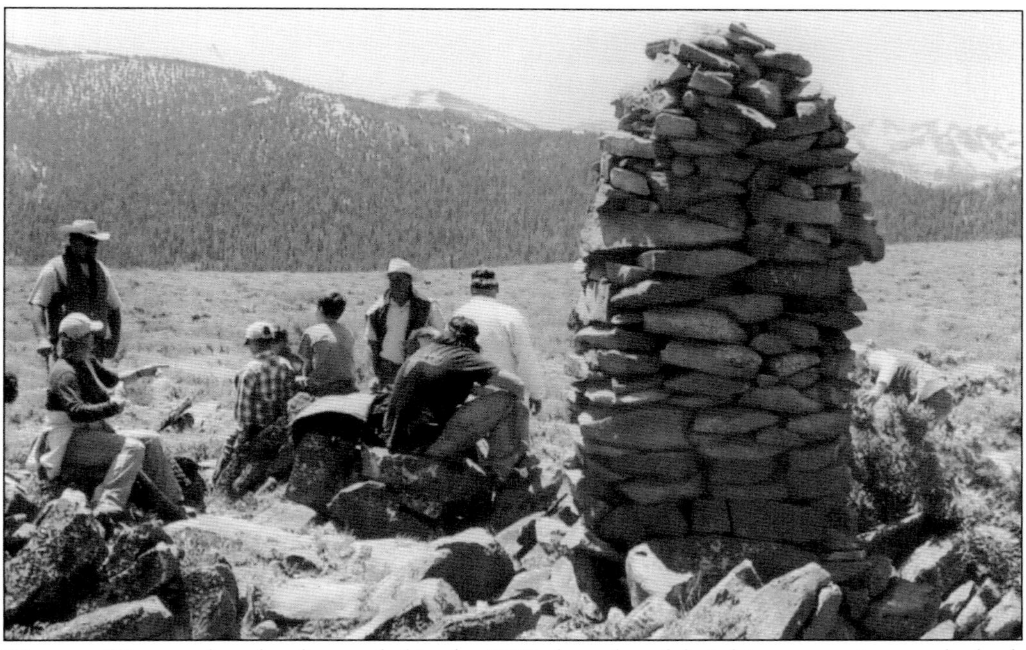

The era of Basque sheepherding ended in the 1970s, but a lot of their history survives on the bark of thousands of aspens. Sheep camps and bread ovens are the other tangible evidence of their labors on the range, and if someone is prepared to really hike, he or she can see something like this, a *harri mutil* (stone monument or marker), standing like a lonely sentinel of the range.

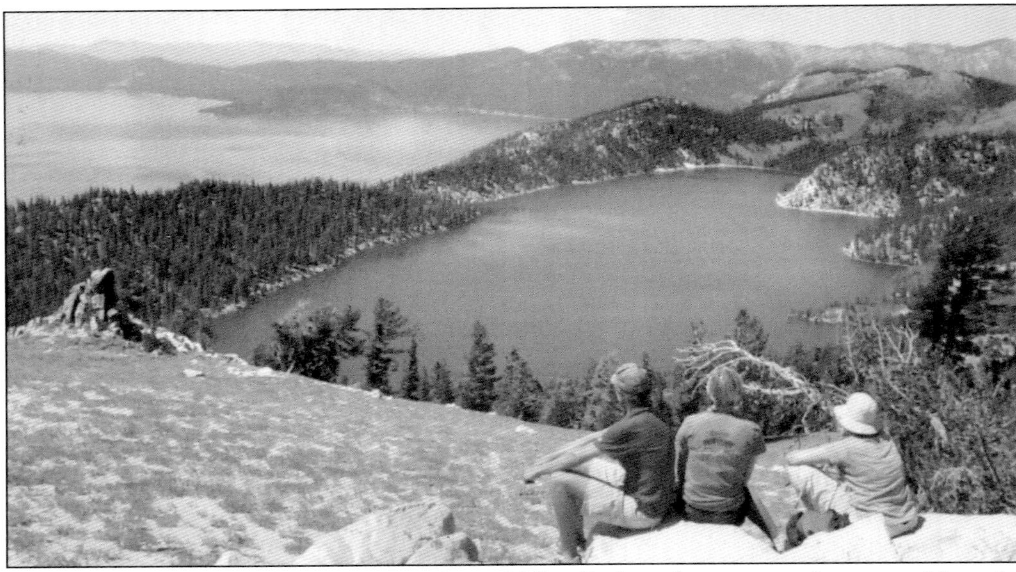

Three hikers of Basque descent sit near Snow Valley Peak as they contemplate, speechless, the beauty of Marlette Lake below. Marlette and Lake Tahoe appear almost connected, but in fact, the latter is 1,600 feet lower. It is no wonder President and Nancy Reagan visited this place with Sen. Paul Laxalt.

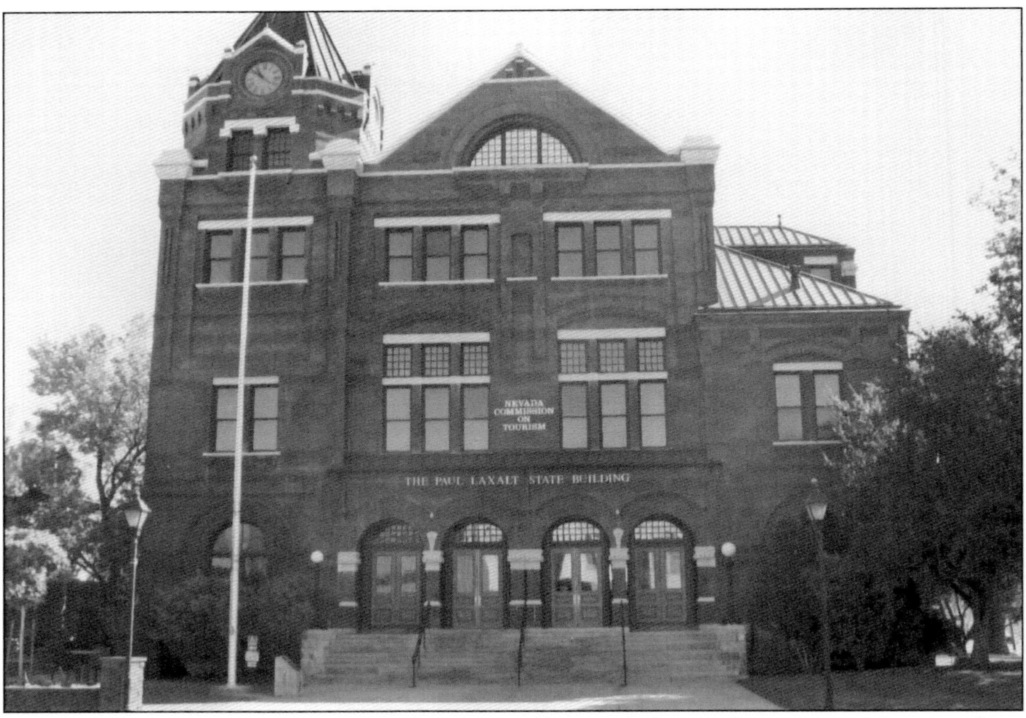

This is the newly designated Paul Laxalt State Building and Plaza in Carson City, Nevada, where Laxalt grew up. As Ronald Reagan's right-hand man and chairman of his election campaigns, Laxalt briefly tested the waters for a presidential run. No other person of Basque descent has achieved the national status and recognition that Paul Laxalt has.

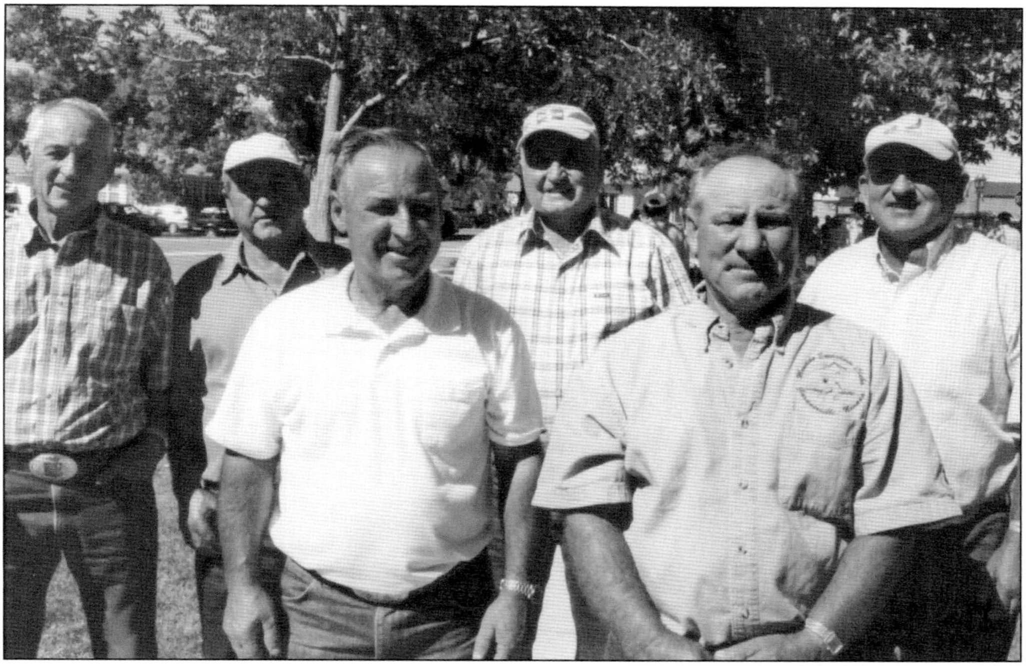

Basque peasant families were large, but having six brothers migrate to America as sheepherders was out of the ordinary. In August 2008, the Sarratea brothers attended the Gardnerville Basque Festival. From left to right are Anastasio, Tiburco, Pedro, Eugenio, Ignacio, and Fulgencio Sarratea.

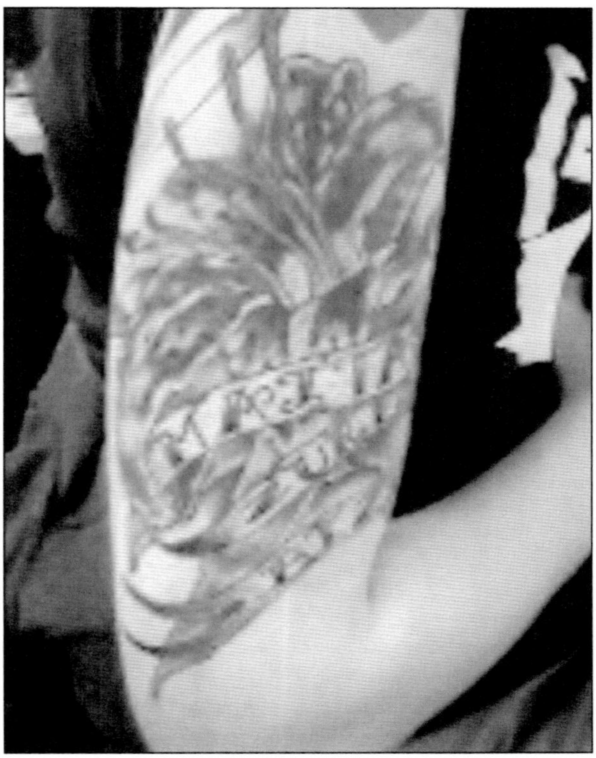

Most do not see everyday a message tattooed in Euskara. Naturally the colors used were appropriate, mostly reds and greens, and the message on her arm states, "*Maita zure bizia*" (love your life).

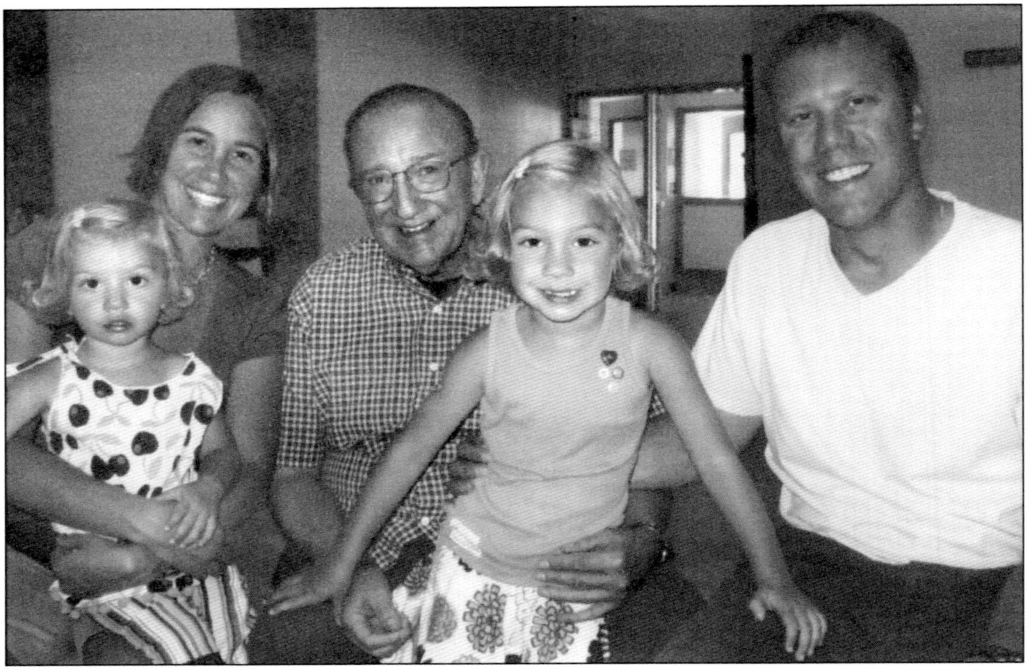

Three generations of Basques are, from left to right, Amaya Aramini, Christine Arrascada, LeRoy Arrascada, Elena Aramini, and John Aramini, Christine's husband. The Arrascadas—father and daughter—are lawyers and for years have been active members of the Reno Basque Club.

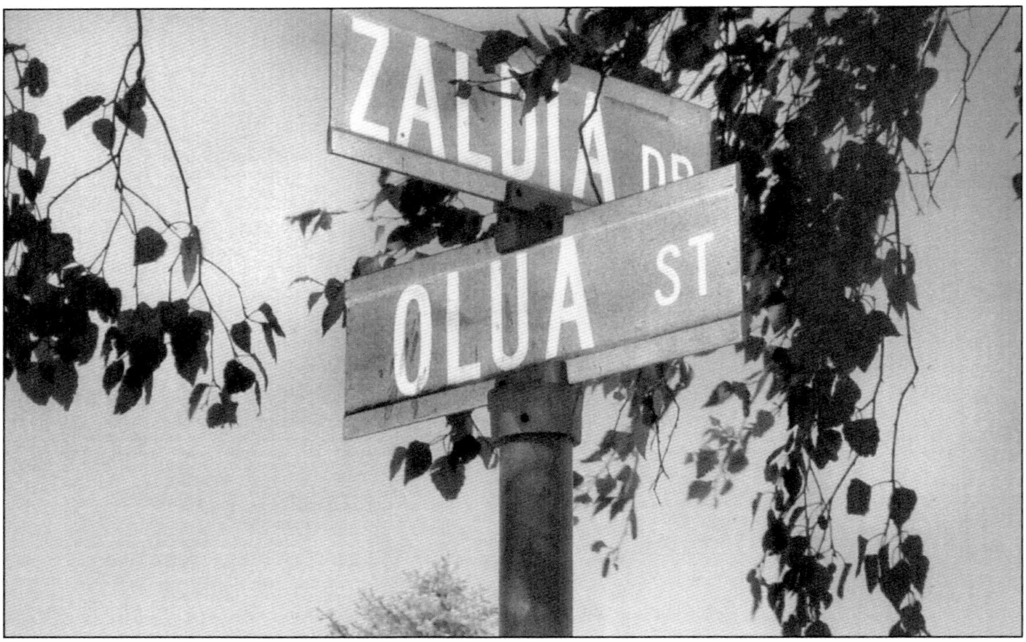

Minden, Nevada, a German town, has a subdivision with Basque street names. *Zaldia* means the horse, *olua* is oats, and there are several others like *barrukia* (corral), all associated with ranching and farming activities. Apparently the man in charge of the street-naming project was Jean Lekumberry of nearby Gardnerville.

A person doesn't have to be Basque to fire up a sheepherder oven, but if he or she wants to eat at noon, the fire better be started at 9 a.m. When cooking in an outdoor oven, a steady heat of embers, not flames, is optimal. A culinary group from San Francisco has been celebrating its Burning Lamb cookout since 2001; in the photograph are Louis Cohen and Sheryl Koehler.

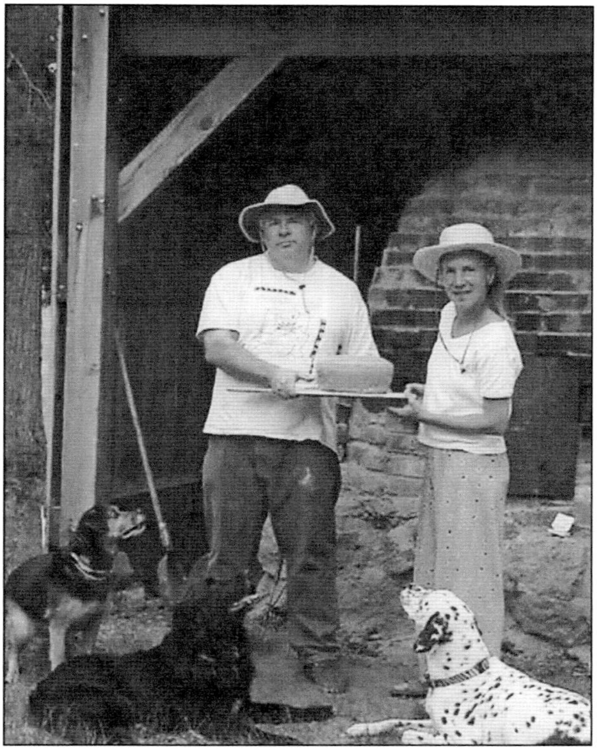

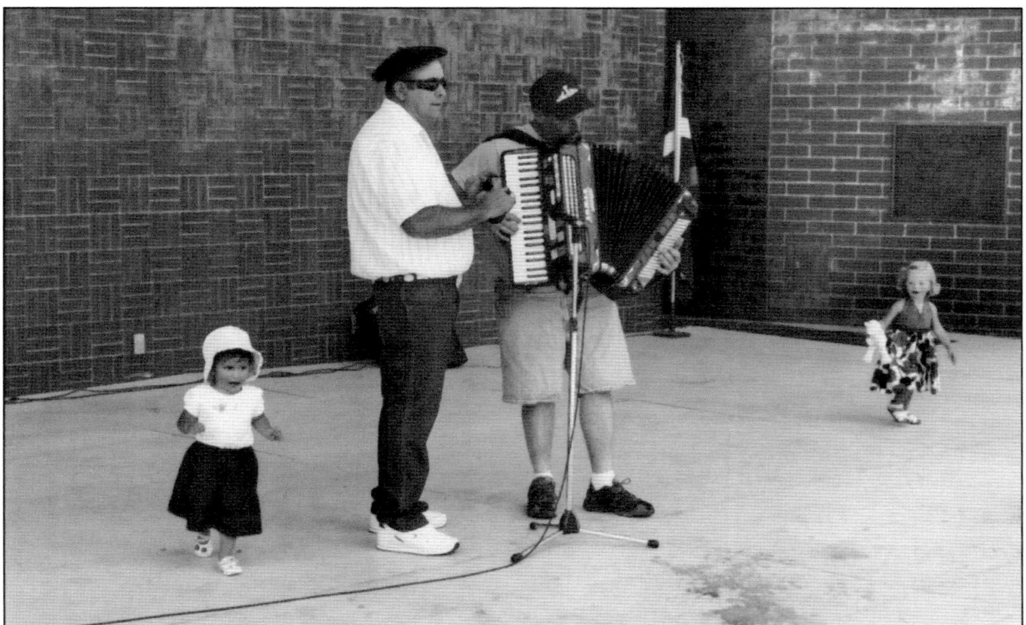

While accordionist Jean-Louis Curutchet of San Francisco, California, played and Jess Goñi of Reno accompanied him with the castanets, Sabrina Arrascada (left) and her cousin, Amaya Aramini, could not just watch. The two precocious dancers jumped on the stage, twirling and chasing each other around the two performers, having the time of their lives.

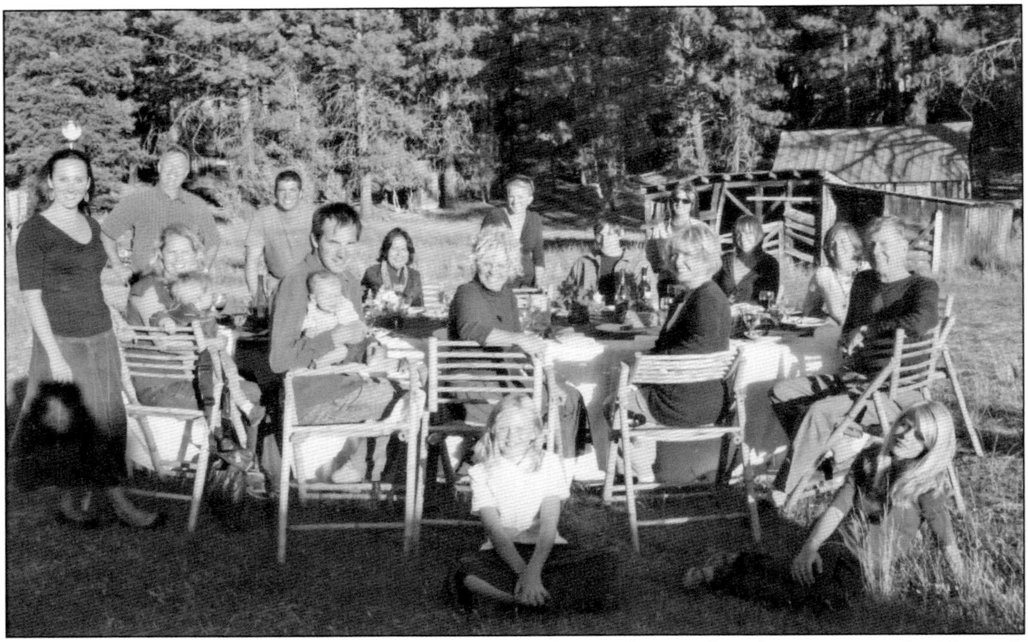

This fancy feast, prepared by a professional chef and served on a white linen–covered table with various wines and champagne, was recorded by a professional photographer. Readers would never guess that this Sierra setting was an abandoned sheep camp and that the chef prepared all the food in a sheepherder oven. The event was the idea of the *Tahoe Quarterly* staff.

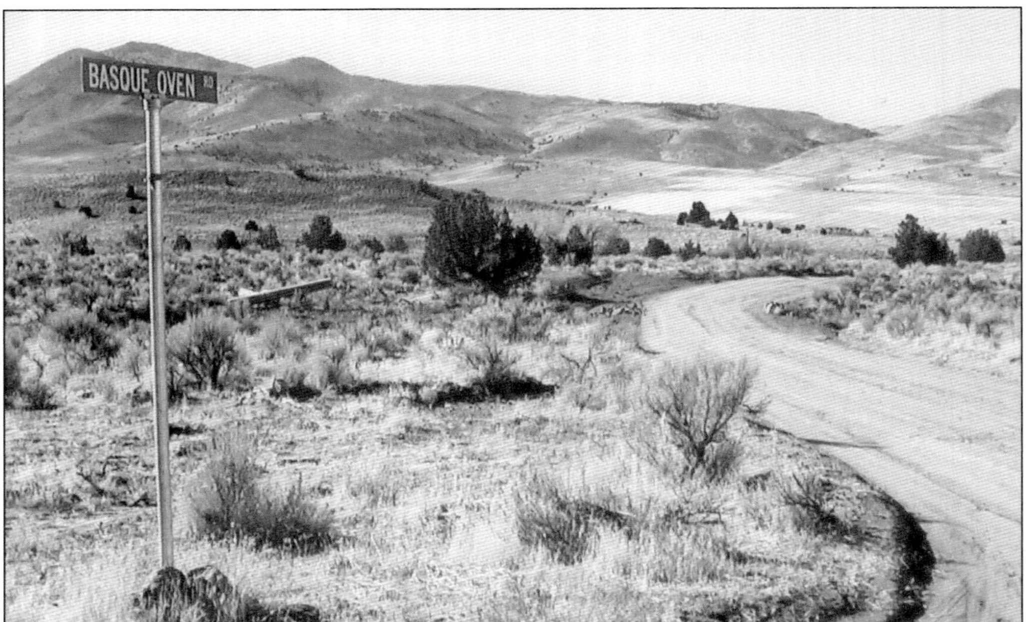

On a topographic map of Nevada are place names like Heguy Reservoir, Basque Summit, Bascoville, and such, all in very remote areas. As subdivisions expand into old sheep corrals, a few historically minded developers are preserving the past. This sign is not far from Sparks, and the road indeed goes to a sheep camp with a well-preserved oven.

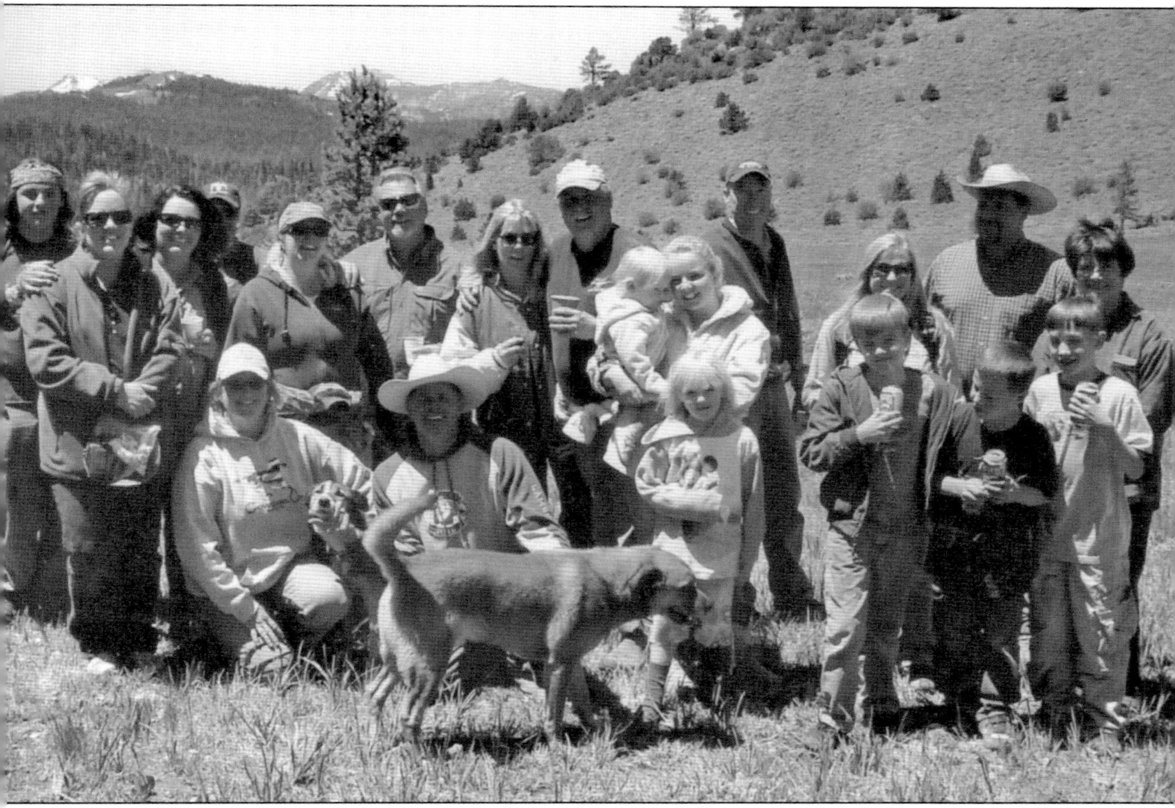

You can take the Basques out of the mountain, but you cannot take the mountain out of the Basques. However, today they do not pack the burro; they take a huge fancy trailer, which is parked at 8,600 feet. Photographed during a celebration of Basque Heritage in June 2008 are, from left to right, (first row) Lisa Lekumberry, J. B. Lekumberry, Shay Lynn Walters, Etienne Lekumberry, Levi Costa, and Ryan Slack; (second row) Dolton Tutt, Sherri Walters, Kim Speer, Richard Speer, Sue Etchegoyhen, Jerome Etchegoyhen, Karen Manning, Bud Rinez, Anna Lekumberry (holding Whitney Walters), Sam Slack, Erin Costa, Joe Cereghino, and Anita Izoco.

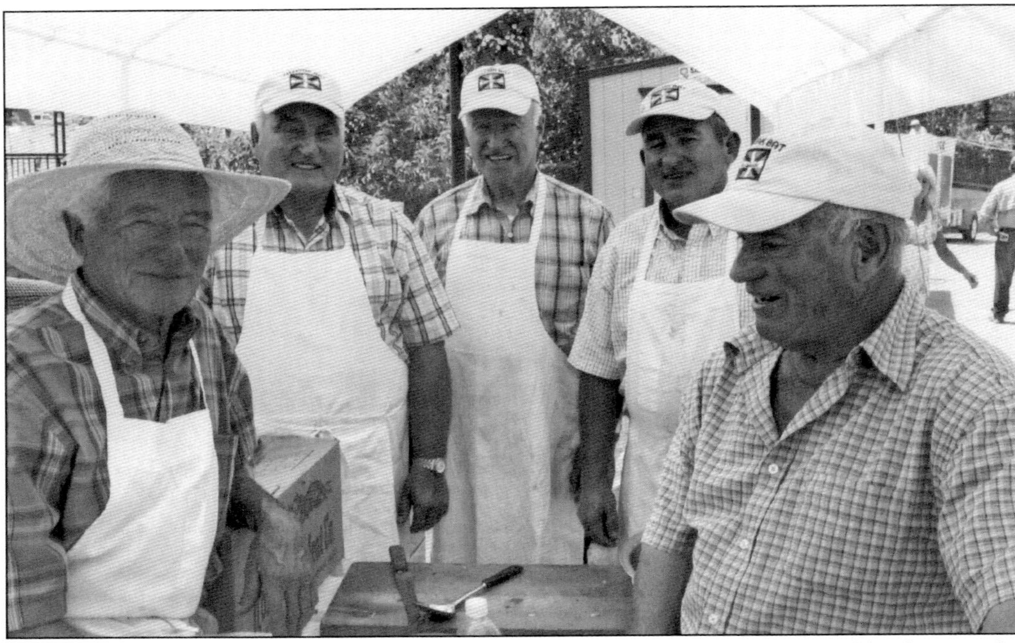

For years, Reno picnickers have been enjoying the beans and the steaks prepared by these cooks. From left to right are Jean Jaureguy, Eugenio Sarratea, Mike Mocho, Fulgencio Sarratea, and Pierre Calleja; two others, Antonio Villanueva and John Etcheto, were out of camera range during the July 2008 festival.

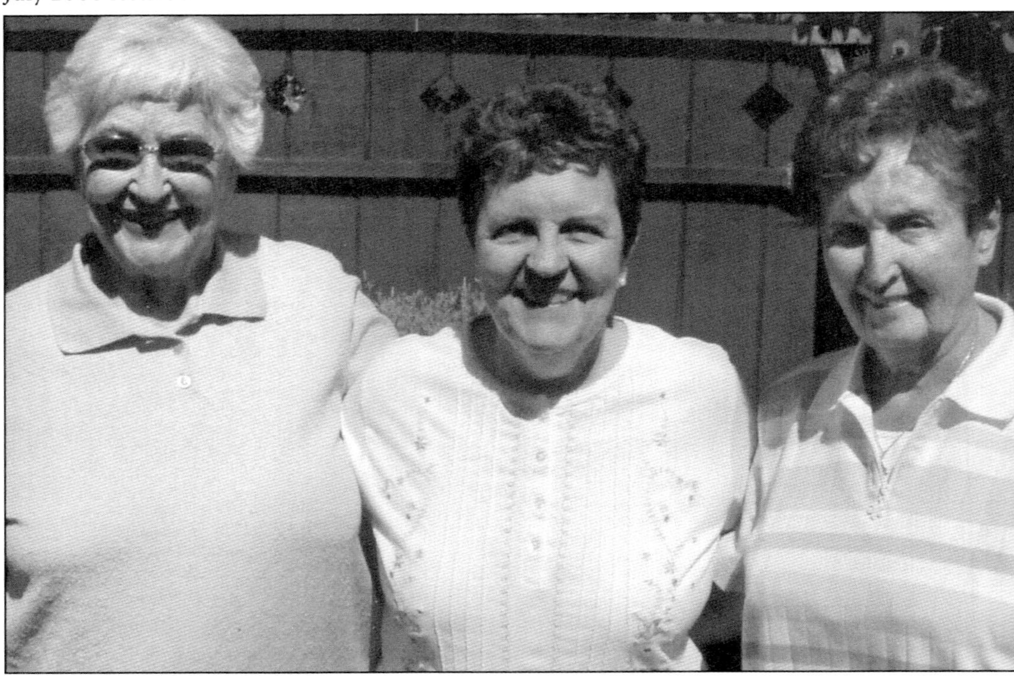

In general, women seem to remember more detailed stories about the past, and Irene Orriaga Arbeloa (left), Helen Jaunsaras Chapell (center), and Lucille Arregui Landa (right) are good proof of it. Irene and Lucille live in Reno, and Helen, who is Lucille's sister, lives in Gardnerville, Nevada.

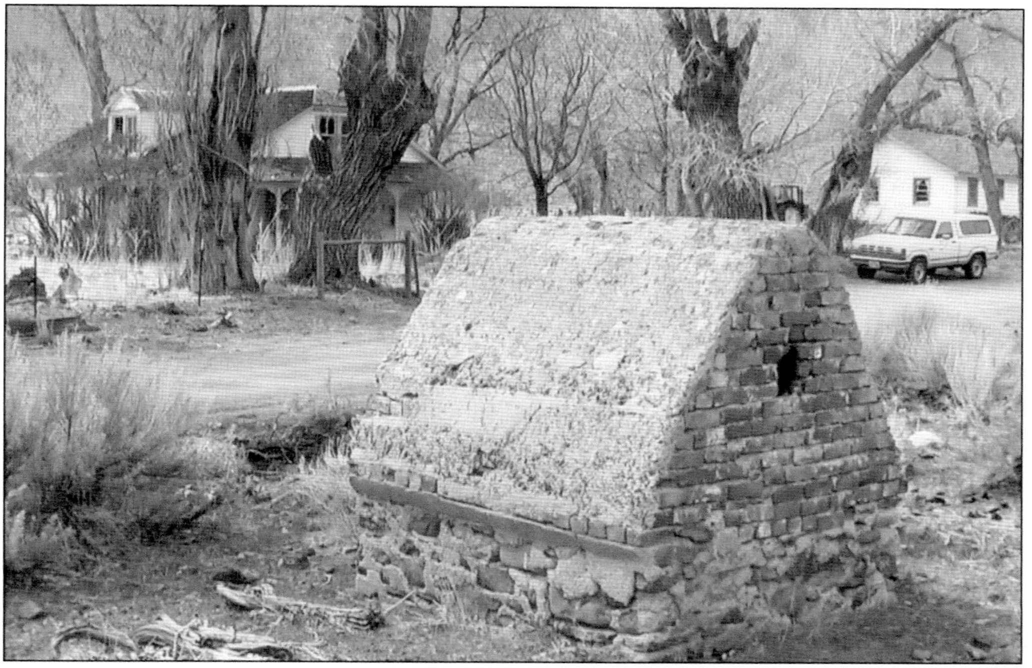

Neal Lemerise informed the author of the original location of this sheepherder oven that now is part of the Basque Exhibit at Rancho San Rafael in Reno. Its owner John Marshall and LeRoy Arrascada, both lawyers, sealed the deal of the donation, and Q&D Construction donated the equipment to dig it up and transport it to the park. Juan Braña made the repairs.

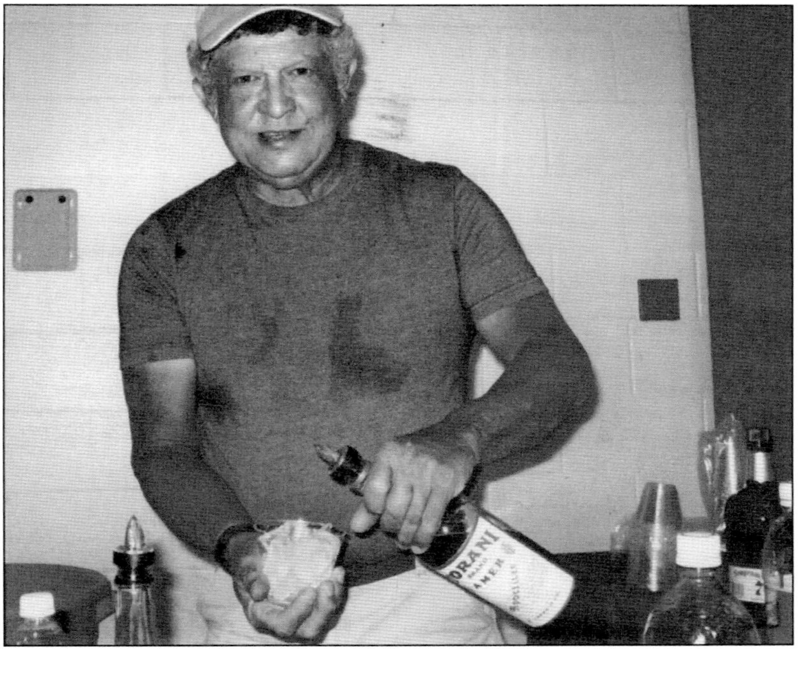

Many people know Gerard Garra, who has been bartending at Basque festivals for over 12 years. He is holding the picon bottle as he is about to mix the popular picon punch. He buys the supplies, files timely reports, and tends bar without fuss. He is one of the many heroes who quietly go about serving the club.

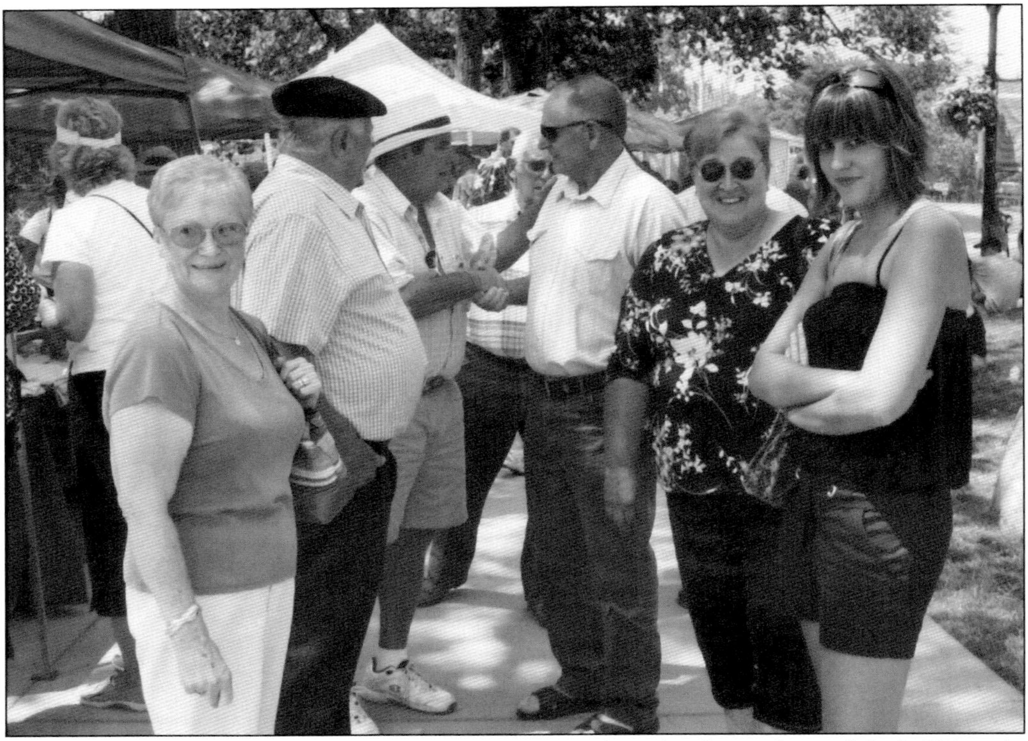

Basques in the West travel many miles to attend picnics where they know they will find old friends, and at times unexpected ones. In this photograph of the Reno Basque Festival are, from left to right, Nekane Gabikagoxeaskoa, Michel Inda, Rob Iturbide, Jerry Etcheverry (half hidden), Patxi Txurruka, Begoña Azkaiturrieta/Txurruka, and Rosana Marquez, who was visiting from France.

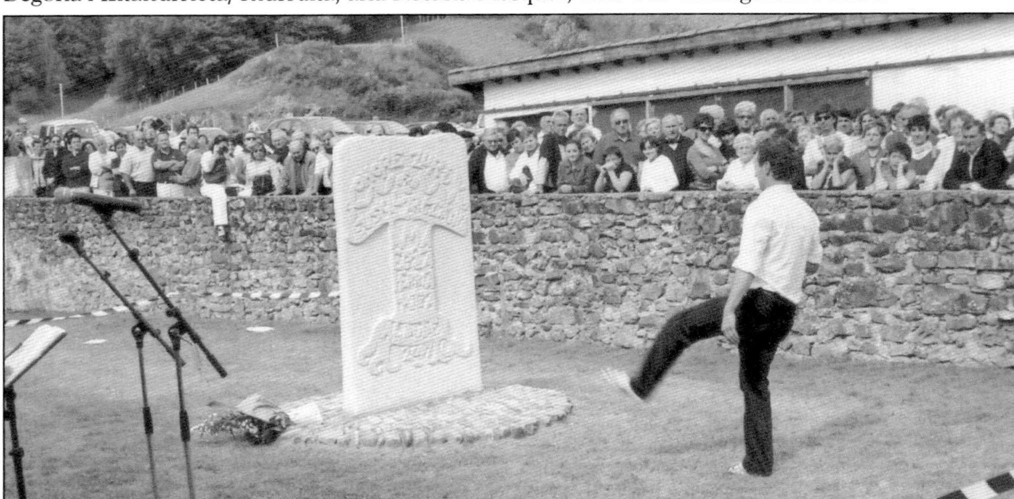

The organization Artzain Mundua of the Basque Country, dedicated to advancing sheepherding in the world, erected two stones in honor of the sheepherders of the American West. On September 30, 2007, an *artzain harria* (sheepherder stone) was inaugurated in Aldude and the following day another one in Gernika. The photograph captured the Aurresku dance, which is de rigueur on such occasions.

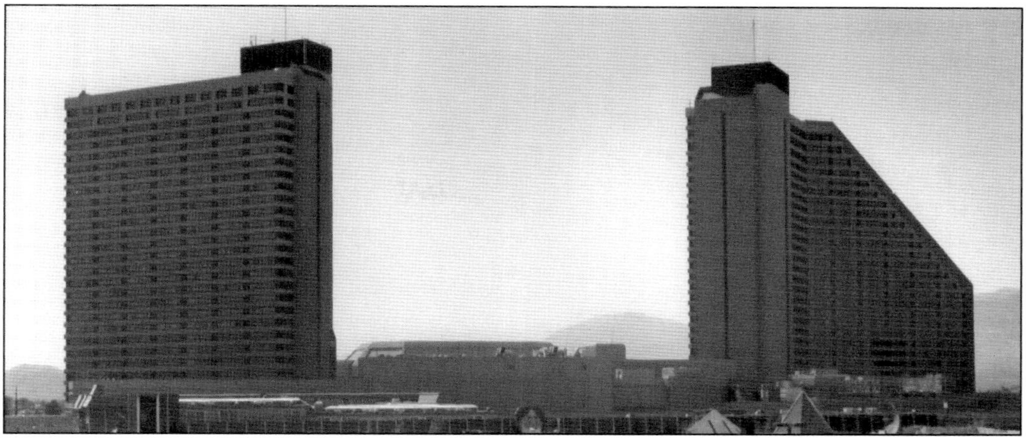

The Nugget Hotel Casino has over 1,700 rooms, nine restaurants, and high-rise parking towers over the skyline in Sparks, Nevada. It is probably the biggest Basque-owned casino in the world. John Ascuaga, whose father was a sheepherder in Idaho, bought the original Nugget in 1960 from Dick Graves. Today John is semiretired, and his daughter Michone Ascuaga runs the business.

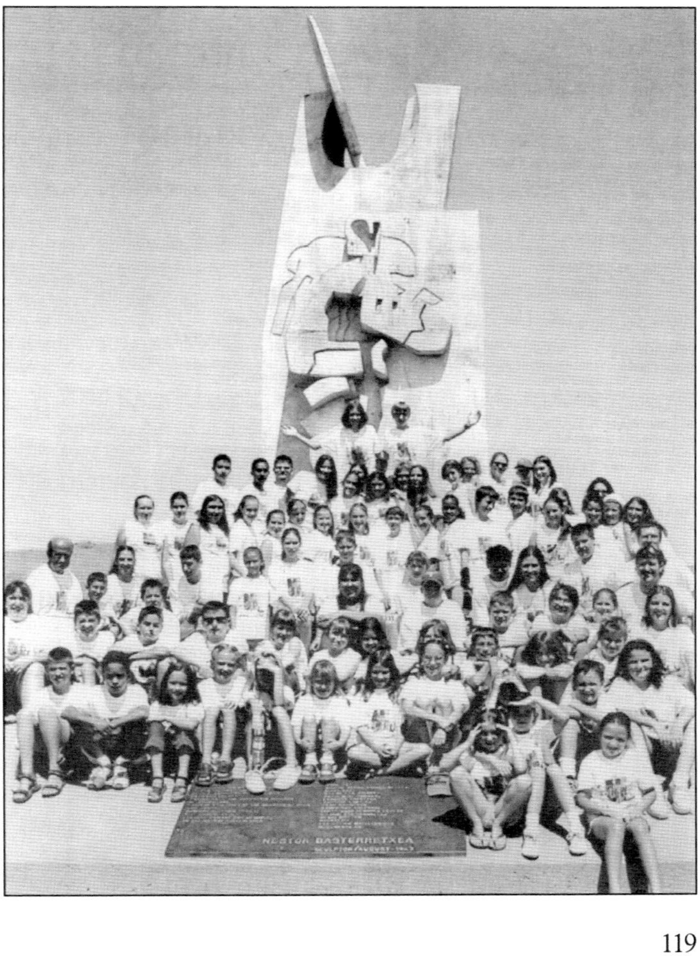

One of the activities NABO sponsors is the annual Music Camp for boys and girls interested in immersing themselves in Basque culture. In 2002, it was Reno's turn to host Music Camp, and as the photograph illustrates, they are very popular events. Here dozens of happy teenagers pose by the Sheepherder Monument at Reno's Rancho San Rafael Park.

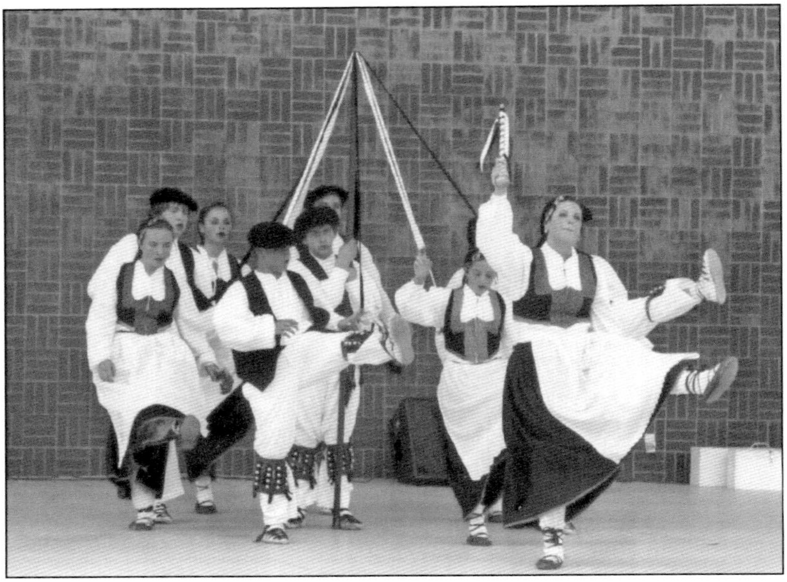

Even girls kick their feet up in some of the Basque dances, though usually it is a modest kick. These are the Gauden Bat Chino Dancers in Reno performing the Zinta Dantza (Ribbon Dance). In most Basque dance groups today, girls outnumber the boys.

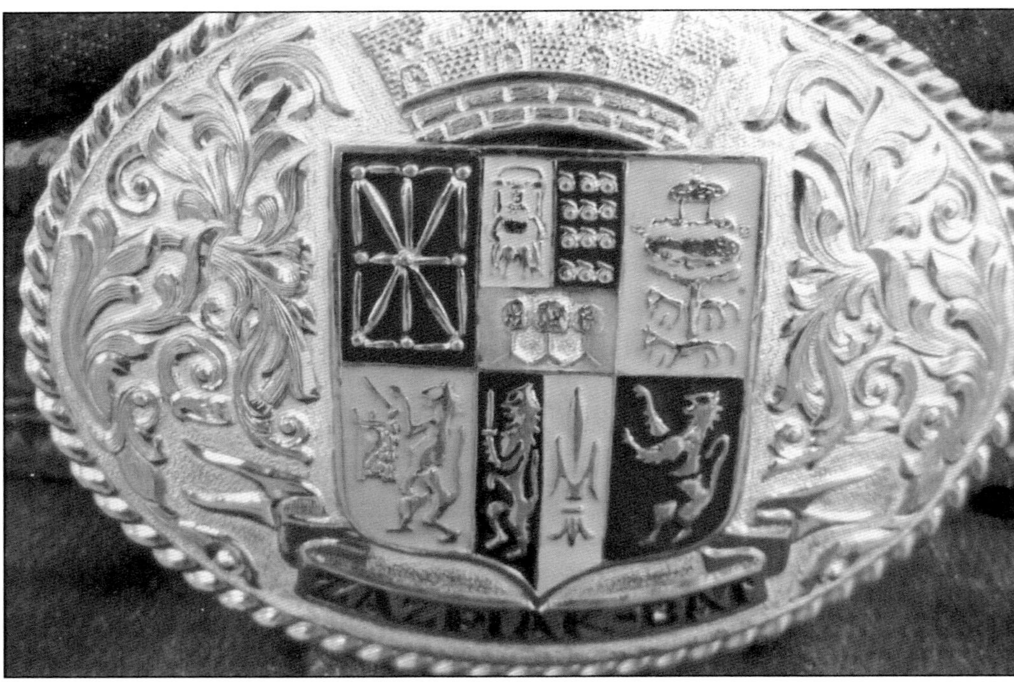

Historically Basque people have held on to their symbols tenaciously. Euskara is number one, followed by the *etxe* (house), and the coat of arms. Many Basque Americans have a display of their coat of arms in their living room, but this fancy and expensive gold-and-silver belt buckle, studded with stones, worn by a proud Navarrese Nevadan, is something else.

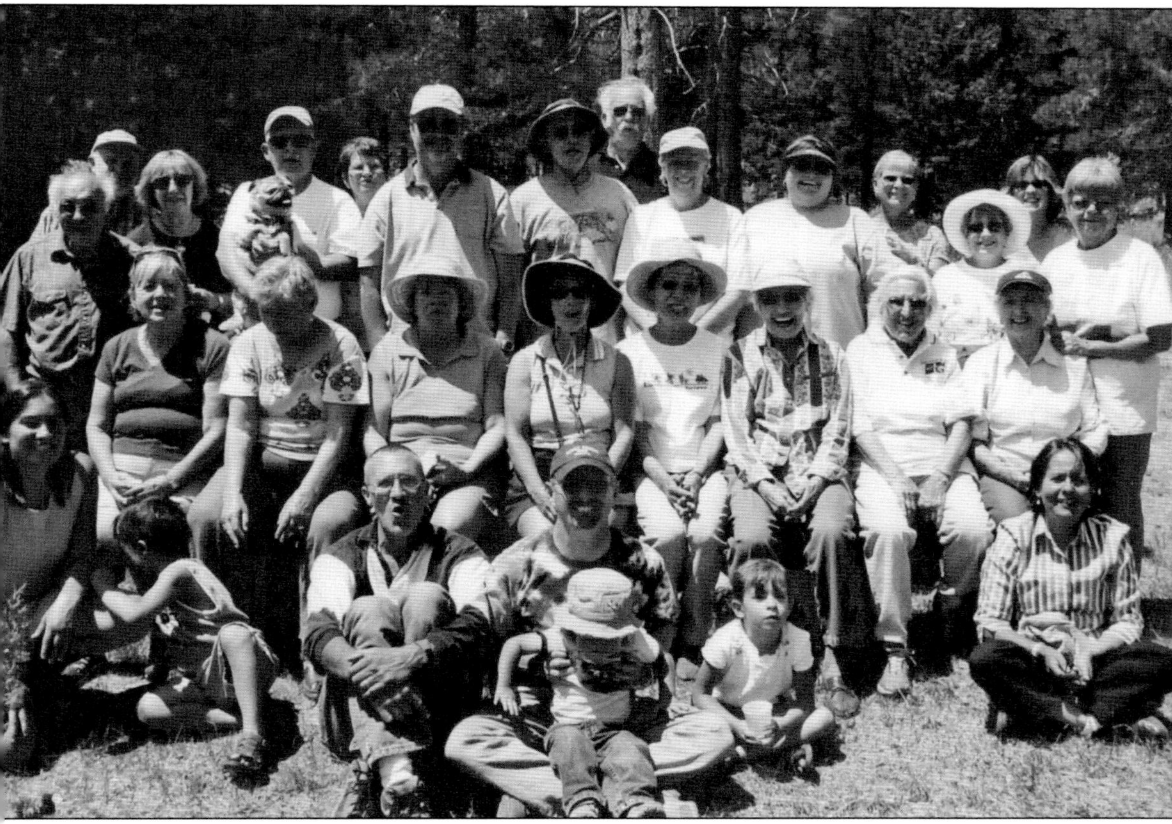

The old sheepherder would never have suspected that one day discriminating Nevadans and Californians would drive up and hike into abandoned sheep camps, rebuild the ovens, and put them back in operation to bake bread, cook Basque dishes, and celebrate the Old West heritage. It is history brought back to life, and it is the spirit of *Eman ta zabal zazu* ("Give forth and spread around"), which is what many Basques have done. The group photographed here gets together every year to celebrate Ogi (Bread) Bash at the Kyburz Flat Sheep Camp in California.

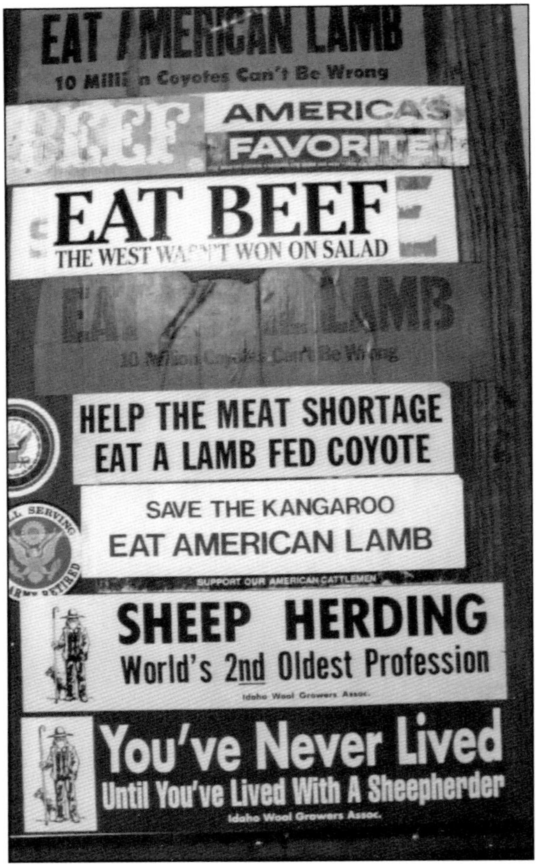

This board covered with bumper stickers is displayed prominently at the bar of the Overland Hotel-Restaurant in Gardnerville, Nevada. There is no doubt that at least here sheepmen and cattlemen are a band of brothers, something that a few decades ago would have been unlikely. The Overland was the first local Basque restaurant to start serving lamb in 1980.

The Arrizabalaga House located near the Truckee River in Reno is of historic significance, according to Neal Cobb, a local history buff. The Arrizabalagas owned ranches and hotels in the Fallon, Nevada, area, and their granddaughter Joan Arrizabalaga owns this house, which she is restoring.

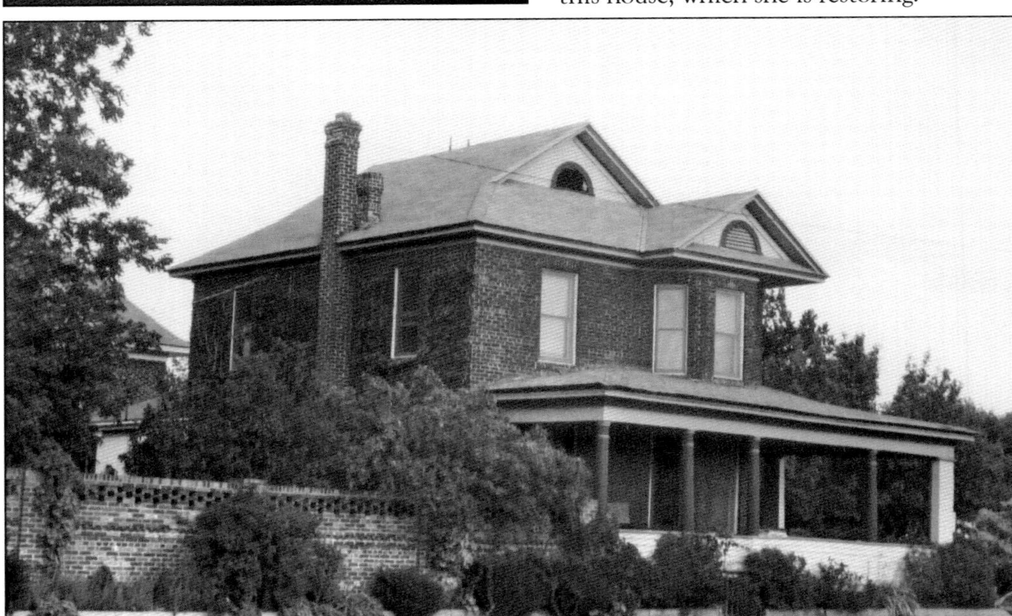

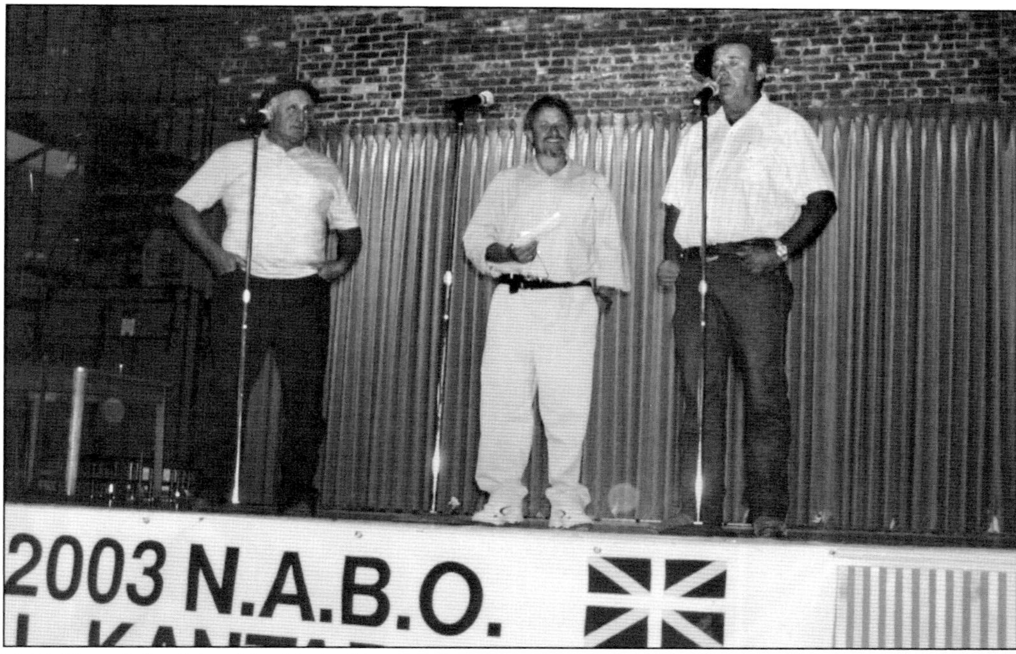

NABO and the Mendiko Euskaldun Club of Gardnerville, Nevada, sponsor an annual day for singing Basque songs and improvisational poetry, which started in 1988. The young and old walk up to the microphone and sing away to enthusiastic applause from the audience. In the picture, poets Jean Curutchet (left) and Jesus Goñi (right) sing verses with the moderator (the author) in the middle.

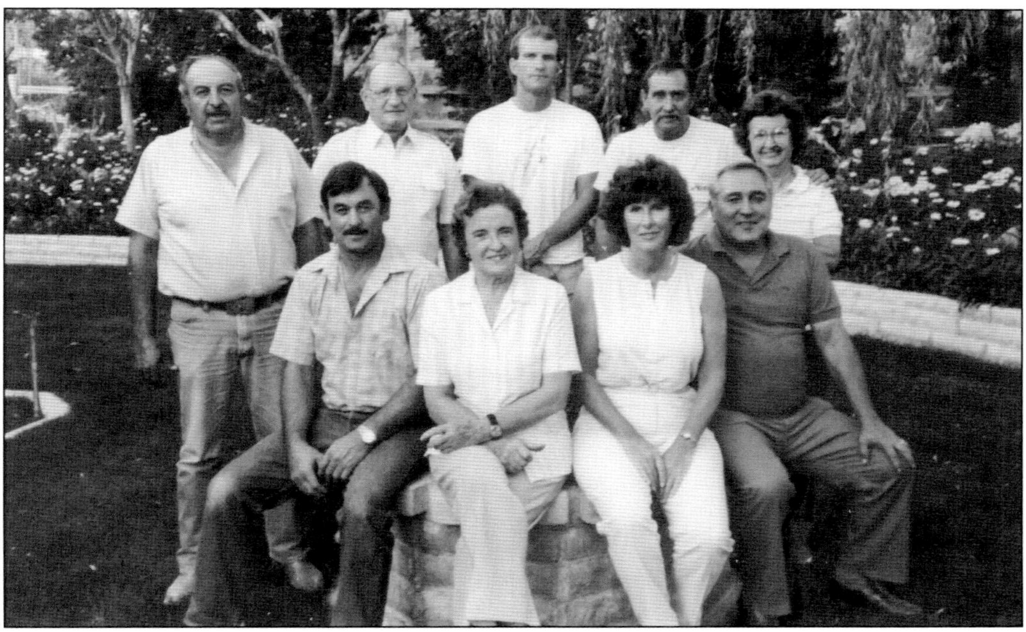
This is the Zazpiak Bat Reno Basque Club board in 1987. Pictured from left to right are (sitting) Jess Arriaga, unidentified, Carmen Landa, and Louie Ecenarro; (standing) John Jauregito, Tony Laca, unidentified, Jim Dufurrena, and Virginia Argoitia. (Courtesy Zazpiak Bat Archive.)

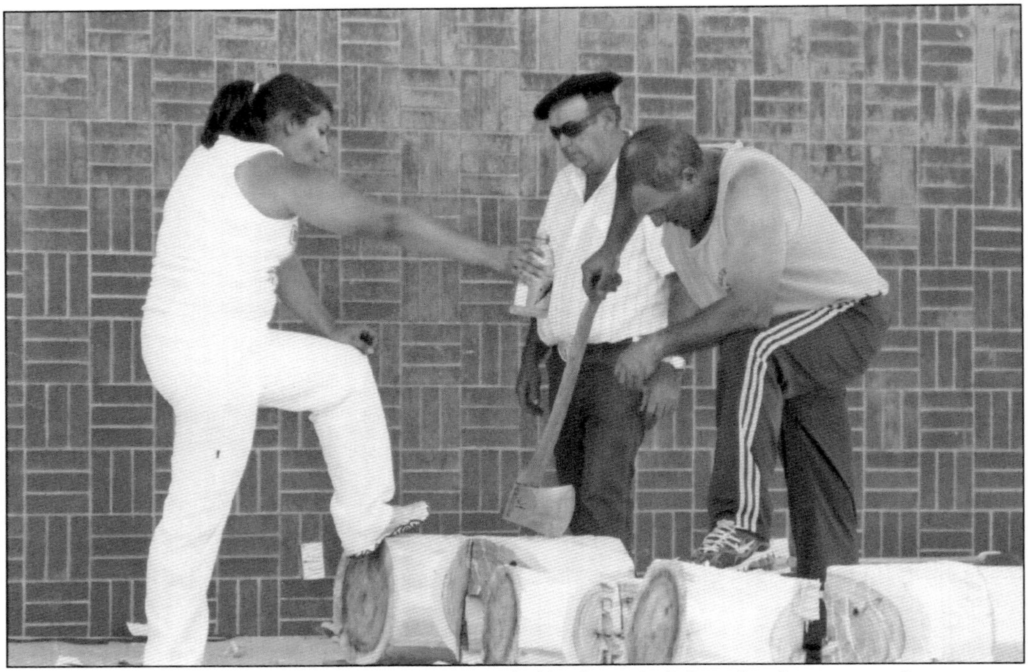

Juan Braña and Stephanie Braña of Reno are probably the only father-daughter team who compete in the wood-chopping world. Females are a rarity in this sport, but Stephanie has won in several university meets. In this photograph, taken right after a contest, Stephanie hands her dad a drink. In the middle is assistant Jess Goñi.

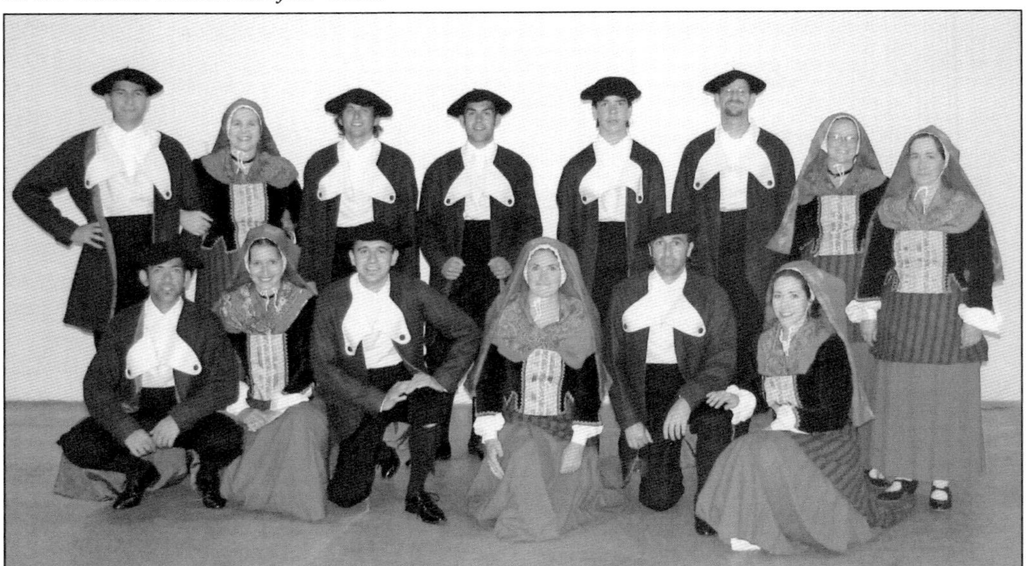

Zenbat Gara (How Many Are We?) is Reno's Basque Folk Dance Assemble that has earned many accolades. Pictured from left to right are (kneeling) Ander Zabaleta, Carolyn Van Lydegraf, Mikel Irizar, Noel Arraiz, Enrike Corcostegui, and director Lisa Corcostegui; (standing) John Ysursa, Denise Inda, Aitor Laca, Yulen Kortabarria, Asier Alonso, Paul Woodin, T. J. Mains, and Amagoia Gezuraga. (Courtesy Lisa Corcostegui.)

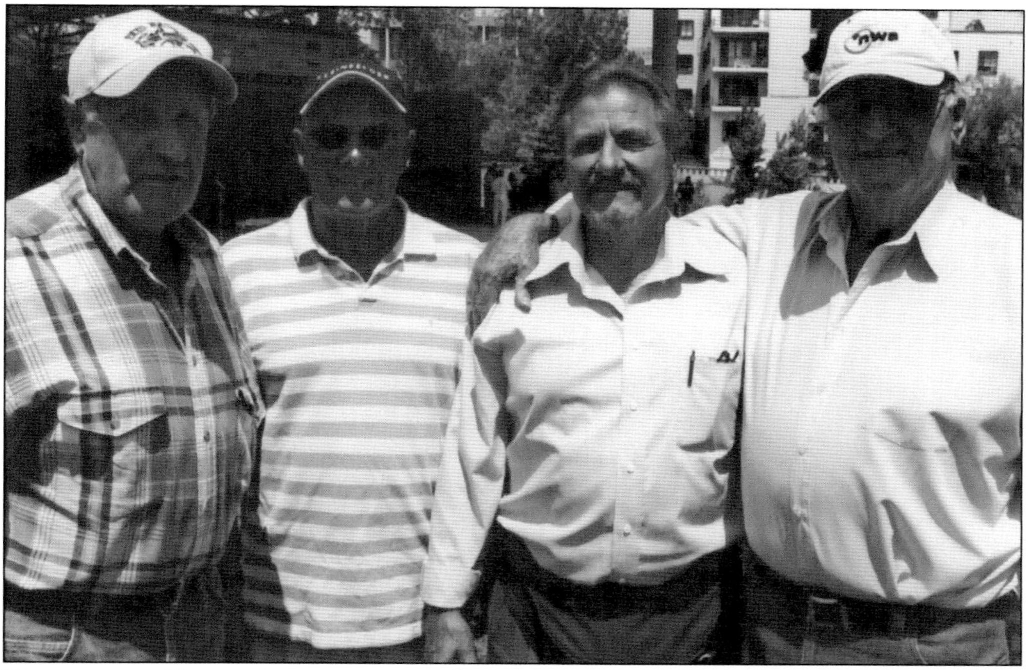

The patterns of Basque immigration entail following kinfolk (the uncle brought the nephew, for example) or proximity (neighbors brought other neighbors). In this photograph, taken during the 2008 Festival of Reno, the cameraman found four men who were all born within a half-mile radius in Bizkaia. From left to right are Louis A. Jayo, Joe Eguen, J. K. Mallea, and Ray Jayo.

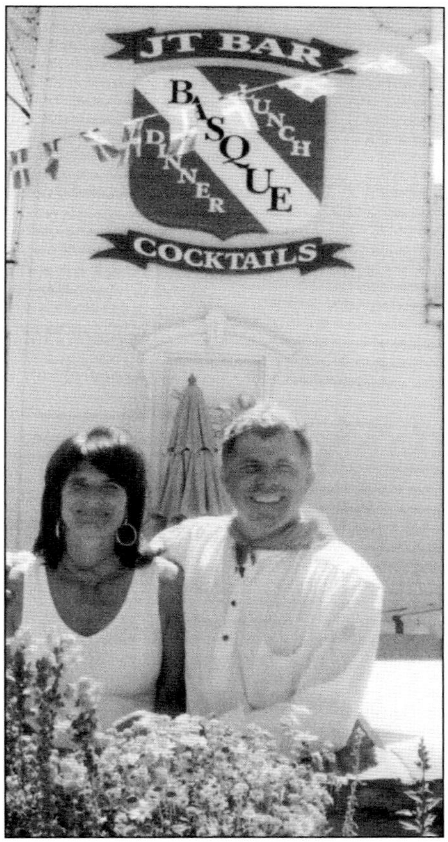

Marie Lekumberry and her brother Jean-Baptiste (everyone calls him "J. B.") own and run the Gardnerville JT Bar-Restaurant, following in the footsteps of their popular father, Jean. The place is filled with Basque memorabilia, with dollar bills stuck to the ceiling, all enhanced by Linda Dufurrena's wonderful photographs exhibited on the walls.

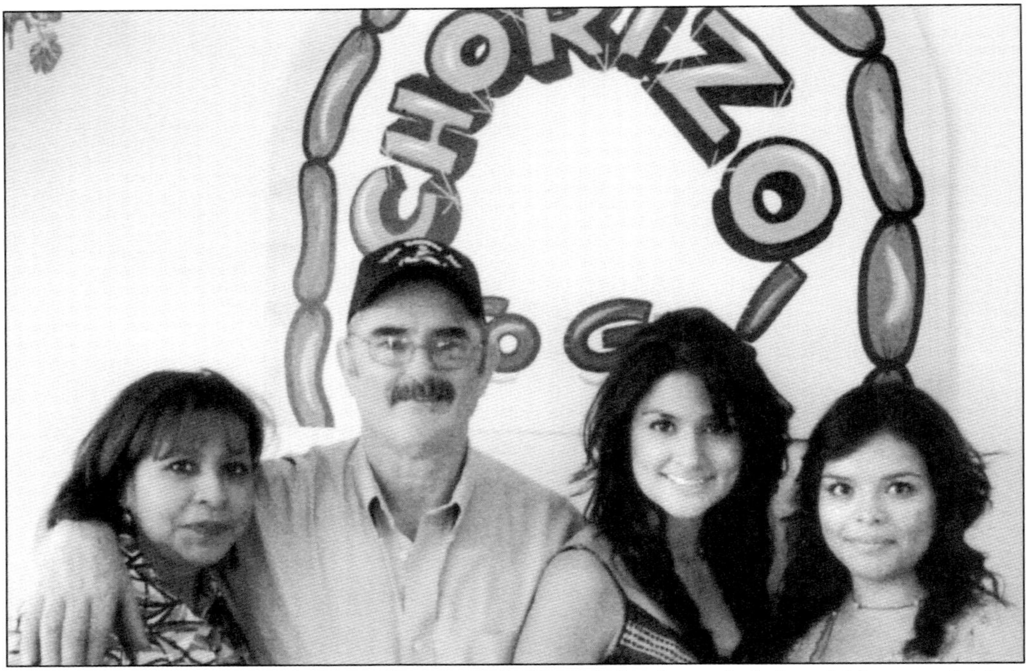

This is Pete Coscarart with his wife, Marta (left), and daughters Isabel and Veronica (right), standing inside their Villa Basque Café and Deli in Carson City. Coscarart became well known for his Basque chorizos in Battle Mountain, Nevada, which he left over 10 years ago. In Carson City, chorizos are still his specialty, but his wife cooks Hispanic dishes as well.

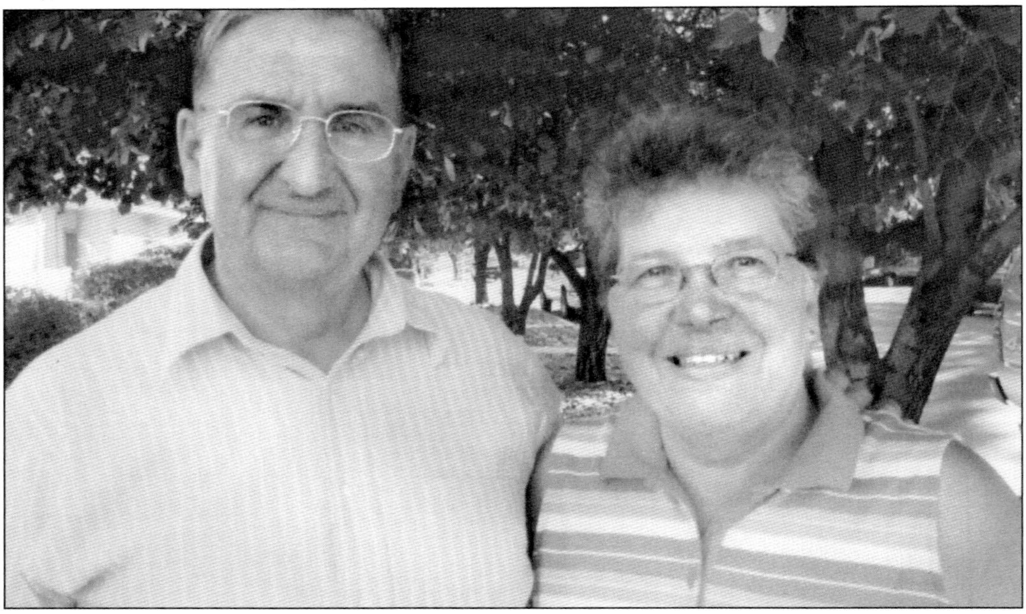

After a sheepherding stint in the Pine Nut Mountains, Jesus Pedroarena moved to Carson Valley, where he still resides with his wife, Frances. Both work tirelessly in the Gardnerville Basque Club activities like Kantari Eguna. In 2001, Anita Izoco and Frances collaborated in the publishing of a book on the local Basque families.

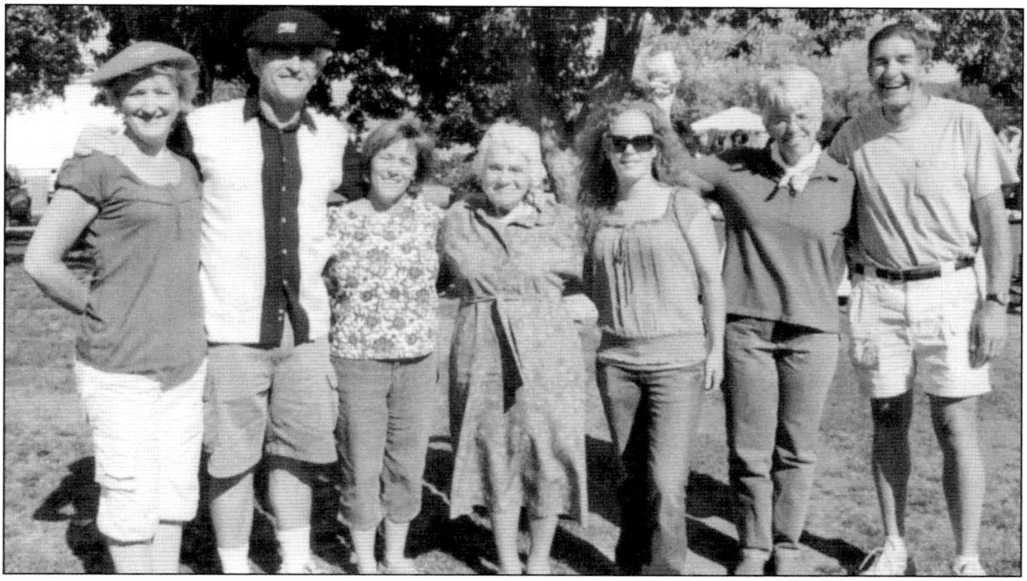

The Borda tribe, which numbers more than 90 members, is known for raising sheep, a tradition that Ted Borda of Topaz, California, continues. This photograph was taken during the 2008 Basque Festival in Carson City. From left to right are Natalie Holman, Richard Borda, Joyce Borda/Gavin, Helen "Txiki" Oxoby, Kedra Gavin, Darleen Borda/Nevin, and Dan Nevin.

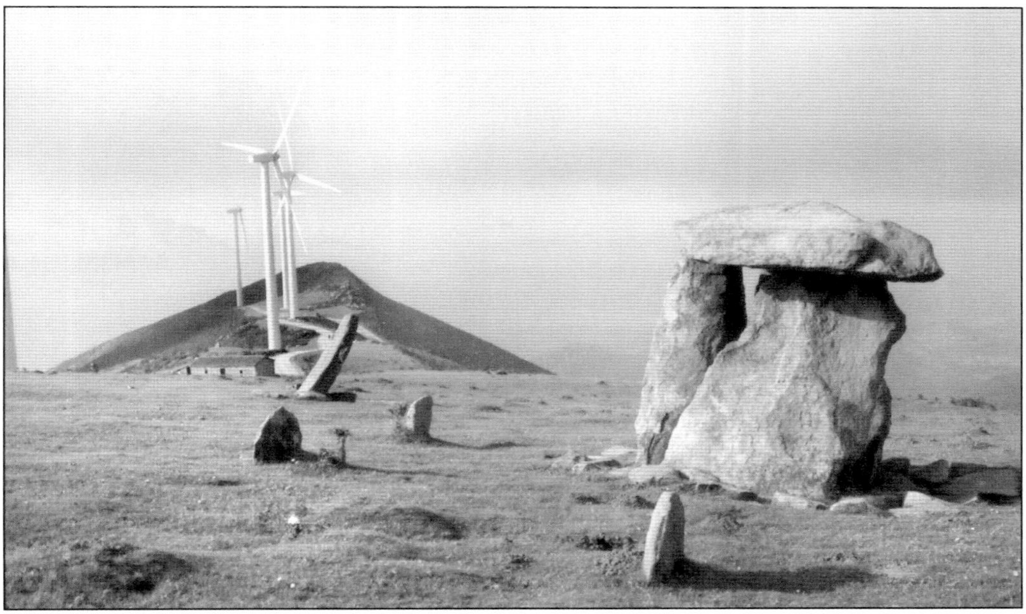

There must be a reason why the Basques—a tiny minority—have survived for so long without surrendering their identity. This photograph of the top of Oiz Mountain, in Bizkaia, provides a clue. The Basques cling to the past but seek the future; thus, a prehistoric dolmen and giant wind generators share the mountain with the sheep.

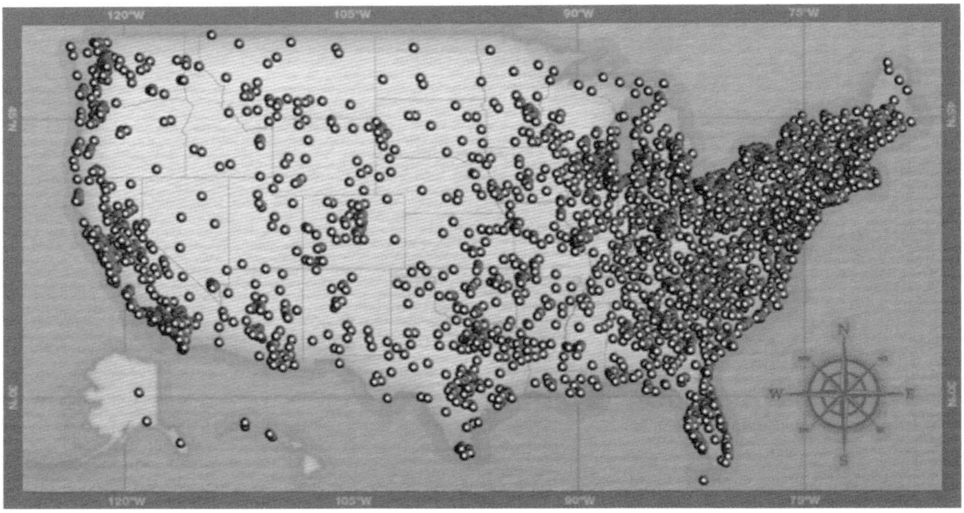